# THE GENESIS OF RENO

Frontispiece
Fuller's Crossing, early 1861. C. W. Fuller built his rustic inn and tavern during the winter of 1859–60 and the bridge over the Truckee River in late 1860. The two structures were the ancestors of the Riverside Hotel and the Virginia Street Bridge, and were the genesis of Reno, Nevada. Reno artist and historian Loren Jahn drew this representative illustration from all of the known written historical references to that first inn and bridge that were written by early Nevada historians and pioneer Truckee Meadows settlers.

The

# GENESIS

## OF RENO

The History of the Riverside Hotel
and the Virginia Street Bridge

JACK HARPSTER

UNIVERSITY OF NEVADA PRESS   Reno & Las Vegas

WITHDRAWN
UTSA LIBRARIES

University of Nevada Press, Reno, Nevada 89557 USA
www.unpress.nevada.edu
Copyright © 2016 by University of Nevada Press
All rights reserved
Cover photos: (*top left*) courtesy of Jerry Fenwick; (*top right*) courtesy of Special Collections
Department, University of Nevada, Reno Libraries; (*bottom*) Tim Dunn.
Cover design by Rebecca Lown

LIBRARY OF CONGRESS CATALOGING-IN-PUBLICATION DATA
Names: Harpster, Jack, 1937- author.
Title: The genesis of Reno : the history of the Riverside Hotel and the Virginia Street
Bridge / Jack Harpster.
Other titles: History of the Riverside Hotel and the Virginia Street Bridge
Description: Reno, NV : University of Nevada Press, [2016] | Includes bibliographical
references and index.
Identifiers: LCCN 2016009429 | ISBN 978-1-943859-23-8 (cloth : alk. paper)
Subjects: LCSH: Reno (Nev.)—History. | Riverside Hotel (Reno, Nev.)—History. | Hotels—
Nevada—Reno. | Bridges—Nevada—Reno. | Reno (Nev.)—Buildings, structures, etc.
Classification: LCC F849.R4 H37 2016 | DDC 979.3/55—dc23
LC record available at http://lccn.loc.gov/2016009429

The paper used in this book meets the requirements of American National Standard
for Information Sciences—Permanence of Paper for Printed Library Materials,
ANSI/NISO Z39.48-1992 (R2002).

21 20 19 18 17  5 4 3 2

Manufactured in the United States of America

Library
University of Texas
at San Antonio

*For Cathy*
(1952–2015)

*My wife, best friend, inspiration,*
*and fellow researcher.*

# CONTENTS

List of Illustrations · xi

Acknowledgments · xiii

Introduction · 3

1. The Genesis · 5

2. The Birth of the Biggest Little City · 23

3. The Wooden Bridge Goes Public · 42

4. Bridging Two Centuries · 60

5. Betwixt Heaven and the Hot Place · 71

6. A Modern Caravansary · 85

7. The Delmonico of Reno · 106

8. Death and Rebirth · 114

9. The Great Depression · 128

10. Top Hats and Ten-Gallon Sombreros · 142

11. It Was the Best of Times: The 1950s · 154

12. It Was the Worst of Times: The 1960s · 172

13. The White Knight · 191

14. A Decade of Reckoning · 208

15. Resurrection · 218

16. One of the Worst Bridges in the Country · 225

17. "Let's Get This Bridge Built" · 232

Bibliography · 239

About the Author · 247

Index · 249

# ILLUSTRATIONS

Frontispiece: Fuller's Crossing, early 1861 · ii
Lake's Crossing, 1862 · 29
Lake House Hotel, Reno, 1868 · 50
The Hanging of Louis Ortiz, 1891 · 63
Riverside Hotel Dining Room, 1890s · 67
Frederic J. DeLongchamps, mid-1900s · 72
Riverside Hotel and Reno Trolley Tracks, 1905 · 80
Riverside Hotel, Registration Desk and Bar, early 1900s · 87
New Riverside Hotel, 1907 · 93
Circus Day on the Virginia Street Bridge, 1915 · 107
Riverside Hotel Inferno, 1922 · 117
George Wingfield, 1928 · 119
Wingfield's New Riverside Hotel, 1927 · 122
Reno: Divorce Capital Postcard, 1930s · 136
Riverside Hotel Soda Fountain, mid-1940s · 146–147
Reno's Thanksgiving Day Flood, 1950 · 156
Virginia Street, 1955 Flood · 157
Riverside Hotel Grand Re-Opening, 1963 · 181
Truckee River Island Park, 1930s · 202
Riverside Artist Lofts Resident, 2015 · 220
Virginia Street Bridge, Pony Truss Design, 2015 · 234
Construction of Virginia Street Bridge, 2015 · 235

**Photo Gallery**
Virginia Street Bridge and Downtown Reno, 1868 · 98
*Reno Twenty Years Ago*, Painting, 1882 · 98
Iron Virginia Street Bridge and North Virginia Street, 1890s · 99
Iron Virginia Street Bridge and Planked River Walk, 1899–1900 · 99
Design Specs, 1905 Concrete Virginia Street Bridge · 100
Virginia Street Bridge and Riverside Hotel, 1910 · 100
Riverside Hotel Banquet Room, 1913 · 101
Riverside Hotel Fire, 1922 · 102
Chateau-esque Riverside Hotel Under Construction, 1926 · 103
Mapes Hotel, 1947 · 104
Demolition of the Virginia Street Bridge · 105

# ACKNOWLEDGMENTS

As with any expansive nonfiction book on history, there were a number of people who graciously stepped in with advice, research, or words of wisdom whenever I found myself floundering. I thank them each and every one, but special thanks must go to the following people and organizations.

First and foremost I must recognize the help and support of a most unusual group of men and women that I've been fortunate enough to become part of. The "Never Sweats" are a jovial, fun-loving group of top-notch Nevada historians, writers, editors, scholars, hail-fellows-well-met, and merry pontificators who, individually and as a group, have pointed me in the right direction many times as I've sweated over this manuscript. Fellow Never Sweats Guy Rocha, Bob Stewart, Robert Ellison, Mark McLaughlin, and Michael Fischer, among others, were particularly helpful. The Never Sweats' spiritual inspiration comes from Nevada's most famous—or infamous, he would claim—citizen, a young Samuel Clemens, later writing as Mark Twain, who once wrote something that could serve as the unofficial credo of the group: "Good friends, good books and a sleepy conscience: this is the ideal life."

The helpful staff at the Special Collections Department, University of Nevada, Reno Mathewson-IGT Knowledge Center, headed by the capable Donnelyn Curtis, were always there when I needed them. So too were the professionals at our great Nevada Historical Society library. The collections at the Society are unbelievably broad and deep, and the experienced staff doesn't just help when asked, they ask to help. Both of these organizations are staffed with wonderful, knowledgeable folks who always go the extra mile for you.

Nevada State Archivist Jeff Kintop steered me through many dangerous shoals during my research into the Utah and Nevada territorial days; and Patty Cafferata generously shared her expansive Riverside Hotel file with me. The curmudgeonly but extremely helpful Tim Purdy, Susanville, California historian and author, passed on vital information on Lassen County history and Charles William Fuller's relationship to it. Finally, local professional researcher/writer Kim Henrick made a number of vital contributions through her extensive knowledge of early Reno history that saved me from making a few critical errors. I owe all of these people heartfelt thanks.

I also owe a huge thanks to those who volunteered many of the wonderful photographs in the book, especially my friends Jerry Fenwick and Neal Cobb.

Thanks also go out to the City of Reno's Stephen Hardesty, who authored the very helpful 1997 report, "The Site of Reno's Beginning: The Historical Mitigation of the Riverside Hotel/Casino" and Charla Honey, engineering manager of Public Works–Capital Projects. Also to Bryan Gant of Jacobs Engineering, Jonathan Compton at Tuttu Ferro, and Brian Graham at Q&D Construction. And finally, to all the helpful folks at Artspace, City of Reno Public Works Department, and Sierra Arts Foundation.

A hearty "Thank You!" to each and every one of you.

# THE GENESIS OF RENO

# INTRODUCTION

OVER 157 YEARS AGO—before there was a Reno, Nevada, before there was a state of Nevada, and even before there was a Nevada Territory—there was a bridge over the Truckee River at a narrow, deeply rutted cattle and wagon trail that would one day become Virginia Street. There was also a small rustic inn and tavern occupying a plot of ground at the southern end of the log-and-timber bridge that catered to thirsty cowboys, drovers, and miners. The inn and the bridge were the first two structures in what would one day be a bustling metropolitan area, and to this day they still form the nucleus of the city they gave rise to. Men traveled south from farming valleys in northeastern California, crossed the bridge, and drank and supped at the inn, as they transported food supplies to the hungry miners at the Comstock Lode. They were joined by a few prospective miners coming from the east, or coming from the played-out California gold fields and headed to the Comstock mines. Standing at the bridge or the inn, a cowpoke could look around for 180 degrees and see little except the lonely, boulder-strewn Truckee Meadows landscape that surrounded him. Today, descendants of these two structures are known as the Virginia Street Bridge and the Riverside Artist Lofts. The 111-year old concrete bridge that was replaced in 2015–16 by a magnificent new structure was honored for its longevity and unique character by placement on the National Register of Historic Places in 1980, and the Riverside Hotel, the forerunner of the Riverside Artist Lofts, was similarly honored in 1986. This is the remarkable story of these two iconic landmarks around which a major Western city has grown, and of the people, the events, and the community that played an important part in shaping their long history.

# CHAPTER 1

# THE GENESIS

THE CLEAR, COLD SUSAN RIVER begins its life high in the majestic Trinity Alps of north-central California's Cascade Range, where its headwaters percolate up through the porous volcanic aquifer. From the Cascades the river flows eastward, and as it tumbles sharply down rugged Susan River Canyon it forms the northern boundary of the Sierra Nevada. Then the river gently bends southeasterly and skitters through the south end of Susanville, the Lassen County seat, as it enters the Great Basin. Both the river and city take their name from Susan Roop, the daughter of Isaac Roop, who was the first permanent settler in the area in 1853. The little river finally ends its sixty-seven-mile journey as it empties into Honey Lake at the northern end of Honey Lake Valley, which is nestled between the eastern foothills of the Sierra Nevada and the California–Nevada border. The lake is shallow and intermittent, and the water muddy and alkaline. A peninsula—"the island," the locals call it—extends into the lake at its southern shoreline, giving the lake a molar-like shape.

Honey Lake Valley encompasses about 600 square miles with an average elevation of 4,100 feet. It is an extraordinary place in many ways. A traveler, John Dreibelbis, passed through the valley several times during the summer and fall of 1853, and he penned a description of the place for *Hutching's Illustrated California Magazine*.

> This valley is beautifully picturesque and fertile...being about fifteen miles southwest of the great Sierra Nevada chain.... Surrounded, as it is, by high, bold, and pine covered mountains of irregular granite, over thirteen hundred feet in height from the valley; and which on the south side are nearly perpendicular.

This is a delightful valley, its soil is the most productive kind...
and covered with clover, blue-joint, red-top, and bunch grass, in great
abundance. The stream abounds in mountain trout, which are easily
taken with hook and line.[1]

The lake and the valley got their names from the honeydew—a sweet,
sticky substance excreted by aphids, cicadas, and insects on plant leaves—
that was found on many indigenous trees, shrubs, and grasses. But it was
Honey Lake Valley's fertile soil and high-quality pasture grass that earned
mid-nineteenth-century pioneer settlers the sobriquet "Never Sweats."
Unionville, Nevada's *Humboldt Register* of April 30, 1864, suggested that
farming and cattle ranching were so easy in Honey Lake Valley because
of the richness of its soil and vegetation that the people acquired indolent
habits, thus their nickname.[2]

These Never Sweats were an independent-minded lot, even to the point
of creating their own unofficial kingdom—Nataqua Territory, they called
it—prior to the official 1861 creation of Nevada Territory. In truth it was only
a ploy to avoid having to pay county taxes in California, but the Never Sweats
were dead serious about it. So serious were they about their cause that they
even went to war over it, a comical twelve-hour standoff with Plumas (today
Lassen) County officials that went down in history as the Sage Brush War.[3]

Lassen County historian Asa Fairfield wrote, "The Sage Brush War was a
queer one. Honey Lake valley at this time had...a population of only forty or
fifty men [and] the 'war' was a good deal like two men fighting in the street,
and while some few people looked on and took sides in the matter, travel
along the street and business went on as usual."[4] Today visitors to Lassen
County can still see the site of the Sage Brush War at Roop's Fort—often
called Fort Defiance—at the County Museum in Susanville, a reminder of
the West's friendliest little war.

In 1857, in the middle of all this flapdoodle, John E. Fuller settled in Honey
Lake Valley.[5] The following year, Fuller and local physician Dr. Zetus N.
Spalding—one of the Never Sweats who would participate in the Sage Brush
War six years later—jointly claimed 480 acres of land on the north side of the
Susan River. The Fuller ranch was a half-mile wide and extended a mile and
a half along the river, about seven miles southeast of Susanville. At some un-
recorded point in time, Fuller's mother Frances and his two brothers, James

and Charles William (Bill or C. W.; hereafter, C. W. Fuller) Fuller, joined him at the ranch.[6]

Like most Honey Lake Valley residents, the Fuller brothers were an independent lot, each man going about his own business. John and his Welsh mother Frances ran the ranch. In 1858 James erected a crude board shanty on ranch property, on the north side of the road near the river and not far from Dr. Spalding's house, where he opened a small store. "Perhaps his brothers, John E. and C. W., were in with him," historian Fairfield speculated. Soon a blacksmith shop opened across the road—perhaps, according to Fairfield, also owned by one of the Fuller boys—and other small businesses including a gristmill soon followed. The area grew into a small settlement, first known as Toadtown and eventually renamed Johnstonville.[7]

In the spring of 1858 gold was discovered on the Fraser River in British Columbia. When word trickled down to the Honey Lake Valley, Fairfield wrote, "Some of the Never Sweats felt their blood warm up with the old time [gold] fever." James Fuller sold his interest in the store, and along with some of his neighbors he headed north for the Fraser River. Within a year, however, the men would return with empty pokes, except for one unfortunate member of the group who had been killed on the road.[8]

James's brother, C. W. Fuller, is an important but often neglected figure in early Nevada history. He was one of the earliest men to settle on the land that would eventually become Reno, Nevada, and he was the very first to settle in what became the nucleus of the city, the very core of Reno. The modest inn and tavern he built in the winter of 1859–60 on the south side of the Truckee River at today's Virginia Street, and the log bridge he built across the river in late 1860, were the roots of two of Reno's most iconic and enduring institutions: the venerable Riverside Hotel and the Virginia Street Bridge. These two structures are considered the birthplace of Reno.

Fuller was born in the mid-1830s, although the few extant historical records about him are murky and often conflicting.[9] He, like his brothers and their mother, emigrated to California from Ohio, but it appears that C. W. was the first to come west.[10] An 1868 bankruptcy petition for C. W. Fuller, filed in Lassen County District Court, recorded that he had arrived in the West in late 1855. That date is confirmed by an article in the October 22, 1855, *Alta California* newspaper of San Francisco that states that C. W. Fuller was a passenger aboard the Nicaraguan steamship *Cortes* that had arrived in the city the previous day.[11] The *Cortes* had come in from San Juan, Puerto Rico, which would have been the final leg of Fuller's trip from the east coast, and

he was traveling alone, which meant that his mother and brothers had probably come later.

From San Francisco Fuller headed for mountainous Sierra County, California, which is adjacent to Lassen County, where he hired out as a teamster
and muleskinner, a man whose chief task was to keep the ornery animals on
the move. Following that he went to work in a general merchandise store in
the Sierra County gold-mining camp of Pine Grove.[12] The store was owned
by another set of Fuller brothers, James P. and W. L. Fuller from New York,
to whom Bill may or may not have been related.[13] It is also possible that
James P. and W. L Fuller were, in fact, the same Fuller brothers as our Honey
Lake men. The initials are different but similar, and the Pine Grove brothers
were supposedly from New York, not Ohio. Still, it is possible that this may
be the same set of brothers, as mid-nineteenth-century records are often
ambiguous and subject to error.

Pine Grove, a ghost town today, was a thriving Gold Rush town of 400
to 500 inhabitants when C. W. Fuller went to work in the store. "Its growth
and development have kept pace with the rest of this region, being a place of
considerable importance," one historical source said of the town.[14]

By 1859 C. W. Fuller had lost all the money he had earned in Sierra County
through bad mining stock investments and some bad debts, and in the fall
of 1859 he relocated to the Truckee Meadows in western Utah Territory.[15]
C. W. Fuller was about to embark on a new adventure that would one day
earn him a few well-deserved lines in Nevada history books.

Prior to the March 1861 creation of Nevada Territory, the western portion of
Utah Territory was commonly called Washoe (meaning "people from here")
after the indigenous Indian tribe that had occupied the Great Basin for at
least 6,000 years. Located roughly in the north–south center of Washoe, on
its western edge, is the Truckee Meadows, a triangular shaped depression
bracketed by the eastern face of the pine-laden Carson Range—an outlier of
the Sierra Nevada—and the western face of the barren Virginia Range. Give
or take a little, the Truckee Meadows is ten miles long by sixteen miles wide
at its widest part, and covers about ninety-five square miles. Bisecting it is
the sparkling little Truckee River—technically a stream—that tumbles from
Lake Tahoe north, then east through the Truckee Meadows, then north again
where it empties into Pyramid Lake. The river is 120 miles long, and the
water is cold and pure throughout its entire course and flows with a rapid
current. Before men intervened with their dams, canals, and flood walls,

and devoted their misguided energies to straightening the river's course, the Truckee River followed a serpentine course through the meadow, and flooded almost every spring with the Sierra Nevada snowmelt.

Few white men came into the Truckee Meadows during the first half of the nineteenth century. A few trappers ventured through, however. The Truckee River, called the *a'waku wa'ta* by the indigenous Washoe tribe, had few fur-bearing beaver, so these men came, they saw, and they moved on, as such men tended to do. A few wagon trains also ventured through in the mid-to-late 1840s, but all in all, recorded traffic was sparse in the Truckee Meadows.[16]

All that would change with the discovery of gold in California in 1848. Almost overnight thousands of fortune seekers began making their way west to the Mother Lode Country in large cumbersome wagons, in two-wheeled carts, on horseback, or afoot. Many of the emigrants who followed the California Trail eventually found their way to the Truckee Meadows as they approached the fearsome Sierra Nevada. By this time a number of passes over the rugged mountain chain had been discovered, but the middle routes became the favored passes for most emigrants for a short while. The first of these was the Carson Pass route, named after explorer Kit Carson and first crossed in 1844 by the Fremont Expedition. The second one was the Truckee River route. It passed through the Truckee Meadows and followed the river to a low notch in the mountains that became known as Donner Pass. Alternatively, emigrants who used the Truckee River route could choose to follow the Henness Pass toll road after it was laid out in 1852 over Henness Pass.[17]

The first wagon train to pass through the Truckee Meadows following the Truckee River route was the Stevens-Townsend-Murphy party from Missouri in 1844, led by Elisha Stevens and guided by Caleb Greenwood. One early emigrant who traversed the Truckee Meadows described his impression of the place: "We emerged in a beautiful, green, velvety valley, which, upon first coming in view, presented a most cheering appearance.... We passed over [the Truckee River] in safety & encamped in this lovely valley, with blue grass to the horses' knees." Despite the luxuriant grasses, the emigrant pointed out that the Truckee Meadows was bereft of lumber-producing trees, which would be a major problem for the area's early settlers. Later emigrant wagon trains entering the Truckee Meadows from the east did not follow the serpentine course of the river directly to the Sierra Nevada. Instead, having survived the barren north-central Nevada wasteland known as the Forty-Mile Desert, they stopped to refresh their supplies and rest their livestock.

Then they followed the emigrant road that looped about four miles to the south of the Truckee River, and eventually followed one of the trails that led back up to the river. This diversion was necessary in order to avoid the extensive sloughs, swamps, and marshes that inundated much of the Truckee Meadows in a wide belt along the river.[18]

During the California Gold Rush period a number of men had put down roots along the Truckee River to service the hopefuls as they passed through. A Mormon trader named H. H. Jamison (often spelled Jameson) had been first when he established a trading post on the emigrant trail in 1852, likely east of today's Sparks. Jamison traded with the emigrants as they passed through; he bought their lean, exhausted cattle and oxen at a bargain, fattened them up on the Truckee Meadows' rich grass, and resold them to later emigrants who passed by. Other men set up similar enterprises along the river at Drytown, today Wadsworth, where the Truckee River turns north toward Pyramid Lake; at Huffaker's Station, today south Reno; at Hunter's Crossing (later Mayberry Crossing) near the River School Farm off White Fir Street; and at O'Neill's Station in Crystal Peak, near Verdi.[19]

In early 1859 gold and silver were discovered on the Virginia Range's Sun Mountain, on the southeastern edge of the Truckee Meadows. Some emigrant wagon trains were still heading for California, the reputed land of milk and honey, despite the waning fortunes in the goldfields. But now many were heading the other direction, leaving the California goldfields to try their hands in the newly discovered Comstock mines. One local historian wrote, "History records few migrations of men equal to that produced by the discovery of the Comstock Lode. The placer mines of California had begun to fail and the Washoe excitement captured the coast and a tide of men poured over the Sierra Nevada range in a perfect torrent."[20] This human avalanche of men heading for the Comstock became known as the Rush to Washoe.

After this horde of miners crossed through the Truckee Meadows and arrived at the Comstock mines in Virginia City, Gold Hill, and other Sun Mountain settlements, they found there was little food available on the steep, arid mountainside, or in the barren, largely unpopulated valleys below. But less than 100 miles northwest of Sun Mountain lay the fertile lowlands of Sierra and Plumas Counties in California, Honey Lake Valley and Sierra Valley chief among them. An article in the *Territorial Enterprise* newspaper in late 1859 described the bounty in Honey Lake Valley: "There are some 500 or 600 inhabitants in the valley, mostly farmers. The soil of the valley is excellent for wheat, oats and Indian corn.... The oat stalks grow quite high, and the grain itself is plump and heavy. Indian corn is very fine.... Wheat, also, is of excellent quality. Vegetables of all kinds are excellent there."[21] Thus a new commerce quickly developed. From these fertile valleys teamsters with their heavily laden wagons and drovers with their fat cattle and sheep began making the trip to Sun Mountain to meet the miners' critical need for food. It was a difficult journey but well worthwhile, as the farmers and ranchers were able to charge handsome prices for their goods. Hay sold for $30 a ton, flour for $28 for a hundred-pound sack, and potatoes for 12¢ a pound. One Honey Lake Valley farmer said, "There was a demand for almost everything—even jackrabbits—and the prices would satisfy almost anyone."[22]

This new north–south traffic through the Truckee Meadows, like the earlier east–west traffic of Gold Rush days, provided another opportunity for visionary entrepreneurs. Most of the Truckee River station keepers had established their enterprises at fords—shallow spots along the river during the summer and early fall—but crude bridges or ferries were necessary despite the shallow waters. One early Truckee Meadows traveler explained why: "We crossed the river today 7 times [due to the river's serpentine course].... Some of them were...very rocky, with a swift current, so much so as to take some of our mules off their feet.... The current is so strong that a man can but with difficulty walk across, & consequently it is very dangerous to be thrown in." Another traveler echoed those sentiments, writing, "The fords are all very bad, the river being a rapid stream, and its bottom covered with large rocks."[23]

Most of these earlier enterprises along the river had been built to accommodate the east–west traffic of the earlier Gold Rush period. Now, with that traffic seriously eroded and the new north–south traffic becoming predominant, it opened an opportunity for other station keepers to serve this burgeoning new trade. One was already in place: In 1857 John Stone and Charles Gates had built an inn and trading post called Stone & Gates Crossing. It was located on the north side of the Truckee River near where today's South McCarran Boulevard crosses the river in Sparks. Stone & Gates, however, had no bridge, but did operate a rope-hauled ferry across the river. But in the spring and summer of 1860 Stone & Gates began building a bridge to serve this burgeoning north–south trade.[24]

The 1860 U.S. Census painted a bright picture of the growing Truckee Meadows. Census takers counted ninety-seven males and eight females living in twenty-two dwellings, a 420 percent increase from only two years earlier.[25]

This was the scene on the Truckee Meadows when C. W. Fuller arrived to try his hand at a new enterprise. Fuller would have been well aware of the large movement of people back and forth across the Truckee Meadows. He would have undoubtedly heard about it from the folks he served at his brother's store in Toadtown, and earlier at the Sierra County Pine Grove store where he had worked, or perhaps co-owned. Searching along the river, Fuller found a lonesome ford that struck his fancy. It was about four miles west of Stone & Gates Crossing and about the same distance east of Hunter's Crossing (later Mayberry Crossing). The site he chose for his inn, trading post, and tavern was a mound of high ground on the south side of the river at or very near what is today Virginia Street, which at that time was only a wispy, rutted cattle trail.[26]

For the past century and a half, ever since C. W. Fuller first settled on what would one day become downtown Reno, Nevada, there has been disagreement among historians and writers about his activities. The first difference involves when he arrived on the Truckee River. Written dates vary from 1859 to 1862, and much of the confusion is the fault of Fuller himself, because in his various legal filings he provided conflicting dates for his initial arrival. In *Fuller vs. His Creditors*, his bankruptcy petition filed in Lassen County, California on July 1, 1868, he provided testimony that in the fall of 1859, after he had lost all his money in Sierra County, California, he "then removed to the Truckee River in Nevada." However, in his February 20, 1861, petition to the County of Carson, Territory of Utah, for a charter for a toll bridge at Fuller's Crossing, he provided testimony that "in March 1860 [I] settled on the Truckee at what is now known as Fuller's Crossing." Thus through Fuller's own words the question arises: Did he arrive in the fall of 1859, in March 1860, or somewhere between the two?[27]

Historians will likely never be certain, but we do know for sure that he arrived before the March 1860 date he testified to, thanks to an item in the *Territorial Enterprise* on February 18, 1860: "Perhaps it may be of interest to the traveling public to state that Mr. Fuller, of toll-gate canyon, is now engaged in erecting a hotel on the Truckee, and building a free bridge across it, some 8 miles above [Stone &] Gates. [It was actually four miles.] His idea is to make a direct route from Dog Valley to [Steamboat] Springs, which in connection with the road to be made by the Truckee Turnpike Company, through Dog Valley, will shorten the distance to Downieville [California], at least 35 miles." The article makes clear that Fuller had relocated to the Truckee Meadows prior to March 1860 if, on February 18, he was already engaged in building his hotel. But how long he had been there before the newspaper noted his presence we cannot know. So taking all these things into consideration, it isn't far-fetched to believe that Fuller had, as he wrote years later, been at work in the Truckee Meadows as early as the fall of 1859.

The first thing Fuller would have done after arriving on the Truckee River and selecting his site was to claim his piece of barren land. Most land in unpopulated or lightly populated areas of the American West could not be owned by anyone until the land had been surveyed and offered for sale by the General Land Office of the United States. What people did instead was to simply claim their land as squatters. The Truckee Meadows' first minister, Reverend F. M. Willis, who arrived in 1853 on a wagon train, described this land situation: "Truckee Meadows was settled in the main by land grabbers [i.e., squatters]...nearly every man in the valley had more land than he could legally hold.... If anyone else undertook to file on any of the government land [that someone else had squatted on] he did it at the risk of his life." So in a sense the land was held simply by civilized agreement, or in some cases, by force of arms.[28]

Because of the absence of official land-claim records, it's impossible to know how much land Fuller staked out, but he would not have required much. We know he claimed land on both sides of the river. His plans were to build a small wayside inn that included a trading post, a tavern, and an adjoining corral (the ancestor of today's Riverside Artist Lofts) and then a bridge (the ancestor of today's Virginia Street Bridge), much like some of his competitors along the river had done. Thus he could have easily claimed enough land for his minimal needs. Once the enterprising Fuller had done this, it was time to begin building his hotel.

There is only one firsthand written, oral, or pictorial description of Fuller's hotel, and it is only a scant few words in the lengthy, contentious 1879 divorce petition between the hotel's second owner, Myron Lake, and his wife Jane. Because of that, early state, county, and city histories are vague when describing Fuller's hotel. *Thompson & West's History of Nevada, 1881* wrote only, "The house was kept as a wayside inn for the accommodation and refreshment of travelers." N. A. Hummel's 1888 *General History and Resources of Washoe County, Nevada*, uses basically the same description, but in more flowery prose, writing, "With his ax he entered the virgin forests which clothed the mountain side, leveled the towering pines, and from their trunks hewed out the logs for his habitation. In this wayside inn he stored goods brought from California." Finally, early-twentieth-century Reno historian Annie Estelle Prouty described Fuller's hotel as "only a dugout and shack," a description she had received in a personal interview with Mrs. F. (Florence)

Thompson of Reno. Mrs. Thompson was the eldest stepdaughter of Myron Lake, and had lived in the Lake House—as Fuller's hotel would later be named—for a few years with her family in the mid-1860s.[29]

Another hint of what the hotel may have looked like can be found in the description of another early hotel in the region. In March 1860, about the same time Fuller opened his hotel, John L. Moore opened the first hotel in Virginia City. Moore had crossed the Sierra with a pack train of supplies from San Francisco with all the supplies he would need for his new enterprise on the Comstock. His inn and tavern was a large canvas tent partitioned into a barroom and a lodging room. The lodging room was fifteen feet by thirty feet in size, and slept thirty-six guests at a charge of $1.00 per night. Each guest received a pair of blankets, and if one was still available, a grain sack stuffed with hay for a pillow. As Reno historian Prouty noted, "Travelers did not expect elegance or comfort in those days."[30]

It is Prouty's description of the hotel that has most frequently been picked up by writers and historians when recording Reno's beginnings. John M. Townley, in his 1983 book *Tough Little Town on the Truckee: Reno, 1868–1900*, is generally considered the most reliable source on the early days of Reno, and he used Prouty's description, although he added his own flourish to it, writing, "Fuller built a primitive station, half logs and half dugout...[and] gave little more time than needed to tack a canvas roof on the dugout."[31]

But in the end we must finally look at Myron Lake's words, cited above, as they are the only firsthand description we have of what the hotel built by C. W. Fuller, which is present-day Reno's first structure, actually looked like. According to Lake's sworn testimony in his wife Jane's 1879 "Petition for Divorce," he had purchased Fuller's Crossing on June 22, 1861. As he described the hotel, it was "[a] way-side hotel for teamsters with a barn connected with it.... It was a pretty fair hotel, a little frame house 1–1/4 story's [sic] high." The half- or quarter-story in early western hotels was the space under the roof rafters that was normally planked and rented as dormitory-style sleeping quarters. Two days before his actual purchase, on June 20, 1861, Lake had published an ad in the *Territorial Enterprise* announcing his ownership. In the ad he described the hotel a little more positively as "large and roomy, [with] the table and bedding...of the best quality." However, he likely took a little creative license with this description.[32]

It is important to remember one phrase in Lake's description—"a little frame house 1–1/4 story's high"—as this will be an important piece of information in chapter 2.

Despite what the hotel looked like, C. W. Fuller and his hired hands would have had a difficult time building this inn and tavern over the winter of 1859–60. A newspaper article noted that a "pogonip"—an extremely cold, icy fog—descended on the Truckee Meadows for six weeks over that winter, and that the river was frozen from bank to bank, which was very unusual for the rapidly flowing water. The *Sacramento Daily Union* wrote, "The Governor [Nevada Territory's new governor, Isaac Roop] reports the snow as very heavy.... The Truckee river is frozen over hard enough to bear up loaded teams." An old settler named Charley Chase verified the bad winter of 1859–60, saying it had snowed in the meadow for ten days without interruption, leaving forty-two inches of snow on the ground.[33]

Another common theme that has become accepted as historical fact is that Fuller also had a trading post or store at Fuller's Crossing, although he never mentioned a store in any of his legal documents. This makes sense, as his main competitor, Stone & Gates Crossing, had a very successful store just four miles downstream and Fuller also had previous experience operating a trading post. We also see firsthand evidence of this trading post from the words of an 1862 Truckee Meadows settler, Edwin Stauts, who told the newspaper during a later interview, "A trading post stood where the Riverside Hotel now is situated." Finally, N. A. Hummel, in his 1888 *General History and Resources of Washoe County, Nevada*, backs this up, stating, "In this wayside inn he [Fuller] stored goods brought from California," likely from his family's ranch.[34]

One thing we can be certain of is that Fuller had a barroom in his hotel. Every nineteenth-century hotel or inn in Nevada—and indeed throughout most of the West—included a room, or at the very least a small corner, where liquor and beer were sold. Writing on December 16, 1918, on the brink of Nevada's historic entry into Prohibition—the state would precede the rest of the nation's entry into Prohibition by more than a year—the *Reno Evening Gazette* wrote, "Without a doubt, the first place where liquor was sold in Reno was the Old Lake House...which was built by C. W. Fuller.... Fuller conducted a primitive tavern at the crossing...[and] in those days the river had to be forded at the point where the bridge is now. Sometimes the water ran high and a party would get wet and chilled in the icy waters and then the liquor that Fuller sold would be in demand."[35]

The February 18, 1860, *Territorial Enterprise* article mentioned earlier also noted that Fuller was "building a free bridge." What the newspaper was referring to were posts and stringers that Fuller had installed across the river shortly after his arrival. We know of this through a rare firsthand story about Fuller's early activities. Thomas K. Hymers—a man about whom much will be said later—arrived on the Truckee Meadows in April 1860 from Wisconsin. As Hymers related the story some years later, when he first arrived at the Truckee River C. W. Fuller was operating a ferry. Hymers told Fuller that he would like to cross the river, and Fuller demanded "four bits" (fifty cents) for the crossing. Hymers related that Fuller was making preparations to build a bridge and had the posts and stringers—which were used to provide a handhold while constructing the bridge—already in place. So Hymers, with characteristic Yankee thrift and ingenuity, walked down to the riverbank and "cooned the timbers," pulling himself along the stringer from post to post until he ended up on the opposite bank, saving his four bits for another day. Since we know from his petition for a toll bridge charter that Fuller did not actually begin building the bridge itself until October 1860, he had obviously installed the posts and stringers earlier in the year to assist in pulling the ferry across the river by rope, much like his nearby neighbors at Stone & Gates Crossing had been doing since 1857.[36]

Hymers's story also provides proof that Fuller operated a ferry at his crossing, as some historical accounts have claimed. Since Fuller's hotel had been open since spring, it would make sense that he would want to provide some sort of interim service for those wishing to cross the river before his bridge was built, and a log raft, or ferry, would provide a simple and inexpensive answer. We also see verification of a ferry from a February 29, 1860, Marysville, California, newspaper, the *Marysville Daily Appeal*, in an article written by a gentleman who had walked from Smith's Flat (today Placerville, California) to the southern end of the Truckee Meadows. He wrote, "The trail on this road over the mountains for persons on foot is in good condition.... There are three crossings now established on the Truckee River on this route, viz: Fuller's, Harrison's, and Stone & Gates. Fullers probably is a savings of some few miles."[37]

Although he had accomplished a lot in a relatively short time, C. W. Fuller still had a long way to go. According to his 1861 petition for a toll bridge charter, after he had finished building the hotel and the ferry Fuller wrote that he "thereafter constructed a Wagon Road, leaving the Old Beckworth [Beckwourth] Route at a point 4 miles from said River [Honey Lake Road in today's Panther Valley] running thence to said River and crossing the same at Fuller's Crossing, thence through 'Truckee Meadows' about six miles and terminating at Huffaker's [today south Reno] where it unites again with the Old Emigrant Road."

In stating his case for a toll bridge charter, Fuller claimed that his bridge and his ten-mile wagon road would save farmers and ranchers from the California valleys five or six miles of unnecessary travel when crossing the Truckee Meadows on the way to the Comstock. Additionally, his road, in conjunction with a road being built by the Truckee Turnpike Company that began in North San Juan near Nevada City, California, would save travelers thirty-five miles when traveling from Downieville, the county seat of Sierra County and a major Gold Rush town. John Townley, noted historian on early Truckee Meadows history, explained that the north–south traffic using Fuller's road would also avoid the oppressive bogs at Stone & Gates Crossing, and was also a shorter, less-hazardous, and easier route for heavily loaded wagons making the north–south trip through the Truckee Meadows.[38]

In laying out and clearing his wagon road, Fuller should be recognized for accomplishing yet another pre-Reno first, in addition to his hotel and bridge. Parts of the road he created eventually became Virginia Street, Reno's main north–south thoroughfare.[39]

Toll roads and their cousins, stage roads and freight roads, were an integral element in the development of the West from the 1850s to the 1890s. They were the only means of connecting the growing network of towns, villages, and mining regions to one another prior to the advent of the railroad. In the earliest days there was no formal process for charging tolls; the toll road operator simply put up a gate at some impassable spot on his road, like a narrow canyon or a bridge crossing, and demanded payment for passage over the road he had paid out of his own pocket to clear. Then at some point in the 1850s in Utah Territory, the Territorial Government was given the authority to grant toll franchises and set rates, and that passed on to Nevada Territory at its founding on March 2, 1861. The toll road operator was responsible for clearing the road to make it passable, and keeping it passable through all seasons, all at the operator's own expense. As for this toll road maintenance, however, one toll road historian wrote that in reality it usually amounted to "a lick and a promise," meaning most roads were not maintained at all. As western states developed in the 1870s and beyond, counties generally took over those roads and bridges and converted them into public passages.[40]

We see evidence of Fuller's early success in an 1860 *Territorial Enterprise* article. It boasts of a new settlement named Janesville (long since disappeared) nearby to Steamboat Springs between Reno and Carson City. In describing the location of the settlement the article notes, "[It is] ten miles south of the crossing of Truckee River and Stone's Ranch [Stone & Gates

Crossing] and about fourteen miles from the main crossing of Truckee [Fuller's Crossing], saving thereby fourteen miles for the travel on the road north of Marysville."[41]

On February 20, 1861, Fuller filed his petition in the County Court of Carson County, Utah Territory, for a toll bridge franchise across the Truckee River at Fuller's Crossing, explaining, "On account of the rapid current & high floods of the Truckee River, it is essential that good & substantial bridge be built across the same." On March 5, 1861, he secured a $3,000 bond, the next step required in obtaining the charter. The underwriters for Fuller's bond were William Alford, an attorney and a selectman in both Utah and Nevada Territories, and George C. Pringle. The bond was necessitated by the fact that toll road and toll bridge operators were taxed 10 percent of their gross toll revenue by Carson County—it would soon become Washoe County—and the bond ensured they would meet that obligation.[42]

In his petition for the toll bridge charter, Fuller claimed to have settled on the Truckee River in March 1860, and to have built a hotel and a wagon road. Most importantly, he wrote, "In October 1860 your petitioner commenced the building of a bridge across said river, at said crossing, and completed the same within three months, at an expense of three thousand dollars." He described the bridge as "a good substantial structure, consisting of good heavy timbers securely bolted, & planked with a track eleven feet wide in the clear, and 148 feet in length, planked; and stands about four feet higher than high water mark of said river." Fuller also noted that his bridge had to be tied down during high water, indicating that the ends of the bridge were simply resting on each shoreline. In 1937 the Nevada Department of Highways described Fuller's bridge as "a low bridge of the angle-arch type."[43]

Fuller's petition was granted on March 5, 1861, with the added condition that no other bridge could be built closer than three miles in either direction. The court also established the following tolls:

| | |
|---|---|
| For pack animals or loose stock of any kind, | 10¢ per head |
| footman | 25¢ each |
| horseman | 50¢ each |
| one or two horse wagon or pleasure carriage | $1.00 |
| four horse or ox wagon | $1.25 |
| for every additional span of horses or yoke of oxen | 25¢[44] |

As a further condition of the charter, Fuller was obligated to pay to the Carson County treasurer at the end of each month a tax representing 10 percent of the net amount collected during the preceding month.[45]

Fuller's bold action of building a bridge probably caused his nearest competitors at Stone & Gates Crossing to do the same. They had survived nicely with only a rope-hauled ferry since opening in 1857, but with all the new north–south traffic they decided it was necessary to compete head-on with Fuller. Unlike Fuller, however, they got the county to agree to install the bridge at their crossing. Since it was a public bridge, passage was free and the station keepers received no revenue from it, but John Stone and Charles Gates earned good money with their lively and popular Farmers Hotel and their busy trading post.[46]

Despite these humble beginnings, C. W. Fuller's little bridge would eventually morph into Reno's iconic Virginia Street Bridge, where many decades later recent divorcees were rumored to have thrown their wedding bands into the cold, tumbling waters of the Truckee River to celebrate their newly won independence.

Considering all the foregoing information, two lingering questions remain. First, Fuller testified in his 1868 Lassen County, California, bankruptcy petition that immediately before coming to Nevada from Sierra County, California, he had "lost all that he had made up to that time." If that was true, a question arises: Where did C. W. Fuller get all the money he was spending on this new enterprise? Building the hotel and the wagon road would certainly have cost him some money, and he would also have had his own normal living expenses, Spartan as they may have been. And finally, he claimed the bridge had cost him $3,000 to build, and he had also accrued attorney's fees for his petition. We can only speculate where all that money came from.[47]

It is likely that one or more of Fuller's brothers, or his mother from Honey Lake Valley in eastern California, assisted him financially in these endeavors. Nevada history book editor and newspaper owner Sam P. Davis suggests this, writing "Lakes Bridge was first known as 'Fuller's Crossing,' from the fact that it was owned by two brothers named Fuller." We know from his various legal documents that C. W. Fuller was the sole *legal* owner of the enterprise, but it's probable that his family provided some or most of the funding. Two facts give credence to this possibility. First is the fact that on October 19, 1860—just when Fuller began building his bridge—he, his brother James, and another man jointly purchased a lot on "C" Street in Virginia City for $700, likely as a mining claim. James Fuller, along with his brother Bill, is described in the deed for that property as living at Fuller's Crossing. The second fact is that when C. W. Fuller traded Fuller's Crossing to Myron Lake (an event discussed in chapter 2) the ranch he received in trade was actually deeded in his mother Frances's name, not his.[48]

One last question is why C. W. Fuller would have traded his promising enterprise to Myron Lake in mid-1861, barely eighteen months after he had launched it. As if his property did not already have fabulous profit potential, it only got better when in early 1861 Sierra Valley Road (now South Virginia Street) was completed from Virginia City to the Truckee River, at Fuller's Crossing. It is likely that in addition to wanting to be closer to his family, Fuller saw financial incentive in owning the Honey Lake Valley farm that he traded for. East of the Sierra in California, farmers from Honey Lake Valley and nearby Sierra Valley were experiencing a boom of their own. Droves of cattle and sheep and tons of produce were being sent over the bridge at Fuller's Crossing to Virginia City to feed the mob of miners who were arriving daily. So perhaps Fuller didn't believe he was giving up on a great opportunity, but simply getting involved in a different one.[49]

Chances are we'll never have a definitive answer to any of the lingering questions that C. W. Fuller left in his wake, thus preserving the mysterious aura surrounding the history of pre-Reno days in the Truckee Meadows.

### Notes

1. Dreibelbis, "A Jaunt to Honey Lake Valley and Noble's Pass."

2. Fairfield, Fairfield's Pioneer History, 363.

3. Anonymous, Illustrated History of Plumas, Lassen & Sierra Counties, 346–47, 352–53.

4. Fairfield, Fairfield's Pioneer History, 315–16.

5. Fairfield, Fairfield's Pioneer History, 67.

6. Fairfield, Fairfield's Pioneer History, 99, 316. Fairfield wrote that John E. Fuller settled in Honey Lake Valley in 1857, but he makes no mention of when Fuller's mother and brothers arrived. His first mention of the two brothers is in 1858 (p. 101) and of the mother in 1861 (p. 241), so whether they all arrived at the same time or separately is not known.

7. Fairfield, Fairfield's Pioneer History. Quote on pp. 101–2.

8. Fairfield, Fairfield's Pioneer History. Quote on p. 145.

9. There are five California voter registration documents for William C. Fuller of Johnsonville, Lassen County, California, from 1868 through 1875, listing four different birth years. California Great Registers 1866–1910, "Charles William Fuller: Image 00007."

10. California Great Registers 1866–1910, "Charles William Fuller: Image 00008." United States Census, 1880, "John E. Fuller"; Rocha, "The Mystery of Reno's Beginnings," 35.

11. "Memoranda: Passengers," Alta California, 10/22/1855.

12. Lassen County, "William Fuller vs. His Creditors, Schedule A."

13. Garvis, Roar of the Monitors, 337–40, 379; author interview with Jann Garvis, 12/13/2012; "California State Census, 1852, James Fuller, Sierra, CA," FamilySearch.org, https://familysearch.org/pal:/MM9.1.1/V4NX-N3F

14. Anonymous, Illustrated History of Plumas, Lassen & Sierra Counties, 477.

15. Lassen County, "William Fuller vs. His Creditors, Schedule A."

16. Prouty, "The Development of Reno," 17.

17. Coman, Economic Beginnings of the Far West, 2:234.

18. Townley, *Tough Little Town*, 26–27; Potter, *Trail to California*, 196–97.

19. Fey, *Emigrant Trails*, 60, 61, 62 (map inset); Hummel, *General History and Resources*, 5; Angel, *History of Nevada*, 623.

20. Fulton, "Reminiscences of Nevada," 83. Fulton moved to Reno in 1875 and took a position as land agent for the Central Pacific Railroad. He also owned and operated the *Reno Evening Gazette* for nearly a decade in the early 1900s, and was an avid amateur historian and writer about early Reno history.

21. "Honey Lake," TE, 12/31/1859.

22. "The Development of Reno," *Nevada State Historical Society Papers*, vol. 4, 1923–24, 71.

23. Geiger, *Trail to California*, 197–98; Curran, *Fearful Crossing*, 154.

24. Fey, *Emigrant Trails*, 60 (map inset), 61; Jeffrey Kintop, Nevada State Archivist, e-mail to the author, 10/24/2013; "Important Enterprise," TE, 02/18/1860.

25. Jackson, "A History of Reno," NSJ, 03/27/1976.

26. Townley, *Tough Little Town*, 52; Hardesty, "The Site of Reno's Beginning," 1.

27. Lassen County, "William Fuller vs. His Creditors, Schedule A," bankruptcy petition; Territory of Utah, County of Carson, "Petition of C. W. Fuller for Bridge Franchise."

28. Communication to the author from Jeffrey Kintop, Nevada State Archivist, 02/08/2013; quote from Willis, "Truckee Meadows Memoirs."

29. First quote from Angel, *History of Nevada*, 634; second quote from Hummel, *General History and Resources*, 30; third quote from Prouty, "The Development of Reno," 4, 28 (fn1).

30. Lord, *Comstock Mining and Miners*, 66–67; quote from Prouty, "The Development of Reno," 28.

31. Townley, *Tough Little Town*, 52.

32. Lake, "Petition for Divorce," 17, lns. 5, 6, 27, 28, with quote on lines 12–14; "Bridge and Hotel at Fullers Crossing," adv., TE, 06/20/1861.

33. "Fog," NSJ, 01/14/1874; n.t., *Sacramento Daily Union*, 12/24/1859; "Charley Chase," NSJ, 11/18/1884, 3.

34. Price, "90 Active Years in Nevada," NSJ, 11/16/1952; Hummel, *General History and Resources*, 30.

35. n.t., REG, 12/16/1918.

36. Hymers's story, "Beauty of Scene on Truckee River," NSJ, 10/03/1905; Stone & Gates ferry, Hummel, *General History and Resources*, 17; Angel, *History of Nevada*, 634.

37. Among the accounts of a ferry at Fuller's Crossing are Fairfield, *Fairfield's Pioneer History*, 243; and Prouty, "The Development of Reno," 27. Prouty, writing in the second decade of the twentieth century, cited R. L. (Robert Larkin) Fulton of Reno, Nevada (p. 27, fn4) as the source for the information about the ferry. For information about Fulton, see Fairfield, *Fairfield's Pioneer History*, 67.

38. Territory of Utah, County of Carson, "Petition of C. W. Fuller for Bridge Franchise"; n.t., TE, 02/18/1860; Townley, *Tough Little Town*, 52.

39. "Grants and Permits for Toll Roads and Bridges," Records of Carson County, Utah & Nevada Territories, 1855–61; Townley, *Tough Little Town*, 52.

40. Goodwin, "Nevada's Toll, Freight & Stage Roads," 458–59.

41. Thompson, *Tennessee Letters*, 114, quoting from the TE, n.d.

42. Quote from Territory of Utah, County of Carson, "Petition of C. W. Fuller for Bridge Franchise"; Territory of Utah, County of Carson, "Bond, C. W. Fuller for Toll Bridge on Truckee River."

43. Territory of Utah, County of Carson, "Petition of C. W. Fuller for Bridge Franchise"; "Reno Constructs Two New Bridges," *Nevada Highways and Parks*, 2, no. 2 (March 1937): 15.

44. Territory of Utah, County of Carson, "Petition of C. W. Fuller for Bridge Franchise."

45. Territory of Utah, County of Carson, "Petition of C. W. Fuller for Bridge Franchise."

46. Trego, "Glendale Once Came Close to Being What Reno Is Now," *NSJ*, 10/08/1950.

47. Lassen County, "William Fuller vs. His Creditors, Schedule A."

48. Davis, *The History of Nevada*, 2:1031; Territory of Utah, County of Carson, "Deeds, Vol. A, 1860–61," 327–28; Townley, *Tough Little Town*, 63 (fn1).

49. "The Development of Reno," Nevada State Historical Society Paper, vol. 4, 1923–24, 71–72; Rowley, *Reno*, 16; Rocha, "Reno's First Robber Baron," 28. Studying early maps of the area, it appears that Sierra Valley Road, which ran from Virginia City to Fuller's Crossing, may have preempted a portion of Fuller's wagon road that ran from his crossing southeast toward Huffaker's.

# CHAPTER 2

# THE BIRTH OF
# THE BIGGEST LITTLE CITY

By early 1861 Fuller's work had been completed. His inn and tavern, Truckee River toll bridge, and ten-mile road were finished, and the winter of 1860–61, while a cold and wet one, was not severe enough to cause any appreciable damage to any of Fuller's structures during the spring thaw.

In California, ninety miles away from Fuller's Crossing, C. W. Fuller's brothers and their mother Frances continued to work at their ranch on the Susan River. One of their Honey Lake Valley neighbors was a man named Myron Charles Lake, an irascible fellow whose small ranch was located on the west branch of Baxter Creek adjoining the Fuller property. Lake had purchased the property from Frances Fuller in September 1860; it was part of the original 480 acres the Fullers and Dr. Spalding had purchased in 1858. Lake would later say of the purchase, "I got a farm by giving fifty dollars and a horse for it. There was a cabbin [sic] on it but no improvements."[1]

Lake, thirty-three years old at this time, was a native of Cayuga County, New York. As a young boy he had moved with his parents to a ranch in DeKalb County, Illinois; years later, he proudly claimed, he had served with the Fifth Regiment of Illinois Volunteers in the Mexican-American War (we discuss that claim in detail in chapter 3). Returning from the war, Lake established a large ranch in Illinois, the nucleus of which was a 160-acre tract he had received as a federal land grant for his war service. In 1852 he left his Illinois ranch and moved to California to join the Gold Rush. He spent the next five years mining for surface gold in and around the gold camp of Rabbit Creek, on the border of Plumas and Sierra Counties. Eventually giving up his dream of riches, he relocated to Honey Lake Valley where he purchased the small farm from the Fullers and again began working the soil.[2]

An early historian who lived in nineteenth-century Reno affirmed Lake's poverty during his early farming days, writing, "At that time he was very poor, and actually sold the coat off his back to buy seed for his farm." Despite a slow start, however, Lake's farm did have promise, and before long he was managing to make ends meet as a farmer, although he never prospered at the trade.[3]

Shortly after purchasing the small farm, the hot-tempered Lake joined other valley residents in a fight against the local Indians who had been stealing potatoes from their gardens in what became known locally as the Potato War. This band of farmers eventually grew into a full-fledged vigilante group. Later, in 1857, a county sheriff arrived just in time to stop the lynching of the Lowery gang, a gang of murderers whom Lake had captured.[4]

Lake was an avaricious and ambitious man by nature, and he was always on the lookout for a better life. At some point he had either had conversations with C. W. Fuller during one of C. W.'s visits to the family's ranch, or perhaps he had visited Fuller's Crossing to see C. W.'s Truckee Meadows enterprise firsthand. In either case, he saw a grand opportunity in station-keeping on the Truckee River, a vision that had apparently eluded C. W. Fuller. Thus during the summer of 1861 Lake and Fuller reached an agreement whereby Lake would trade his Honey Lake Valley farm to C. W. Fuller for his Fuller's Crossing enterprise. The trade appears to have taken place soon thereafter, although Lake's quitclaim deed titling the farm to Fuller was not filed in Lassen County until September 28, 1861. In addition to trading his Fuller's Crossing enterprise, C. W. Fuller was also to pay Lake $1,067 for the farm, although Lake would brag years later in his divorce petition that he was paid an additional $1,500.[5]

In one of those odd situations that often cloud historical research, there is another Lassen County deed on file dated December 7, 1861, that states that "M. C. Lake" sold the same piece of property to Frances Fuller, C. W. Fuller's mother. One possible explanation for that would be that C. W. Fuller had not been able to complete the original transaction with Myron Lake because he did not have the $1,067, so his mother repurchased the property for her son C. W. later in the year.[6]

Regardless of how it happened, we see the first public announcement of Lake's takeover of Fuller's Crossing in an ad he placed in the June 20, 1861, edition of the *Territorial Enterprise*, although his ownership would not be official until the second deed on the ranch was filed on December 7. It does appear that in his ad Lake exaggerated the size and quality of the inn he had purchased from Fuller:

Bridge and Hotel

AT FULLER'S CROSSING

The undersigned would respectfully inform the traveling public that he has purchased the hotel and bridge at Fuller's Crossing on the Truckee river, and is now prepared to offer excellent accommodations to all who may favor us with their patronage. The house is large and roomy, and the table and bedding will be of the best quality. The road from the Northern mines to Virginia and Carson cities is much nearer by this than by any other route.

Good stables are attached to the establishment and a good supply of hay and grain is kept constantly on hand.

M. C. LAKE.[7]

As for Fuller, he may or may not have stayed around to help Myron Lake get started. In any event, he soon moved to Lassen County where he made his new home on the small farm he had received from Lake. Little is known about Fuller for the remainder of his life. We know he was forced into a bankruptcy petition in 1868, swearing in that petition that "he engaged in the stock business, since which time he has lost everything by the depreciation in the price of stock and losses in farming." He also shows up in California voter registration records a number of times while living on the farm in Johnstonville—formerly called Toadtown—in Lassen County, California, the latest such voter record being in 1875. On May 2, 1877, "Charles William Fuller" sold the Johnstonville farm to "A. S. Wright." That is the last we know of C. W. Fuller, the founder of what would later become known as the Riverside Hotel, and of the Virginia Street Bridge and, some historians believe, the founder of Reno as well.[8]

Myron Lake's first year on the Truckee Meadows was not an easy one. His hotel, which had been known simply as the Fuller's Crossing Hotel, was now called Lake's Hotel, and the entire enterprise was dubbed Lake's Crossing. A few years later the name of the hotel would be changed to Lake House. Lake may have enlarged the hotel somewhat, and he established a postal station inside. When the Lake House was torn down forty-six years later to be replaced by a grand multistoried brick hotel, an article appeared in the *Nevada State Journal* on May 29, 1907, describing what business at the original hotel, under both Fuller's and Lake's ownership, would have been like:

In those early days the "hotel life" was of a very primitive order. The drovers and other struggling travelers prefered [sic] to camp out in their tents and cook their own grub, and little effort was made to entertain them except in the barroom. This was a little stuffy room that in the evenings would be thronged with a rough crowd, thirsty and tired after weeks on the desert. They would fill up on tanglefoot [a strong, cheap whiskey made of deerweed] at "two bits" a glass, of the kind that tears a hole in the handkerchief when one sneezes…. The menu was not very varied but made up for that in the price charged for vitals [sic]. Beans was the staple article of diet and they were not served in any appetizing style…. But the guests were not of the fastidious kind, and complaints to the "manager" were few and far between.[9]

Little did Myron Lake realize that in less than a year's time his new enterprise would disappear in the blink of an eye.

In recent years, scientists with the U. S. Geographical Survey have identified a new type of super-storm they named ArkStorm, bringing to mind Noah's biblical flood. Whereas most flood concerns today are centered on 100-year storms that occur on average once a century, an ArkStorm (Ar for Atmospheric River) is even more rare, occurring only once every 300 years or so. The last ArkStorm to hit California and the Sierra Nevada foothills of Nevada Territory occurred in the winter of 1861–62. During the thirty-day period from Christmas Eve 1861 to January 23, 1862, it snowed and rained for twenty-eight days. San Francisco tallied thirty-four inches of rain and Sacramento thirty-seven inches during the two-month period. Statistics were not kept for Nevada Territory at the time, but rain and snow in the Truckee Meadows certainly approached California's figures. Even the faraway *New York Times* wrote of the storm and its resultant floods: "The Pacific Slope has been visited by the most disastrous flood that has occurred since its settlement by white men. From Sacramento northward to the Columbia River, in California, Nevada Territory, and Oregon…[the floods] inundated towns, swept away mills, dams, flumes, houses, fences, domestic animals, ruined fields and effected damage, estimated at $10,000,000."[10]

One poor fellow caught up in this super-storm and its resultant flood was a young Samuel Clemens, later writing as Mark Twain. He was relatively new to Nevada Territory and possibly wondering why he had ever left Missouri.

In his own inimitable style, which must be taken with a grain of salt, he wrote, "We rode through a snow storm for two or three days, and arrived at 'Honey Lake Smith's,' a sort of isolated inn on the Carson River.... There was not another building within several leagues of the place."[11]

Clemens wrote that a group of Indians warned him and his companion that they should immediately leave the area because heavy rain was expected, but they ignored the warning. The two men made a bed under the rafters of the hotel roof that night and soon joined the cacophony of snoring travelers. But after a while they heard turmoil outside, and looked out the small window, where they witnessed the raging waters of the Carson River approaching their hotel. By 11:00 PM, Clemens wrote, "Our inn was on an island in mid-ocean.... We remained cooped up eight days and nights." By the ninth day Clemens and his companion had had enough of the stuffy inn and their prickly companions, and in the midst of a heavy snowstorm they launched a canoe and eventually made it to safety.[12]

Many Truckee Meadows residents and travelers also experienced Clemens's misfortune during the ArkStorm of 1861–62. Because the Truckee Meadows was so thinly populated, no news of the flood's effects on the area apparently made it into print. However, on January 13, 1862, the *Territorial Enterprise* dispatched a story on flood damages on the Comstock to San Francisco's *Alta California* newspaper of January 27, 1862. These tales of woe were similar to what was experienced by Samuel Clemens, by Virginia City residents, and by those living at Lake's Crossing, Stone & Gates Crossing, and other Truckee River settlements:

> The greatest damage of the flood as far as was heard was done in Gold Hill Canyon near Dayton.... Very little had escaped without...injury. At Gold Hill several houses have been considerably damaged...[and] the new two story brick building of Mr. Marglot is almost a total ruin. The Nevada mill was saved by the greatest exertion.... The North Wall of Golden's Hotel fell down, and a [nearby] wooden building was completely demolished. At the Devil's Gate the entire bed of the ravine is gullied out some twenty-five feet deep rendering it impassable even to footmen. The mill [of the Washoe Gold and Silver Mining Company] is badly injured [and] the foundation of the boiler room is swept away, and the boiler lies in the ravine.... Two stone cabins belonging to Phillip Agusner, are washed away.... Mr. Blumsfeld's adobe dwelling was carried away together with Mark Ferris' and Mr. Park's adobe dwellings.[13]

Myron Lake suffered his share of grief from the ArkStorm. When C. W. Fuller had built his bridge, he testified that it rose four feet above the river's depth, even when the water ran high, but it did have to be tied down on both ends during extremely high water. But despite Fuller's good intentions, when the ArkStorm floodwaters roared down the Truckee River, Fuller's bridge—now Lake's bridge—was not spared.

Once spring set in, Lake began rebuilding the bridge. Over the years some Reno historians have suggested that Lake moved the bridge site six to eight feet upstream from Fuller's original bridge site to a spot he likely considered safer, and every Virginia Street Bridge built since then has occupied basically the same location. But is the claim of Lake moving the bridge site historically accurate? Many latter-day writers have cited Effie Mona Mack's 1936 *Nevada: A History of the State* as the source for that claim. Mack, in turn, cited early-twentieth-century Reno historian Annie Estelle Prouty's 1917 University of Nevada master's thesis, "The Development of Reno in Relation to its Topography," as her source. Continuing to move back in time, Prouty cited the oral claim of moving the bridge site as having come from pioneer Reno resident and businessman Robert L. Fulton, one of the city's leading citizens. However, Fulton didn't arrive in the Truckee Meadows until 1875, as a land agent for the Central Pacific Railroad, so he would not have had firsthand knowledge of where the initial bridge had been located. Thus he, too, received the information second hand, or perhaps even third hand, from somebody else. So as we sit today listening to the claim that the original Virginia Street Bridge site was different from today, we are getting this "fact" fifth hand, at least. So did Myron Lake relocate the bridge site when he built the second iteration of what we know today as the Virginia Street Bridge, or did he not? We simply cannot be certain.

Lake's new span was described as a log queen-post structure; it used two central supporting posts on each side for added strength and stability, rather than one as before. As related in chapter 1, many historical accounts say that Fuller still owned the bridge during the heavy winter of 1861–62, and that it was he who rebuilt the bridge after the floods. That is inaccurate: Lake owned the bridge by that time, and it was he who rebuilt it.[14]

Although we know of the bridge's fate through a number of historical accounts, nothing was recorded about the crude hotel that Fuller had built that stood precariously near the riverbank. It is nearly certain, however, that the hotel, like the bridge, would have been destroyed during the flood. We even see evidence of this in the first image ever produced of the Fuller's Crossing–Lake's Crossing pre-Reno era. It is an oil painting entitled *Reno Twenty Years*

Lake's Crossing is shown here in Cyrenius McClellan's oil painting entitled *Reno Twenty Years Ago*. This version of the painting was commissioned in 1882 by Myron Lake, who is standing in the foreground with some Washoe Indians. The bridge, and likely the hotel and tavern in McClellan's painting, had just been rebuilt following a major ("300-year") storm and flood the preceding winter. Construction lumber and building stones are stacked next to the hotel awaiting use. Courtesy of Very Special Arts of Nevada.

*Ago*, painted in June 1882 by Cyrenius B. McClellan, northern Nevada's most renowned painter during the last half of the nineteenth century.

McClellan's biographer wrote that the artist arrived in Nevada from eastern California in 1862. Soon after he arrived he drew a sketch of Lake's Crossing, which is verified in the boulder in the right foreground of the painting where he noted the date, "June, 1862." In the painting we clearly see Lake's brand new bridge. We also see that a hotel is obviously under construction, with a huge pile of lumber and stones nearby. What we don't see is any evidence of "a primitive station, half logs and half dugout," as historians Townley and Prouty described Fuller's hotel. It is even more convincing that the hotel was washed away when one compares the hotel in McClellan's painting to Myron Lake's firsthand description of Fuller's original hotel as being "1-1/4 story's [sic] high." Myron Lake's new hotel in the painting was quite obviously one and a half stories high. All of this leads to the conclusion that Fuller's inn—the original forerunner of the Riverside Hotel—was, like the bridge, lost to the ArkStorm flood.[15]

As for McClellan's painting, it would be twenty years before the artist completed the most recognized of the oil paintings from his initial 1862 sketches. In that rendering, which was commissioned by Myron Lake himself, Lake and a group of Washoe Indians appear in the foreground. That painting ended up in the hands of Lake's stepdaughter, Florence Thompson, and today hangs in the Very Special Arts of Nevada (VSA) Lake Mansion in Reno, which serves as the headquarters and gallery for the nonprofit arts foundation. McClellan also painted an unknown number of other original oils from these 1862 sketches, but with slight variations in content and rendered in different sizes. Some were signed; some were not. Another of the paintings, on display at the Nevada Historical Society in Reno, is quite different from Myron Lake's version. A black-and-white version of that one is featured in the photo gallery in this book.[16]

---

Despite all the work Lake put in during the spring and summer of 1862 rebuilding his bridge and hotel, he never took his eye off the big prize: soliciting the new Territory of Nevada for a revised toll franchise for the bridge and permission for an adjoining toll road. On December 17, 1862, Lake was rewarded for his efforts. The statute granted him a ten-year monopoly on the toll bridge, and along the route of the toll road he was given permission to build, much of which would shadow Fuller's earlier road. While Fuller had requested and received a charter only for a toll bridge, Lake had received charters for both the road and the bridge. Lake's toll road, when completed, would be twenty miles long—twice as long as Fuller's road had been—and would run from a point near today's South Virginia Street and Peckham Lane to the California border, crossing the Truckee River at his bridge. In a slight that would have irritated the arrogant Lake, the statute referred to the bridge as "Fuller's Bridge." Offsetting the affront, however, was the fact that Lake was taxed at only a 2 percent rate, while Fuller had been taxed at 10 percent, although it's doubtful if either man ever paid those taxes, as most did not.[17]

Early Reno historian Annie Estelle Prouty described Lake's Crossing in the early 1860s: "The two corner stones of the future metropolis were the bridge and the tavern [hotel]. The little tavern in the midst of sagebrush with great boulders strewn around it had many guests. Ranchers came for their mail from over the valley and it was a long journey to Virginia [City]. Mr. Lake kept a small store where they could get some supplies." An 1862 Census of Nevada Territory recorded five people, including M. C. Lake, living at Fuller's Crossing, indicating that he had hired a few hands to help him run his business.[18]

Despite having gained a local monopoly in late 1862 with his bridge and road, Lake's Crossing was slow to develop as a settlement site with ranches, homes, and commercial enterprises surrounding his structures. Stone & Gates with their free bridge, Junction House, and Huffaker's remained the primary settlements on the Truckee Meadows. But Lake was undeterred, and year by year Lake's Crossing gained momentum. His monopoly on the use of Sierra Valley Road (now South Virginia Street) and the valuable Comstock traffic it carried was the driving force behind his enterprise, and he knew a bustling settlement would eventually grow up around it. Whatever small profits Lake realized from his toll business and hotel–tavern clientele he wisely invested by buying the land on which the bridge and hotel sat, and other land that surrounded his businesses through the 1820 Sale Act and the 1862 Homestead Act, indicating that Lake was looking toward the future.[19]

In 1864 the once-divorced Lake became a husband again, and an instant father, when he married the daughter of a neighboring rancher he had known in Honey Lake Valley. Jane Conkey Bryant, a widow who had lost her husband in the Civil War Battle of Shiloh, had come to California with her three young children to live with her parents; after the marriage to Lake the new family made their home in Lake's Hotel at Lake's Crossing. Six weeks after their marriage, the entire family joined in the celebration when Nevada gained its statehood.[20]

It was clear from the outset that this was a marriage of convenience only, and both Myron and Jane admitted to that in Jane's petition for divorce some years later. Because Lake's Crossing had yet to become profitable, at the time the marriage occurred Myron was also holding down a number of other jobs. He had begun farming some of the land he had purchased, and the food products from this endeavor were either sold or used in the kitchen at the Lake House. He also testified that he worked as a teamster, and that his work around the hotel amounted to "bossing men and fixing up the road, tending the stable, tending bar [in the hotel] and collecting toll." For her part, Jane put in long hours at the hotel cooking for the dining room, serving as a housekeeper, doing the laundry, making beds, and emptying the slops. Myron also expected her children to work at the hotel.[21]

In the McClellan painting, the brand new Lake House of 1862 looked like a neat, tidy little building with a fresh coat of white paint. But by the mid-1860s, time, weather, and hard use had apparently taken a toll, according to Jane Lake's description of it. She wrote, "[It was] a small frame building upon the river bank…containing a bar-room, dining-room, kitchen and 5 or 6 bedrooms. It was uncarpeted and had little or no furniture. There were no other houses near and the country all about where Reno now stands was unimproved and still covered with rocks and sagebrush."[22] Jane's statement indicates that although the hotel had deteriorated somewhat, the surrounding landscape still looked exactly as McClellan had painted it.

The financial problems the Lake House encountered during the second half of the 1860 decade could not be laid at Myron Lake's doorstep. The primary problem was the traffic across the Truckee Meadows to and from the Comstock mines. It had simply dried up. Borrasca is a Spanish word; one of its definitions is "an exhausted mine." From the peak year of Comstock production in 1864, silver and gold output plummeted by more than 50 percent through the remainder of the decade. Men left the Comstock in droves—just as they had once arrived—and the supply line that serviced the Comstock also withered dramatically. It would be 1870 before rich new veins were discovered at deeper depths, and the Comstock would turn the corner to greater prosperity.[23]

During this period, in order to keep all his business interests and his family financially afloat, Myron developed a plan. The small gold-mining district of Meadow Lake, also known as Summit City, was located in the Sierra at an altitude of 7,400 feet, about thirty miles northwest of Lake's Crossing and northwest of Donner Pass. For roughly three years beginning in 1865, the small settlement enjoyed a boom when gold was found on nearby quartz ledges; it had grown to about 5,000 residents in a short period of time. Myron Lake heard about the hubbub on the mountain and decided to open a hotel there to bolster his disappearing earnings on the Truckee Meadows. He, Jane, and the three children loaded most of their belongings and some of the Lake House's equipment into a sturdy wagon and set out for Meadow Lake. The wagon was so heavily laden, Jane recalled later, that she had to walk up the mountainside for miles at a stretch, causing a dyspeptic and bowel complaint that she suffered with for the rest of her life. When they arrived, they opened a boarding house in a large tent where they boarded fifty to seventy-five men at a time, Jane contending that she did all the work to keep the business afloat.[24]

But Myron was busy too. He was hard at work building a more permanent structure to replace the tent. It was described as "a commodious two-story hostelry," and was but one of a number of permanent structures being haphazardly thrown up in the burgeoning, gold-hungry settlement. Within two years Myron Lake's hotel would be one of ten lodging houses in Meadow Lake. When Lake's hotel was finished in August 1865, Myron celebrated "by giving a ball on the roomy second floor. Only thirteen ladies were present, but they made up for their lack of numbers by good looks and dancing skill; [and] they and the gentlemen footed it in a sprightly way to the music of two violins and a cello." For the brief time that Meadow Lake's promise shined, Lake's hotel would be the settlement's most successful hotel. It became the center of most local festivities and, according to the settlement's biographer, "Thoughtful townsmen took to dropping in…for informal discussions philosophical and scientific." But hard winters and an inability to separate the gold from the quartz on the inaccessible ledges would spell doom for Meadow Lake within three years, and Lake's abandoned hotel mysteriously burned to the ground in 1868.[25]

Whether Myron Lake closed his Truckee Meadows hotel while he was at Meadow Lake, leased it to another innkeeper—which is the most likely scenario—or hired hands to keep it minimally operating while he was away is not known for sure. About the time he returned, however, Lake decided he needed help with his business ventures. An old friend of his from Illinois, Daniel Hickey Pine, had supposedly served with Lake in the Mexican-American War, and they had become good friends. Pine had also moved west, serving as constable, city marshal, and eventually the postmaster in Aurora, a mining town on the California–Nevada border, in the early 1860s. Following that he served for a year or so as a lieutenant in the Nevada Volunteers at Fort Churchill. At some point in 1866 or 1867 Lake hired Pine to serve as toll collector for the Lake's Crossing Bridge, and Pine moved to the Truckee Meadows with his family. It is also possible, but not supported by any known facts, that Pine may have come earlier and run the Lake House for Myron while Myron was at Meadow Lake. What is known for sure is that Pine would spend years working in the small tollhouse on the south side of Lake's bridge. Pine Street, in today's downtown Reno, was named after Daniel Pine when the town was established in 1868.[26]

In the winter of 1867—after the Lakes had returned from Meadow Lake—a flood destroyed Lake's toll bridge for the second time. An article in the *Territorial Enterprise* described the event: "Nearly the whole country [referring to the Truckee Meadows] was under water day before yesterday, the river having overflowed the banks and spread over the bottom land for a width of five miles in many places.… The bridge at Stone & Gates' crossing is gone, in fact all the bridges on the river and small streams except the bridge at Hunter's station [are gone]."[27]

By this time, Lake may have felt that his business was cursed. But cursed or not, the bridge had to be rebuilt. J. S. Sellers who owned a 160-acre ranch outside Stone & Gates Crossing, by now renamed Glendale, had previously worked on the Stone & Gates bridge, and Lake hired him to rebuild the Lake's Crossing Bridge. During the construction, Sellers also built a plank walk across the river for the use of foot passengers who had always been in danger while crossing alongside the ungainly freight wagons, oxen teams, and cattle herds. One day, according to folklore, a large flock of turkeys happened upon the walking bridge, and in single file they crossed the bridge in turkey-trot fashion heading toward Virginia City.[28]

Lake leased the hotel—by now renamed the Lake House—to others off and on from the mid-1860s until the early 1870s. By this time the hotel was beginning to do better, as the Comstock mines began to rebound. It had a few private rooms for guests, in addition to the Lakes's apartment, but most single visitors slept upstairs in a large room under the rafters that was disparagingly referred to as "the corral." Downstairs there was a large barroom—the main attraction for the teamsters and drovers who stopped over—and a hearty meal was served for 50 cents. The outside corral and stables that Fuller had built had been moved to a plot of ground across the river and expanded, and it was now penning and feeding a large number of horses and oxen. When Sellers finished rebuilding the bridge, Lake hired him to raise up the old frame hotel and build another story beneath it, making the hotel two-and-a-half stories high. In an ironic twist, given all his bridge-building experience, Sellers would be killed in 1881 while repairing the Mayberry Bridge.[29]

To further enhance his property, Lake also began work on a large building at the southeast corner of the bridge, across the road from the hotel, with the intention of eventually using it as a gristmill to mill a large field of wheat he had nurtured. However, his interest in the building would be forgotten when the Central Pacific Railroad came to town.[30]

As early as 1859, pioneer Sierra Nevada surveyors had determined that if there ever was a trans-Sierra railroad, it should cross the fearsome mountains at Donner Pass, which had first been crossed fifteen years earlier by the Stevens-Townsend-Murphy party from Missouri, and had later foiled the ill-fated Donner Party. Whether this decision was common knowledge during the mid-to-late 1860s on the Truckee Meadows we cannot know. Perhaps Myron Lake knew it, perhaps not. In any case, when he and representatives of the Central Pacific Railroad would finally make contact to talk about the railroad crossing Nevada through the Truckee Meadows, Lake was aware that the opportunity of a lifetime was knocking at his door. The Central Pacific Railroad had begun laying tracks in Sacramento in 1863, but progress had been slowed by difficult terrain and the instability of the workforce. Still, on December 13, 1867, the work crews crossed the California–Nevada border.[31]

Lake's Crossing was certainly not the only site in the Truckee Meadows that railroad officials considered for their eastern Sierra depot. In fact, it wasn't even the first one, as these men knew they had a number of good options. Crystal Peak, strategically located at the California–Nevada border at the mouth of Truckee Canyon, was a well-established settlement with over 1,500 citizens, and it was the first site considered. Glendale, today Sparks, the site of Stone & Gates Crossing, was also promising, with a popular hotel and a surrounding complement of rich ranches and farms. But both settlements expected the railroad to pay premium prices for their land, and Glendale had the added misfortune of being partially underwater when the railroad party visited: "Water was four feet high in the barroom of the Glendale Hotel and houses were swimming all over the valley," one newspaper reported of the ill-timed storm.[32]

By the time the railroad's advance party finally arrived at Lake's Crossing, the Lake family had moved into a small frame house just south of the hotel, on a fenced site where the Washoe County Courthouse would eventually be built. Remains of that original courthouse, built in early 1872, still stand as an internal component of the present-day building. By this time Lake also owned the majority of lots in the brash, noisy settlement that had sprung up along the river over the past seven years, including the area's most important assets: the hotel, the toll bridge, and the turnpike. Despite treating the settlement's residents fairly—locals were not required to pay a toll for use of the bridge—Lake was still an unpopular presence in the community. He was tactless, overbearing, and tight-fisted. One settler was quoted in the newspaper, saying, "It becomes us…to thank God that he has given us such powerful guardian angels to watch over and protect us against the machinations of that wolf in sheep's clothing, M. C. Lake, who stands ready to gobble up unwary innocents."[33]

Despite the shortcomings in his character, Lake had a sharp mind when it came to business. When the Central Pacific Railroad team arrived at his crossing, he knew he had to trump the competing settlements if he was to gain the agreement—and the huge personal wealth that would go along with it—by being selected as the site where the railroad would establish its eastern Sierra Nevada depot and the vital transfer point for freight destined for Virginia City. He soon struck a deal with Charles Crocker, the superintendent of construction for the Central Pacific Railroad and one of the railroad's four owners.[34]

Over the past century and a half historians and writers have claimed a number of different acreages and different sums of money as having been sold or exchanged in these transactions that created the town of Reno. The figures of 140 acres, 160 acres, 80 acres, and other acreages that have been declared over time have mostly been educated guesses. The truth, of course, lies in the original paperwork—the primary source documents—that are often difficult to locate, and even more difficult to decipher. These are the official deeds, the Federal Land Grant Patents, and the government plat maps. Credit for accurately unraveling this 148-year-old mystery goes to outstanding Nevada historical researcher Kim Henrick, who first published her findings in early 2016. In essence, this is what occurred in the founding of Reno, Nevada.

Myron Lake's original Federal Land Patent #177, issued August 10, 1865, granted him 137.28 acres on both sides of the Truckee River. Of this, 107.34 acres were on the north side of the river and 29.94 acres were on the south side; Lake paid the government approximately $170 for the land. Three recorded deeds between Lake and the Central Pacific Railroad, or one of its four owners, describe how Reno was born. A deed recorded March 27, 1868, shows that Lake sold to Charles Crocker of the Central Pacific Railroad his 107.34 acres on the north side of the river for $200, this land to be divided and sold to create the town that would become Reno.

The second deed, recorded July 7, 1868, describes the sale of land from the Central Pacific Railroad to Myron Lake of 109.98 acres on the south side of the river for approximately $275. This property, when added to the 29.94 acres Lake already owned on the south side from his original land patent, became nearly 140 acres in what would become known as Lake's Addition.

Finally, much has been previously written stating that the railroad had to return to Lake some of the north-of-the-river lots as part of the agreement between the parties. To be more specific, however, in a deed recorded February 1, 1869, Charles Crocker sold back to Myron Lake two large parcels on the north side of the river, one on each side of the bridge, for the grand sum of $1.00.[35]

The earliest public announcement of the deal between Lake and the railroad had been made on February 29, 1868, in the *Eastern Slope* newspaper in Washoe City, then the largest town in the state and the county seat of Washoe County. The small announcement would be prescient: "Location of the C.P.R.R. [Central Pacific Railroad]—We learn from good authority that the Railroad Company will build their depot at Lake's bridge. The citizens of the Truckee Meadows anticipate the building of a great city in that locality.... We think a fine opportunity is now offered them to make it, the said city, a great railroad center. They of course will favor the building of the Virginia and Truckee Road [referring to the soon-to-be-built Virginia & Truckee Railroad]."[36]

In early April 1868, according to a member of one of Reno's pioneer families, "the [Lake House] hotel was filled with these people who were laying out the townsite [sic]. Mr. Hatch was the man who was the head of this group that was laying out the town with his surveyors." Crocker had made the decision on Lake's Crossing quickly and unexpectedly, and Hatch did not have one of his key employees at hand. James M. Graham was the lead surveyor, and he and his party and all their equipment were heading east at the time the decision was made, Graham would recall years later. A messenger was sent to find him and his team and return them to Lake's Crossing, which he did. "The next day we started laying out the townsite [sic] and I drove the first survey stake," Graham recalled. Although he couldn't remember exactly where he had driven that stake, the then ninety-year-old surveyor said he could probably find the spot after a few hours of effort with some old maps. This 1932 visit to Reno had been Graham's first visit since that historic day in 1868, and he said he was amazed to find a thriving and beautiful city where once had stood a "rambling, dust-desert town."[37]

So on May 9, 1868, the Central Pacific land agent banged his gavel while more than 1,000 land-hungry buyers from as far away as San Francisco bid up to $1,000 for a 25-by-100-foot lot that Graham had laid out on the railroad's new property. The first lot sold was on the east corner of Commercial Row and Virginia Street, bringing $600.[38]

The original town site was roughly bounded by today's Valley Road on the east, Ryland on the south, Arlington on the west, and 5th Street on the north. Historian Townley noted that on the portentous day when the auction was conducted to sell off the first town lots, the only substantial structures decorating the town site were the Lake House, the toll bridge, and the partially built gristmill, which by now had become the Alhambra Saloon and Lodging House. Barely six weeks after the auction, the first train passed through the fledgling town, immediately making it the interchange where stages and freight wagons would connect with incoming trains. As further indication of the newly minted importance of the town, the Nevada-California-Idaho Stagecoach line immediately moved its Truckee Meadows interchange to Reno as well. The only sour note to the entire episode was when the Central

Pacific reneged on its promise that Reno would also be made a full-fledged station, with roundhouses and machine shops. The railroad's land agent had made that promise to each of the competing settlements in order to sweeten the deal, when in fact it was planned all along that the station would be located at Wadsworth, the last watering hole before the trains crossed the challenging Forty Mile Desert.[39]

Sierra Valley Road had become Virginia Street, or perhaps Virginia Road, presumably when the town was initially laid out, although the change could have occurred earlier. The name "Virginia" was chosen because the southern terminus of the road was Virginia City. Allan C. Bragg was born in Maine in 1849, and came with his parents to Carson City in 1862 where they engaged in the lumber business. Young Allan traveled often to early Reno in the course of working for his father, and in 1874 he opened his own lumber business in the town. He also owned the *Reno Evening Gazette* for some years, selling it in 1903. In 1914 Bragg was asked to write an article for his old newspaper about Virginia Street, and what it had been like when the town was first chartered:

> Virginia Street…was not much more than a cow trail leading to Lake's Crossing…but with the arrival of freight trains from the west, it bounced into a busy business section of the infant town. The street was lined with eight, twelve and sixteen-animal teams, pulling big prairie schooners, with two and three trail-wagons loaded with goods…and M. C. Lake was piling up gold at the rate of from $100 to $1,000 per day for toll in his little frame toll-house at the southern end of the bridge. That is not all—for large bands of Nevada's and Northern California's juicy beef cattle and flocks of mutton-sheep were frequently driven through town. These, with hay wagons and produce from Honey Lake Valley en route to Virginia City, made an immense traffic on the street. [Note: Needless to say, all of this traffic had to eventually cross Lake's Virginia Street toll bridge as well.]
>
> Square front one story wooden shacks, with wide wooden awnings, and sidewalks of the period were constructed…plank walks with nails sticking up toward the sky from one-eighth of an inch to one inch, pulled out by the genial sunshine and the wonderful climate of Nevada, but we were considered quite citified, and we were, for every stranger within our gates said so.[40]

The only task that remained was to name the new town. Judge E. B. Crocker, the chief legal counsel to the Central Pacific Railroad and the older brother of Charles Crocker, suggested the name "Argenta" (the plural of the

Latin word for silver, argentum), and an appropriate name given Nevada's rich silver heritage, the judge believed. In mid-April 1868 that name had been announced to the citizens of the new town, and they let the word roll around on their tongues. But two weeks later the judge's younger brother Charles overruled his sibling and renamed the town "Reno," in honor of a little-known Union general in the Civil War. Oddly, the *Reno Crescent*, the forerunner of the *Reno Evening Gazette* and the town's first newspaper, stubbornly called the town "Argenti" (the possessive form of argentum) as late as December, even though its masthead carried "Reno" in its name.[41]

Nearly eight months after the founding, Reno celebrated its first Christmas. To outsiders, the new town may have looked like a dismal assemblage of shacks surrounded by a treeless, boulder-studded landscape, but to the local folks it was home. Four days of rain had preceded Christmas and the streets were sluggish rivers of mud; a chilled wind snarled off the Sierra Nevada causing the entire populace to don their heaviest coats. The *Reno Crescent* described the holiday: "Christmas in Reno was spent after the fashion of our fathers. The bars of the town...held forth with tempting freedom their compounds of eggnog, punch and Tom-and-Jerry.... Much feasting was done.... The hotels and restaurants vied with each other in generous rivalry.... Many presents were bestowed, many 'Merry Christmases' said.... The very mud on the streets seemed to add to the hilarity of the merrymakers." A community-wide party had been held on Christmas Eve for all the children in town, and Hook and Ladder Company #1 held a benefit ball at the renamed Alhambra Hall, Myron Lake's old gristmill building. So much fun was had by everyone that talk was already going through town about a New Year's Eve celebration.[42]

Myron Lake had done it! Not only had he established a town, but he had also made a name for himself, earned a tidy sum of money, and set the stage for even greater personal wealth in the years to come. However, lest Lake believe that he was the master of all he surveyed, unforeseen forces would soon set the pompous fellow straight. Before the decade of the 1860s was over, both Lake's hotel and his bridge would prove to him that he was still mortal after all.

## Notes

1. Fairfield, *Fairfield's Pioneer History*, 243; Townley, *Tough Little Town*, 58, 63 (fn1). Townley states in the footnote, without listing a specific deed citation, that Myron Lake had purchased the property from Frances Fuller the previous September [1860]; quote from Lake, "Petition for Divorce," p. 16, lns. 14–20.

2. Lake, "Petition for Divorce," lns. 10–16; "A Pioneer at Rest," *NSJ*, 06/21/1884; "Myron C. Lake," *REG*, 06/20/1884; Cafferata, *Lake Mansion*, 29.

3. Quote from "Myron C. Lake," *REG*, 06/20/1884. Some writers have attributed this statement to C. W. Fuller when he started out on the Truckee Meadows, but that is incorrect. It originally came from Lake's obituary in the above-mentioned newspaper, and refers to his own early penury, not Fuller's.

4. Fairfield, *Fairfield's Pioneer History*, 83–93; Townley, *Tough Little Town*, 93.

5. Lassen County, California, *"Book A of Deeds,"* 27, filed 09/28/1861; Lake, "Petition for Divorce," p. 16, lns. 14–20.

6. Lassen County, California, *"Book A of Deeds,"* 34, filed 12/7/1861. Like many things connected to C. W. Fuller's activities in the Truckee Meadows, there was a long-standing disagreement over when he traded properties with Lake, and perhaps it was the aforementioned double sale of the Lake farm that caused this confusion. Despite that, well-regarded history books have claimed every year from 1859 to 1863 as the date of the trade, but it would be 1980 before then Nevada State archivist Guy Louis Rocha finally brought an end to the controversy by publishing the correct answer of June 1861. Rocha found the information by searching the archives of *TE*.

7. "Bridge and Hotel," *TE*, 07/20/1861.

8. Quote from Lassen County, California, *"Book A of Deeds,"* 27; Lassen County, "William Fuller vs. His Creditors, Schedule A"; Lassen County, California, *"Book C of Deeds,"* 192.

9. "Old Lake House Now Only a Reminiscence," *NSJ*, 05/29/1907.

10. Null and Hulbert, "California Washed Away," 26–31; DeLong, "Nevada's Superstorm Scenario," *RGJ*, 12/01/2013; quote from *New York Times*, "The Great Flood in California," 01/21/1862.

11. Twain, *Roughing It*, ch. 30.

12. Twain, *Roughing It*, ch. 31.

13. Quote from "Flood on the Truckee," *TE*, 01/27/1862

14. Territory of Utah, County of Carson, "Petition of C. W. Fuller for Bridge Franchise"; "National Register of Historic Places Inventory—Nomination Form: Virginia Street Bridge."

15. First quote from Townley, *Tough Little Town*, 52; second quote from Lake, "Petition for Divorce"; Basso, *The Works of C. B. McClellan*, "Introduction."

16. Basso, *The Works of C. B. McClellan*, "Introduction"; "Art Notes," *REG*, 07/25/1881; Earl, "C. B.'s Artwork," *Sparks Tribune*, 06/09/1982; interview with Sherlyn Hayes-Zorn, acting director/curator of manuscripts, Nevada Historical Society, Reno, 12/10/2015.

17. "Laws of the Territory of Nevada, Passed at the Second Session of the Legislative Assembly," 19; Jeffrey Kintop, Nevada State Archivist, e-mail to the author, 02/08/2013.

18. Quote from Prouty, "The Development of Reno," 65; "1862 Census of Nevada Territory," Ancestry.com.

19. Prouty, "The Development of Reno," 53–58; Rowley, "Reno's First Robber Baron," 28; Jeffrey Kintop, Nevada State Archivist, e-mail to the author, 02/08/2013.

20. Cafferata, *Lake Mansion*, 30–31.

21. Lake, "Petition for Divorce," quote on p. 18, lns. 14–19; p. 5, lns. 15–17; p. 6, lns. 24–27.

22. Lake, "Petition for Divorce," p. 4, lns. 18–29.

23. Lord, *Comstock Mining and Miners*, 416.

24. Lake, "Petition for Divorce," p. 7, lns. 1–20.

25. Fatout, *Meadow Lake, Gold Town*, first quote from 40; second quote from 53; third quote from 60; Doten, *Journals of Alfred Doten*, 2:55.

26. Bob Ellison, Nevada law enforcement historian, 04/19/2013 correspondence with the author; Zimmer, "Myron Lake Made a Trade and Founded a City," *NSJ*, 11/02/1958.

27. "The Flood on the Truckee," *TE*, 12/28/1867.

28. Kingsbury, "Pioneer Days in Sparks and Vicinity."

29. Zimmer, "Myron Lake Made a Trade," *NSJ*, 11/02/1958; Kingsbury, "Pioneer Days in

Sparks and Vicinity," 339; Lake, "Petition for Divorce," p. 8, lns. 25–30. For Sellers' death, see Kingsbury, "Pioneer Days in Sparks and Vicinity."

30. Zimmer, "Myron Lake Made a Trade," *NSJ*, 11/02/1958.

31. Townley, *Tough Little Town*, 52; Elliott, *History of Nevada*, 112.

32. Trego, "Reno, the Tough Little Town by the Truckee, Got Going All at Once Exactly 86 Years Ago," *NSJ*, 05/09/1954; quote from n.t., *NSJ*, 08/26/1882, p. 2.

33. Townley, *Tough Little Town*, 146; National Park Service, "Washoe County Courthouse"; quote from n.t., *RC*, 01/21/1871.

34. Myrick, *Railroads of Nevada and Eastern California*, 1:13; e-mail from Nevada historical researcher Kim Henrick, 01/17/2016.

35. Henrick, "Elevenses (or Let's Revisit Reno's Past)."

36. "Location of the C.P.R.R.," *Eastern Slope*, 02/29/1868; BLM, "Military Bounty Land Warrant"; Washoe County, *Book 2 of Deeds, Part 1*, filed 06/02/1868, 360–61; Washoe County, *Book 2 of Deeds, Part 2*, filed 12/28/1868, 673–74; Washoe County, *Book 2 of Deeds, Part 2*, filed 05/09/1868, 430–31; "Town of Reno…1868," Map.

37. First quote from Gulling, "An Interview with Amy Gulling," 3; second quote from "Reno's Original Surveyor Here for Short Visit," *REG*, 07/26/1932; "Man Who Aided in First Reno Survey Visitor," *NSJ*, 07/27/1932.

38. Trego, "Reno, the Tough Little Town," *NSJ*, 05/09/1954; "The Development of Reno," Nevada State Historical Society Papers, vol. 4, 1923–24, 99.

39. Townley, *Tough Little Town*, 67, 70; Goodwin, "Wm. C. (Hill) Beachey, Stagecoach King," 33; n.t., *RC*, 05/15/1869.

40. Davis, *History of Nevada*, vol. 2, 1278–79; quote from Bragg, "When Virginia Street Was a Lane," *REG*, 10/30/1914.

41. Townley, *Tough Little Town*, 147; n.t., *RC*, 12/05/1868.

42. Trego, "Reno's First Christmas Was Liquid, Lively and Gay," *NSJ*, 12/23/1971, quoting from n.t., *RC*, 12/26/1868.

# CHAPTER 3

# THE WOODEN BRIDGE GOES PUBLIC

MYRON LAKE, like many successful hotel owners of the day, often leased the Lake House out to other operators and collected his monthly lease fees without having to face the day-to-day challenges that went with running a busy hostelry. When he was running the hotel he and his family usually lived in the hotel owner's apartment, but when it was leased they lived in their small house on Virginia Road just south of the hotel. That was where they were living on December 4, 1868, when the Lake House, cobbled together from parts of Fuller's original hotel—if indeed any parts had survived the 1861–62 flood—and Lake's own expansions and renovations, burned to the ground. Lake's wife Jane happened to be downtown shopping at the time, and when someone rushed into the store with news of the fire, she exclaimed, "Oh, what a terrible loss of life." When asked if the hotel had been full, she answered, "No, but there are lots of bedbugs!" Jane Lake was a meticulous housekeeper, and bedbugs, which were a scourge in most western towns at the time, were her chief nemesis.[1]

Undaunted by the fire, Lake immediately began to rebuild, rehiring J. S. Sellers of Glendale to do the work. Lake's vision for the new hotel was to provide a friendly family resort, in addition to a place where travelers passing through could bunk down for the night. In less than a week a brand new 74-foot by 34-foot, two-and-a-half-story frame structure was rising phoenix-like from the ashes. A fancy bar was added on the first floor and a large ballroom on the second floor. In addition to the communal sleeping quarters under the rafters, the hotel also had twenty-six individual rooms. The entire building cost $23,000 and was open for business less than ninety days after the fire. A newspaper ad proclaimed, "New and Newly Furnished from Cellar to Garret," and described the establishment as "First Class Accommodations." Lake retained a permanent apartment at the hotel, and he was usually on hand to see that the hotel and tavern operated smoothly—and profitably. It was during this period that the hotel began earning the reputation that it would carry for much of the next century as Reno's premier hostelry.[2]

Years later, on May 29, 1907, when the Lake House—by then, the Riverside Hotel—was torn down to be replaced by a grand new hostelry, the *Nevada State Journal* published a retrospective of the hotel and tavern during its earliest days. At this time there were still some old-timers around who could provide firsthand accounts of what the hotel and the community had been like just after Reno was chartered, and their reminiscences are priceless:

> The hotel was even then a rendezvous for the convivialists of Reno. The barroom was added to and was the scene of much revelry and life, typical of the "wild and wooly west." But it was always an orderly house, until the period when the railroad was shooting its gleaming rails into the heart of the town, when the crews would stir things up a bit.
>
> The fame of the house soon began to spread and as the city of Reno grew, Lake found it necessary to enlarge his building. It began to entertain travelers of note. Men whose names have become [familiar] to millions have rested under the rooftop of the old inn. Its registers, if they [existed] today, would be worthy of a great price and much sought after by autograph hunters.... In its parlors have been held secret political caucuses.... Deals involving millions have been [made] within its walls. Crime has stalked through its rooms and halls and their confines have rung with cheers of victory at polls and hurrahs for leaders. When news reached Reno of some important discovery in the state it was in the new spacious barroom of the Lake House that the people would gather to receive and debate the intelligence.[3]

Another story—perhaps true, perhaps fable—told of an event several years earlier when a miracle occurred at the hotel. There was a severe thunderstorm, and suddenly a bolt of lightning struck the building, piercing the roof and hitting the barroom floor beneath. A toddler had been playing on the floor, and the lightning bolt burned a circle around the little girl, but left her completely unharmed, although severely frightened.[4]

As for the Lake's Crossing Bridge, or Virginia Street Bridge, it too would cause Myron Lake a lot of grief, although much of it was due to his own stubbornness and greed. In 1869 he strengthened the bridge by adding some

heavy new timbers, according to the *Reno Crescent* of June 19, 1869. The article added, "A naughty boy suggested that [strengthening the bridge] was
in consideration of the County Commissioners lowering his toll…at their
last meeting." Actually, the real reason for the structural changes was much
more interesting. San Francisco's Bank of California held a virtual monopoly
on the booming Comstock Lode in Virginia City. In the late 1860s bank
leaders added to that stranglehold by beginning construction on the Virginia
& Truckee Railroad, which was designed to carry lumber and supplies to
their Comstock mines, and unprocessed silver and gold ore to their quartz
mills on the Carson River for refining. The Virginia & Truckee tracks had
reached Carson City, where the railroad would be headquartered, and the
first three locomotives, engines number 1, 2, and 3 (the *Lyon*, the *Ormsby*,
and the *Storey*, respectively) had been ordered from the Union Iron Works in
San Francisco. They were to be delivered to Reno via the Central Pacific Railroad, but then had to be hauled by oxen teams on to Carson City. Only one
thing stood in the way of these plans: getting the heavy locomotives from
the Reno depot back across the Truckee River for the last leg of the journey
to Carson City. The plan was to haul them across Myron Lake's bridge, and it
was in anticipation of that project that Lake had been convinced—and undoubtedly paid by the railroad—to strengthen the bridge so it could carry the
heavy load, which it did without incident. As for the *Reno Crescent*'s charge
about having lowered Lake's tolls, it was true the commissioners had done
that a couple of times, despite the fact that he charged nothing to local residents using the bridge. As for the professional teamsters whose business
depended on the bridge for their livelihood, there were few complains about
high tariffs: "We find, on inquiry, that four-fifths of them prefer a toll road,
kept in good condition, to a country road, which will necessarily be more or
less unfit for travel," the *Reno Crescent* noted.[5]

The teamsters weren't the only ones satisfied to pay Lake a toll to cross
his bridge: the express companies were more than anxious to pay liberally
for the privilege of running their horses at full speed across the Truckee
River on the Lake's Crossing Bridge. The companies would pay weekly so
the riders didn't have to slow down to pay as they raced along. Watching the
pony riders gallop pell-mell across the bridge and through the town became
a public spectacle. Large crowds would show up and cheer the riders as they
sped toward Virginia City. One time, as the Pony Express riders raced over
the bridge, two other horses were right behind them, their riders pretending
to be Pony Express in order to avoid having to pay the toll. But the sharp-eyed
Lake wasn't fooled. He dashed from the crowd in front of the two horsemen,

frantically waving his hat for them to stop, but they were going too fast and charged right past him, knocking him down. Lake tumbled to the ground and rolled over several times through the thick dust, shouting obscenities at the trespassers.[6]

Lake could be unrelenting when trying to collect his tolls. On another occasion a farmer tried to cross the river with his team of horses at the natural ford a short distance below the bridge. Lake rushed into the water and caught one of the horses by the bridle, bringing the team to a stop. Undaunted, the farmer laid his whip to the team—and to Lake as well—and Lake had to let go of the bridle as he tumbled into the swiftly moving current. The farmer continued on his way while Lake angrily shook his fist at the scofflaw.[7]

Many of Lake's problems were caused by the fact that people simply didn't like his haughty attitude, and many were jealous of his success as well. Even the Central Pacific people grew angry with him when he donated a choice piece of his property for the site of the Washoe County Courthouse when Reno wrested the privilege of being the county seat away from Washoe City in 1871. Lake had previously promised the railroad that the courthouse would be located next to its depot, but he reneged when he decided instead to place it closer to his hotel, on the south side of the river. He donated one acre of land and $15,000 in cash for construction of the building, plus the promise of planting shade trees around the premises. It was a generous donation, but as always Lake had an ulterior motive. The donated land was part of his Lake Addition—a section of land owned by Myron Lake that was annexed to the town—and he realized the presence of the courthouse would greatly increase the value of all his surrounding land. The following year, in 1871, Lake also purchased a 554-acre farm about five miles south of Reno, on the west side of Virginia Road, where he would farm hay, wheat, oats, potatoes, Indian corn, and vegetables.[8]

Another event in the early 1870s caused Lake a great deal of unrest. The Virginia & Truckee Railroad had completed its Virginia City to Carson City leg, but the bank's chief man in Nevada, William Sharon, had grander plans in mind: he wanted to take the Virginia & Truckee all the way to Reno where it would connect with the transcontinental railroad. Thus in 1870 construction was started on the Virginia & Truckee's Carson City to Reno leg. By early 1872 the tracks had reached Reno and construction began on a railroad bridge across the Truckee River, about a half mile south of Lake's toll bridge, just east of today's Rock Street. It was completed by September. Normally that would not have raised the hackles of the irritable entrepreneur, but when Lake discovered that the bridge would also be available for pedestrian use, he was not the least bit happy. Worse by far was the fact that thousands of visitors who had previously arrived in town in stagecoaches and carriages, and who had to pay a toll to cross the river, would now be arriving on the train with not a single penny going into his pocket. But Lake's problems would get even worse.[9]

In 1873 Lake's ten-year bridge charter was ready to expire. When he asked county commissioners for a new charter, they refused to grant it, declaring that the bridge would henceforth be a free public bridge, and his toll road a public highway. This was not the first time Lake's bridge had been coveted by the public. Just months after the town was established, a petition signed by Reno citizens demanded that the bridge be converted to public use, according to the *Reno Crescent* of August 1, 1868. Nothing had come of that petition, but for this latest threat Lake responded in January by putting a locked gate on the bridge, forcing all the traffic to use another bridge or ford the turbulent river. He also dug a trench around the approaches to the bridge and stationed one of his employees with a gun to guard it. After a week of this standoff, the Evans brothers with a herd of cattle attempted to breach the gate. When Lake resisted he was placed under arrest and fined $20 for obstructing a public highway, although the district court later found him not guilty of the charge. Finally, in May, after Lake unsuccessfully fought the county commissioners' "free public bridge" edict in the lower courts, the Nevada Supreme Court ruled that the bridge was indeed public property. Lake was beaten. This marked the end of the bridge's thirteen years under private ownership, and began the little structure's 141-year tenure under public ownership. Nevadans would never again have to pay a toll to cross the Virginia Street Bridge.[10]

If a public face could be put on Washoe County's campaign to take over the bridge, it would have been that of Thomas K. ("T.K." to his friends) Hymers, the chairman of the Washoe County Commission. Hymers was born in Delaware County in upstate New York in 1834 of immigrant Scottish parents. In 1859 he crossed the plains to California driving a team of horses, and moved to Nevada in April 1860, settling in Galena. In 1868, just months after the town of Reno was established, Hymers, his wife, and their two children moved there, where he co-owned and operated the very successful Truckee Livery, Feed, and Stable for many years. Extremely active in Republican politics, Hymers served on the Washoe County Commission off and on for more than thirty-five years beginning in 1870, frequently serving as chairman of the group. He also served one term as Reno mayor. He was an active Mason in Reno, a member of the Board of Trustees and chief engineer of the Reno volunteer fire department, and a long-serving director of the Nevada State Agriculture Committee. But it was in his role as chairman of the County Commission in 1873 that he led the effort to wrest the Lake's Crossing Bridge from Myron Lake and make it a public structure.[11]

Once the wooden bridge was in the commissioners' hands, local citizens, the local press, and visitors who regularly used the bridge began to harangue county officials. The bridge was seven years old, it was heavily trafficked, and it was showing wear and tear. It was too narrow, for one thing, and it was getting shakier by the day. The only other bridge across the river between Hunter's Crossing (later Mayberry Crossing) and Glendale's Stone & Gates bridge—a distance of about eight miles—was the Virginia & Truckee Railroad bridge. Although pedestrians could use it, they had to be extremely cautious and stone-cold sober in order to hopscotch across it safely. Commissioners, in response to the complaints, limited the wooden bridge to only twenty-five cattle on the span at one time, and they had to be walked across slowly. Then in September the commissioners passed an ordinance that anyone crossing the bridge by foot or on horseback had to walk rather than run or canter across. In the fall of 1875 a grand jury finally demanded that commissioners do something about the bridge.[12]

Once their hand was forced, commissioners decided the old wooden bridge should be replaced, but still they dithered. In July 1876 the *Reno Evening Gazette* rebuked commissioners, writing, "To-day a ten-horse team, loaded with grain, passed over the old bridge, and the way it creaked and swayed about, was a warning to the county fathers that they have a duty to perform."[13] Finally, in 1877 chairman T. K. Hymers and the county commissioners were authorized by the state legislature to issue $16,000 in bonds for the construction of a new bridge. Most of the bonds would be purchased by the Washoe County Bank. Legislation called for the new bridge to be wide enough for two wagons to pass each other on the carriageway, with planked sidewalks on each side, separated from the carriageways by substantial railings. Bids were solicited, and the firm of King & Wheelock of Des Moines, Iowa, was granted a $15,700 contract, to be paid in gold coins, to build the 190-foot bridge as a preconstructed iron span featuring a "King's Patent Arch." To save $300 commissioners decided to use local pine rather than the superior Oregon pine for the bridge's roadbed, a decision that would be regretted years later. Representatives of King & Wheelock took a room at the

Lake House and set up a model of the proposed bridge in the hotel for public inspection; and T. K. Hymers traveled to California to inspect some of that state's iron trestle spans.[14]

In April, teamsters hired by King & Wheelock began hauling rock from a quarry near Virginia City to the bridge site, and masons of the Gill & Madden Company of Reno began constructing the huge stone abutments that would support each end of the bridge. By late May a temporary wooden bridge had been installed and carpenters began dismantling Myron Lake's 1867 wooden bridge. After inspecting the old bridge, the job foreman told the *Reno Evening Gazette*, "The timbers of the old bridge are being removed today. The soundness of these timbers, after they have so long withstood the weather changes incident to this State, is remarkable." In fact, the timbers were in such good condition that most of them were donated to ranchers who reused them to build a bridge on the Glendale–Huffaker Road, at a spot southeast of Reno known as Boynton Slough where the road had been virtually impassable for years.[15]

The new iron structure would be the fourth bridge crossing the Truckee River at this site, and it would mark the beginning of the end of the Truckee Meadows' historic wooden bridges, although the roadbed of the new bridge would be constructed of four-inch-thick local pine. On May 26 Chairman Hymers received a letter from King & Wheelock stating that all the bridge elements had been built, assembled, and checked for accuracy in Cleveland, and that the bridge was now ready to be disassembled and shipped by rail to Reno. The stone abutments that would support the span at each end were still under construction, but they would be ready when the iron bridge arrived. On July 1 five Central Pacific Railroad flat cars arrived in Reno with the 105,965-pound bridgework, at a freight cost of $3,408.79, and the work of reassembling it began.[16]

Once the bridge was completed, and to the surprise and chagrin of many Renoites, it veered a few degrees to the left after it crossed over the Scott Ranch irrigation ditch, left Virginia Street, and crossed the river, then veered back by an equal distance to the right on the other side of the river, creating a slight skew in the roadway. The *Reno Evening Gazette* wrote, "Much criticism is…justly passed on the action of the Commissioners in having the bridge set 'cat-a-cornered' across the river. The north end of the bridge should have extended at least six feet further down the stream than its present position." The *Nevada State Journal* also chipped in with a tongue-in-cheek comment, laying blame for the crooked bridge directly on Chairman Hymers: "It [the bridge] has only one fault; it stands at an angle to the street. This is entirely due to the crookedsightedness of our worthy county father…Thomas K. Hymers. Tom has a bad habit when playing poker of twisting his head and looking into his neighbor's hand. A long practice of this has ruined his eyesight entirely, and therefore the defect in the bridge." Counting the stone abutments, the slight skew in the bridge, and the approaches, the total span was 240 feet.[17]

The truth is that the skew in the roadway where it crossed the bridge had likely existed since at least 1862, and possibly even earlier. The original 1868 plat map of the town of Reno clearly shows the skew. And the McClellan oil painting of Lake's Crossing from 1862, discussed in chapter 2, appears to indicate that if the line of the roadway crossing the bridge from north to south had followed a straight line, it would have cut right through the front end of Lake's hotel. So the skew was also there in 1862.

It is most likely that C. W. Fuller actually built in the skew himself. He had built the hotel first, then he built the road, and finally the bridge. It's probable that in building the road he had had to move it a little off center on one side of the river or the other—or perhaps on both sides—in order to find the most suitable spots to anchor the bridge to the ground. Huge boulders, underground rocks—any number of things could have forced Fuller to stray from a straight course for the road and the bridge that crossed it. The concrete Virginia Street Bridge built in 1905 has the same skew, but the long-anticipated Virginia Street Bridge being built in 2015–16 will finally eliminate, or at least minimize, the skew, straightening the roadway, according to engineers. But despite the 1877 anomaly, and reflecting the opinion of most people in the community at the time, the *Reno Evening Gazette* lauded the new bridge, writing, "The bridge is very light in appearance…giving it a very cheerful and airy appearance."[18]

When the bridge was finished, a test was scheduled to see if it was up to the task. However, the day before the scheduled test an uninvited out-of-towner happened upon the bridge, and the newspaper reported what occurred: "About 11 o'clock to-day nearly half of the male population of Reno turned out to see Geo. Elder's…10-mule team cross the new bridge. Three large wagons were heavily loaded with barley and the whole drawn by sixteen fine mules…. The total weight of the team…amounted to 72,000 pounds…. Half way across and the bridge scarcely moved."[19]

The following day, during the official test, the bridge again proved its merit: "That band of cattle, 180 strong…were driven across the new bridge… [and] developed the fact that the bridge will hold all the cattle that can get on it." The iron bridge had passed both tests with flying colors, and it would

Myron Lake's brand new hotel, renamed the Lake House after the hotel was destroyed by fire in 1868, was the pride of early Reno. Here, a decade or so later, the hotel and the Virginia Street Bridge, built in 1877, sit cozily side by side as they would for more than 150 years. Special Collections Department, University of Nevada, Reno Libraries.

change little over the next quarter-century. One small safety measure, however, was added in 1880: the embankments leading to the northern end of the bridge were fenced in. It seems that a number of riders, after spending an evening bending their elbows at the Virginia Street bars, would topple off the road alongside the river, horse and rider tumbling pell-mell into the rushing waters below. The fence stopped all that.[20]

Years later, a Reno old-timer said it was actually he and Myron Lake who had taken the first trip over the new structure, not George Elder and his wagonloads of barley. Del Overton, then a Sierra Valley farmer, said that at the time the bridge opened he had been the driver of the Lake House horse-powered bus that ferried visitors from the railroad depot to the hotel. He said he and Lake, with the cheers of an assembled crowd ringing in their ears, had driven across the bridge before anyone else had. Stranger things have happened, so it could be true, and Myron Lake was perhaps entitled to this one small victory.[21]

In 1875, while county commissioners were still dithering about building the new iron bridge, Myron Lake had leased out the Lake House to another operator. The new proprietor was Colonel Horace M. Vesey, a native Vermonter who had previously operated both the Vesey House in Virginia City and the Glenbrook House on Lake Tahoe. Vesey immediately "repainted and refitted" the hotel, and soon had the building in "apple pie order," according to the newspaper. Sadly, the sixty-one-year-old Colonel Vesey died less than three months later, and the hotel business was taken over by his son, Edwin A. Vesey.[22]

Young Vesey, who had trained under this father, proved to be an excellent proprietor. About a year after he took charge of the Lake House, a New York writer headed west to report on the changes that had occurred since the opening of the transcontinental railroad. He was amazed at what he saw, and he wrote one of the earliest coast-to-coast guidebooks on his travels. Entering Reno less than a decade after its founding, the writer was impressed with the growth of the little town on the Truckee River:

> Reno—is 293 miles from San Francisco, situated in the Truckee Meadows, the junction of the Virginia & Truckee Railroad, the first point reached from which there are two daily passenger trains to San Francisco, and the best point of departure for tourists going west to visit Lake Tahoe.

The numerous boulders which...strew the meadows, are built into fences, and alfalfa seed sown after digging out the sage brush, and rich pasturage results on which sheep thrive.

Reno has an altitude of 4,507 feet, and although a railroad town only a few years old, is destined to be the prominent city of the State. It...has now 2,000 people and is a county-seat with a $30,000 court-house.... It has five churches...and ground will soon be broken here for the erection of a Young Ladies' Seminary.... Here are the grounds of the State Agricultural Society and the finest speed-track in the State, two banks, one newspaper...and several factories, a steam fire department and a public library.

There are two Hotels, the Railroad House, which is well kept, and the Lake House, on the bank of the Truckee River, a most desirable place for a few days' rest.[23]

At about the same time the New York writer visited the city, Edwin Vesey ran an ad in the newspaper touting all the advantages of the Lake House: "Comfortable Rooms and the Best of Board.... A Good Stable with Best Feed for Horses.... Finest Brands of Wines, Liquors and Cigars.... Free Billiard Table and every appliance to insure comfort of guests."[24]

On Sunday, March 2, 1879, a devastating fire swept through downtown Reno and the adjacent residential areas. "Fifty Acres of Business Houses Destroyed!," the newspaper lamented, adding that there were five deaths and over 100 residential houses lost in the intense blaze that was centered on the north side of the river on Virginia Street, Commercial Row, and Second Street. Fortunately the Lake House, located across the river, was untouched, but Myron Lake lost six other commercial buildings valued at more than $12,500. Many of the Lake House's competitors were destroyed or damaged, including the Depot Hotel, Railroad House, Granger House, Pollard House, and Shaw Hotel. Both the Central Pacific and Virginia & Truckee Railroads also suffered extensive damage, both concerns losing their ticket offices, freight houses, baggage houses, a number of railroad coaches, and even some track.[25]

During the fire, Lake House proprietor Edwin Vesey proved to be a hero. The entire time the volunteer fire department was fighting the huge blaze, Vesey opened the hotel dining room and fed the firefighters in small groups so they could maintain their strength through the ordeal. He also fed local citizens who had lost their homes, and even his business rivals whose own hotels had been lost. He dispatched his carriages to the railroad depot and brought the passengers to the Lake House to be fed and housed, as space allowed. All of this Vesey did without charge, endearing him and the hotel to the local populace.[26]

Although the Lake House continued to do well as the city recovered from the holocaust, and Myron Lake's wealth was largely unaffected by his loss of the toll bridge and commercial buildings, his personal life was in shambles. His oldest stepdaughter, Florence, had married the prominent Nevada state senator William Thompson, a rancher from Franktown, and in 1875 Myron and Jane Lake had had their only child together, Charles "Charlie" Junior. In 1879 the couple purchased from the Marsh family a house at 469 Virginia Street, and moved into it; the Italianate style house with many Georgian features would eventually become known as the Lake Mansion, which exists to this day. But despite all these signs of domestic bliss, Lake's marriage was deeply troubled. He mentally and physically abused Jane, and had even threatened to kill her on at least one occasion. In fact, his purchase of the Virginia Street mansion was done primarily to make amends. But she had finally had enough, and on December 13, 1879, she filed for divorce.[27]

The divorce trial and the ensuing battle over Lake's extensive wealth was acrimonious; and testimony at trial about Lake's abuse of his wife further blackened his already shoddy reputation. It took two years and a Nevada Supreme Court trial before the mess was untangled, but Myron came through the debacle surprisingly well, keeping title to all of his property, although Jane was awarded $250 a month in alimony and full custody of Charles Junior. In the property settlement filings, the Lake House and its furnishings, the adjoining barn and stables, and the land they all sat on was valued at $15,000 ($340,000 in today's dollars), a significant sum for the times. Although Myron Lake was smugly satisfied at the outcome of the trial, in truth, the battle for his wealth was far from finished.[28]

Myron Lake remarried in 1883, after arranging a very unromantic (for the times) prenuptial agreement, but on June 4, 1884, the widely despised entrepreneur died at his home of a coughing fit brought about by severe asthma. Few people in the city he had founded mourned his passing. His last will was legally voided, and a number of confusing court trials followed. Eventually, Lake's third wife sold her interest in the estate to Jane Lake for $15,000, and William Thompson, Florence's husband, was given the title to the Lake House in return for a judgment he held against the estate. Other real and personal property was granted to Jane Lake in trust for their son Charlie, along with a modest sum for child support. When the estate was finally settled, Lake's only child, Charlie, received "all the [remaining] property of every nature and kind," with the stipulation that he would not receive the inheritance until he turned twenty-one, and could not sell any of the property until he turned twenty-seven. The only exception to this was to be the home that became known as the Lake Mansion, which his widow Jane received.[29]

Myron Lake was never a popular man during his lifetime, due primarily to his selfish, arrogant nature. However, he harbored one secret that, if ever discovered, would have cast an even darker shadow on the man. His reputation as a veteran of the Mexican-American War, fighting unselfishly for his country, was one of the few positive things most folks knew about Lake. One of his obituaries summed up his service, writing, "His boyhood days were spent in farming near his birthplace until the breaking out of the Mexican war, when he joined the Fifth Illinois Volunteers and served throughout the campaign." Even his family believed that story. His granddaughter, Amy Thompson Gulling, in an interview years later, said, "Mr. Myron Lake was a veteran of the Mexican War. He became acquainted with grandmother and they were married...that must have been September, 1864." But Lake's war service was a lie, one that he kept hidden throughout his lifetime.[30]

Here's what really happened, published here for the first time. On May 11, 1846, Congress had passed an act declaring that a state of war existed between the United States and Mexico. The act also authorized the president to raise 50,000 volunteers; and Illinois—where Myron Lake lived at the time—was called upon for three regiments of infantry or riflemen to fill its quota. By July, Illinois had met the quota, and had even volunteered a fourth regiment, and all the men had been mustered into service. The Illinois volunteers served admirably during the war. The first and second regiments served heroically in the critical Battle of Buena Vista, and the third and fourth regiments in the Battle of Cerro Gordo. Around 2,200 men from Illinois served bravely during the Mexican-American War, and 151 of these men paid the ultimate price for their service. Myron Lake was not among either group.[31]

Fighting in the war ended with the Unites States' capture of Mexico City in mid-September 1847, and the war officially ended on February 2, 1848, when Mexico signed the Treaty of Guadalupe Hidalgo. The war was heavily politicized in the United States; thus it would be many months before the

U.S. Senate ratified the peace treaty. During that span of time, in early February 1848, the president was empowered to call up more troops, even though the fighting had ended and the war was over. On February 6, 1848, at Ottawa, LaSalle County, in north-central Illinois near his farm, Myron Lake enrolled as a private in Company D, Fifth Regiment of the Illinois Volunteers. Since the war was over by then, Lake and the Fifth Regiment never saw any action, and Lake and most of the others were mustered out a few months later. However, as a volunteer—even though the war had ended—Lake still qualified to file for a free land warrant, which he promptly did, a 160-acre plot at Dixon Mills, Illinois. It certainly leaves one to question the sincerity of Myron Lake's motivation, his courage, his patriotism, and his honesty.[32]

Immediately upon taking charge of the Lake House, William Thompson, an astute businessman—and no fan of his father-in-law, Myron Lake—changed the name of the hotel to the Riverside Hotel. He hired W. R. Chamberlain, who had served as proprietor of the competing Depot Hotel for the past seventeen years, to be the new manager.[33]

Thompson gave Chamberlain carte blanche to rehabilitate the entire property. On the grounds a stone walk was installed along the riverfront and a dancing pavilion was built in the grove of trees adjoining the hotel. Inside the building, remodeling and renovation was extensive. When the hotel was ready to be introduced to the community, a newspaper reporter penned an essay of flowering prose in honor of the new establishment:

> Every nook, cranny and corner of the large establishment has received due attention, every bed in the house made over, new carpets and furniture placed in every room, and the walls of each peppered in the most beautiful and durable designs. The work of improvement has been impartial and the sleeping apartments in the third story are as pleasant and inviting as those on the second floor.... Bath and patent closets are conveniently located on every floor.... The rooms are so arranged that guests can...view unexcelled...the swift-flowing Truckee, aligned by innumerable ranches which dot the meadows for miles, the whole bordered, as if by a frame, by the lofty mountains which fringe the valley on every side.
>
> On the first floor is located the reception parlor, bar, reading room, dining room and the culinary department, the latter being presided over by that prince of cooks, Charley Legate, the mere mention

of whose name is sufficient to vouch for the excellence of the fare provided for the guests. The dining room...is 46 x 18 feet in dimensions and has a seating capacity of sixty persons. It extends the whole length of the main annex to the hotel proper, opening on the south into the magnificent orchard and gardens...while on the north the Truckee can be seen flowing tranquilly....

The reading room is located on the north side of the ground floor.... Periodicals and papers will be supplied in abundance and scores of easy chairs will invite the weary and indolent.[34]

The renovations came at a very good time, as competition was increasing for the hotel that was once the only lodging house in the area. It catered to visitors, but also housed a number of local residents in its apartments. With the establishment of the town, and the growing traffic the bridge was experiencing, there were ten hotels along with six restaurants in Reno by 1885; by the beginning of the next decade, the annual Nevada State Fair, a new first-class racetrack and grandstand, and a fine opera house were also greeting visitors to Reno.[35]

On the day after Christmas in 1889, the *Reno Evening Gazette* recognized the stature the Riverside Hotel had gained under Thompson's ownership, writing, "Those who have stopped off at the Riverside Hotel do not need to be informed that it is the finest family resort on this side of the mountains."[36]

For years, large, rumbling herds of cattle and sheep had shared the iron bridge with pedestrians, horse-drawn carriages, and huge oxen- and mule-team freight wagons. But in 1886 plans arose for building a cattle bridge that would provide the herds with their very own crossing over the Truckee River. By August of 1886 plans had been approved, and by 1887 the bridge was completed. It crossed the river east of town, at Park Street, today just west of Wells Avenue. In 1915, after years of hard wear, the old cattle bridge would be torn down and a new one built. A poignant little passage in the newspaper some years later described this out-with-the-old-and-in-with-the-new culture of the growing community: "Where the emigrants drove their ox teams down to Lake's Crossing, the trolley car now speeds, and the lowing of the patient beasts that drew civilization to the westward is replaced by the angry clang of the street car bell."[37]

More than three-quarters of a century after the iron bridge was completed, a University of Nevada professor emeritus of civil engineering, Horace Boardman, wrote an article for the newspaper describing how unusual the 1877 iron bridge was for its time. He pointed out that modern metal bridges are built of steel, but the Virginia Street Bridge was built of iron. Coincidentally, the country's first steel bridge was under construction over the Missouri River at the same time the iron bridge was being built over the Truckee River. The interesting thing about the iron bridge from an engineering standpoint, Boardman wrote, was that it was a very unusual parabolic bowstring truss bridge. The arched iron spans on top were connected to the horizontal iron spans on the bottom by evenly spaced vertical rods. That tended to uniformly distribute the weight of the load on the bridge over the entire length of the roadbed, which was perfect for a herd of cattle or a large flock of sheep passing over the length of the bridge. Another advantage, according to the professor, was that the design was such that the bridge merely rested on the stone abutments at each end, instead of pushing against them as would have been the case with a true arch bridge. Professor Boardman remarked, "For many years I took my classes of structural engineering students...down to inspect the novel and rather unusual bridge at Rock Street where the iron bridge would be relocated when the new concrete bridge was built in 1905. Probably very few, if any, parabolic bowstring bridges have been built in the United States since the year 1890."[38]

## NOTES

1. Townley, *Tough Little Town*, 148; quote from Gulling, "An Interview with Amy Gulling," 6.

2. Townley, *Tough Little Town*, 148; n.t., *RC*, 12/05/1868; Hardesty, "The Site of Reno's Beginning," 22.

3. "Old Lake House Now Only a Reminiscence," *NSJ*, 05/29/1907.

4. "Old Lake House Now Only a Reminiscence," *NSJ*, 05/29/1907.

5. Quote from n.t., *RC*, 01/21/1871; Sampson, "Memoirs of a Canadian Army Officer," 67–68.

6. "Memories of Old Bridge," *NSJ*, 11/25/1905.

7. "Memories of Old Bridge," *NSJ*, 11/25/1905.

8. Hardesty, "The Site of Reno's Beginning," 8; "The Development of Reno," Nevada State Historical Society Papers, vol. 4, 1923–24, 114; "Pen and Scissors" column, *TE*, 08/01/1871.

9. "The Virginia & Truckee Railroad," *NSJ*, 09/16/1871; Trego, "Old Span Was Second That Had Stood There," *NSJ*, 08/12/1951.

10. n.t., *RC*, 01/23/1873, 01/30/1873; n.t., *NSJ*, 01/25/1873; n.t., 02/01/1873; n.t., *NSJ*, 02/08/1873; n.t., *NSJ*, 05/08/1873; Hardesty, "The Site of Reno's Beginning," 8; Townley, *Tough Little Town*, 147; McDonald, *History of Washoe County*, n.p.

11. U.S. Census, 1880, https://Familysearch.org; "Mr. Thomas K. Hymers," *NSJ*, 01/04/1873; "Eventful Life of Pioneer Has Closed," *NSJ*, 02/27/1909; Peckham, "Reminiscences of an Active Life," 14, 49; "Laying the Cornerstone," *REG*, 10/04/1879; "Thos. J. Hymers Placed Under Arrest," *NSJ*, 08/20/1903."

12. "Reno's Iron Bridge of 1877," *NSJ*, 08/08/1954.

13. "That Bridge," *REG*, 07/20/1876.

14. Statutes of Nevada 1877, ch. XXIX, pp. 71–72; Angel, *History of Nevada*, 627–28; "The New Bridge," *REG*, 07/31/1877; "Our Bridge," *REG*, 04/06/1877.

15. "The Masonry," *REG*, 06/12/1877; "Bridge," *REG*, 04/06/1877; "The Timbers," *REG*, 06/29/1877.

16. "Our New Bridge," *NSJ*, 05/27/1877; "The Masonry," *REG*, 06/12/1877; "Iron Bridge," *REG*, 07/02/1877.

17. First quote from "Bridge Comments," *REG*, 07/11/1877; Townley, *Tough Little Town*, 85–86; "The New Bridge," *REG*, 07/31/1877; second quote from n.t., *NSJ*, n.d.

18. Bryan Gant, transportation program manager, Jacobs Engineering Group, private correspondence with the author; quote from "The New Bridge," *REG*, 07/31/1877.

19. Quote from "First Test of the New Bridge," *REG*, 08/01/1877.

20. Quote from "First Test of the New Bridge," *REG*, 08/01/1877; "Stood the Test," *NSJ*, 08/07/1877; "The Embankments Leading," *REG*, 05/10/1880.

21. "First Man to Cross Bridge," *NSJ*, 08/19/1905.

22. Quotes from "Special Notices: LAKE HOUSE," *NSJ*, 12/21/1875; "Letters from Glenbrook," *NSJ*, 05/14/1873; "Death of Colonel Vesey," *NSJ*, 03/21/1876.

23. Williams, *The Pacific Tourist*, 205–7.

24. Adv., "Lake House," *NSJ*, 04/15/1877.

25. "Reno's Ruin," *REG*, 03/03/1879.

26. "A Good Hotel," *REG*, 03/17/1879.

27. Hardesty, "The Site of Reno's Beginning," 9; Cafferata, *Lake Mansion*, 32, 25–26.

28. Cafferata, *Lake Mansion*, 26–27, 32–33; Lake, "Petition for Divorce," 13.

29. "A Pioneer at Rest," *NSJ*, 06/21/1884; quote from "Lake's Will," *NSJ*, 06/24/1884; "M. C. Lake's Will," *REG*, 12/23/1884; Lake, "Petition for Divorce," 34–35.

30. First quote from "An Old Settler Gone," *REG*, 06/26/1884; second quote from Gulling, "An Interview with Amy Gulling," 2.

31. Merry, *A Country of Vast Designs*, 245; Fisher, "Mexican War."

32. Merry, *A Country of Vast Designs*, 426, 428, 434; Elliott, "Record of the Services of Illinois in the Black Hawk War," 215; n.t., *NSJ*, 07/14/1888; BLM, "Military Bounty Land Warrant," 1032:116.

33. "The Riverside," *REG*, 07/06/1888.

34. "The Riverside," *REG*, 07/06/1888.

35. "The Old Lake House," *REG*, 06/05/1888; Hummel, *General History and Resources*, 36; "To-Day's Race," *REG*, 09/22/1891; "Opera House," *REG*, 09/22/1891.

36. n.t., *REG*, 12/26/1889.

37. "Jottings," *REG*, 08/15/1886; n.t., *REG*, 08/11/1915; quote from "Another Landmark Doomed," *NSJ*, 01/07/1905.

38. "Engineering Expert Points Out Why Reno's 'Iron Bridge' Was Unusual," *NSJ*, 08/15/1954.

CHAPTER 4

# BRIDGING TWO CENTURIES

THE FINAL DECADE of the nineteenth century would be noteworthy for both the Riverside Hotel and the Virginia Street Bridge. Had it been human, the bridge would likely have suffered an identity crisis. Long after Myron Lake bought it from C. W. Fuller, local folks, and even the local newspapers, still called it "Fuller's Bridge" or "Fuller's Crossing Bridge," a fact that would have been a constant irritant to the prideful Myron Lake. Not too long after folks finally got it right—Lake's Crossing Bridge—the town fathers took it away from Lake and rebuilt it. For the next decade or so it was simply referred to as "the iron bridge." Finally, in the late 1880s folks occasionally started calling it the Virginia Street Bridge, the name that would stick to the historic structure for at least the next 125 years.

Regardless of what the bridge was called, shortly after midnight on Friday, September 18, 1891, it was the scene of one of the most lawless and grisly events in Reno history. The town had been in a festive mood that day; the eighth annual State Fair was due to open the following Monday, and the whole town was awash with an air of gaiety. A man known in Reno as Louis Ortiz (real name, Louis Bravo), twenty-seven years old, had just arrived back in town that day after a judge had banished him a month earlier for assault and battery on a fellow citizen. Upon his return Ortiz had immediately headed for the bar at the O'Keefe brothers' Grand Central Hotel on Plaza at Virginia Street where he spent the evening sharing libations with other bar-room habitués. The Grand Central Hotel was certainly not a genteel place; in fact, the O'Keefe brothers themselves were said to have taken a few potshots at one another on more than one occasion, and it was often said that there was always a fight by 4 PM at the Grand Central. Dan O'Keefe began to close the bar at midnight, and he asked all the customers to leave. A few stragglers, including a very intoxicated Ortiz, headed to the front porch to finish their beverages. But as soon as he reached the porch, and without warning, Ortiz pulled out a revolver and fired a shot that struck one of the other men in the buttocks. When he was challenged, according to the local newspaper, which allowed no profanity in the day, Ortiz yelled, "I want to kill some s__ of [a] b____," and he fired again. The second bullet went through the coattails of a nearby man and then struck sheriff's officer Richard Nash, who was hurrying to the scene to quell the problem, in the groin area. Despite his injury, Nash and a few of the other men finally subdued Ortiz and dragged him to the jail.[1]

Nash was a very popular peace officer in Reno, and he was certainly worth every penny of the $13-a-month salary he was paid. He had come to town in the 1870s and had been connected with the police force ever since; he had even run unsuccessfully for sheriff five or six years earlier. "There are no better officers than Dick Nash," the newspaper wrote. "He is strictly temperate in all his habits and in every respect a model man.... [He] is fearless as a lion...but last night the drunken brute he was trying to arrest came near getting him." Ortiz, meanwhile, talked to the same reporter the next morning at the jail and said, "I don't know what I did.... I was drunk yesterday all day and I don't know nothing.... I don't know why I was arrested."[2]

That night, according to the newspaper, "Prominent citizens were missed from their usual haunts and the town was quiet as a grave.... At 11:45 a hundred or more men were seen coming down First Street." It was a vigilante mob. The men were all masked, and they ordered people off the street as they passed by, most folks hurriedly scuttling out of the way. Across the iron bridge they marched, and headed for the courthouse where the jail was located. When the group arrived, a number of the men held the deputy at bay with revolvers, took the cell keys from his pocket, pulled Ortiz out of the cell and led him back to the iron bridge. Ortiz, sensing his fate, asked for a glass of water and a priest. He was given the water, along with a flask of whiskey that he gulped down quickly, but there was no priest offered. The mob put a rope around Ortiz's neck and began to throw it over one of the bridge's outside arches, but some in the group pointed out that if the rope broke the victim would fall in the water. So the rope was pulled down and thrown over the crown of the arch in the middle of the bridge. "At the command of 'Haul away' he was soon suspended between heaven and earth," the newspaper reported. As quickly as they had come, the vigilantes quietly dispersed and returned to their homes, leaving Ortiz dangling high overhead in the middle of the Virginia Street Bridge. The headline in one of the newspapers reflected the feelings of many in the town:

ORTIZ HUNG!
The County and Town Well
Rid of a Worthless Vagabond.
The Man Who Was So Handy With His
Gun Departs This Life at the
End of a Rope.[3]

A coroner's inquest was held the following day, and it quickly found "that the deceased came to his death at the hands of parties to the jury unknown." And that was the end of it. No one was ever brought to justice for the lynching. Officer Nash's wound was serious, but not fatal. A month later the town commissioners granted him a bonus of $150 for his exemplary service in the capture of Louis Ortiz. More than a half-century later a Reno old-timer, Mrs. John T. Read, reminisced about this example of frontier justice: "I did not see him up there," she recalled, referring to the hanged man, "but only because I was too young.... On the way to school the following day, though, all of us went past the bridge to stare at the scene."[4]

As is often the case, some good did eventually come out of the Ortiz hanging. Reno town fathers were disturbed by the vigilante action, fearful it would give the town a black eye and perhaps even hurt their chances for eventual cityhood. So an effort was unofficially launched to publicize the activities of another group of local young men, Company C of the Nevada State Militia, more commonly known as the Reno Guards. The group, which had been in existence since the early 1880s, was given uniforms, praised often in the local press, and encouraged to participate in every local holiday celebration, shooting matches, parades, and drill exhibitions. Eventually, in 1891, the state formally recognized October 31 as Admissions Day, the forerunner of today's Nevada Day celebration. "[This] of all days in the year is the young men's day," the Reno newspaper proudly proclaimed. "If taken in hand by the young men, with proper support from the citizens, the celebration will be one that will reflect credit upon the young men of Reno."[5] In short order the local populace was paying tribute to their Reno Guards, and the story of Luis Ortiz and the vigilantes was quickly forgotten.

The bridge was also recognized by local folks in the late nineteenth century for another sordid reason. The area's original settlers, the Washoe Indian tribe, were never integrated into the community; they were still looked upon by many as indolent savages, and were not welcome in most stores and homes in Reno. In 1904, in one of the earliest books on Nevada history, edited by former judge Thomas Wren, he remarked that the bridge served another

Drunken gunslinger Louis Ortiz is depicted hanging from the uppermost supports of the iron bridge in this 1891 drawing that appeared in the *Reno Evening Gazette & Stockman*. Ortiz's hanging was a classic example of Old West justice in the raucous railroad town. From *Reno Evening Gazette & Stockman*, 09/24/1891.

important function: "Even above drinking the Indian likes gambling. They are inveterate poker players, and the bridge, or rather under it, at Reno, is known as the 'Indian Monte Carlo.' Male and female alike play, and no small sums are wagered and lost. The Indians always have plenty of money."[6]

The year 1891 also had its prouder moments. The late nineteenth century was a time when many western cities were attempting to attract tourists to the health benefits in their areas. Spring water, mineral springs, salt baths, and a number of other natural cure-alls were being touted from California to Montana to New Mexico. William Thompson, a man who was always on the lookout for a way to keep the Riverside Hotel's business humming, led an effort to promote the health benefits of Reno to tourists. Local business owners formed the Western Nevada Improvement Association to promote the area. A large, colorful brochure was produced promoting Reno as "Nature's Sanitarium," inviting travelers to enjoy all the health benefits Reno could provide. With the help of C. C. (Christopher Columbus) Powning, the owner and editor of the *Nevada State Journal* and one of the town's leading men (Powning would sell the newspaper that year), Thompson spearheaded the construction of a road that would carry prospective tourists directly to Reno from Lake Tahoe and that would, the two men envisioned, tempt San Francisco tourists to venture on to their town.[7]

The newspaper also published a special edition alerting both locals and visitors to what a grand place Reno had become. "The Asthmatic's Haven of Rest" and "A Climate Favorable for Every Form of Invalidism," the paper touted. Pure air, good water, a moderate range of temperatures, and abundant thermal springs were all waiting for tourists to discover. Of course there were also excellent hotels—the Riverside foremost among them—along with marvelous health resorts and high-quality restaurants awaiting discriminating visitors.[8]

The Riverside Hotel's unparalleled location, and promotional programs like this one, kept its rooms and restaurants full most of the time. A few years earlier William Thompson had even struck a deal with town commissioners for the hotel to feed all the prisoners housed at the nearby jail for 50 cents per head per day, an arrangement that would eventually hit a snag. In early 1894 the Toronto Restaurant underbid the Riverside and took the business away from its larger neighbor. However, that didn't last long. In short order the prisoners got fed up with the Toronto's food, and almost staged a riot. They kicked the bottom out of the coffee pot, broke all the dishes, and emptied out all the canned food, then left the following note for the beleaguered person who delivered the food: "This is only a sample of your cans. We want sugar in our tea and coffee; milk, and grub that is fit to eat. We want enough to eat. We want you to understand this or we will break every can you send in here. [Signed] Prisoners. P.S. Send pie sometimes." The contract was soon returned to the Riverside Hotel.[9]

As his business increased, Thompson began to develop plans to tear down the old wooden building and replace it with a grand new brick structure. The first evidence of this plan came at a Reno commissioners' meeting in February 1891, where discussion focused on the possibility of purchasing some sites in the town for public parks. Commissioner R. L. Foley told the others that William Thompson had assured him that if a large parcel of

Thompson's land nearby to the Riverside was bought and turned into a park, Thompson would build a large new hotel to replace the existing twenty-four-year-old wooden structure.[10]

Thompson had the newspaper publish a rendering of his proposed hotel. It was enormous, in many ways resembling a medieval European castle, and it created quite a stir in Reno. The following year the newspaper reported, "It is now almost an established fact that the new $100,000 Riverside Hotel will be built. Mr. Thompson has succeeded in placing a large portion of that amount, and it is said the work will be commenced upon it in a short time." Succeeding reports announced that the new hotel would be built in the rear of the present structure to allow for a large open lawn on the riverfront; and that an architect, Mr. Brown from San Francisco, had been hired to draw up architectural plans for the new hotel. Thompson had supposedly even formed a new corporation, the Riverside Hotel Company, capitalized at $70,000, to move the project forward, according to an article in the *Nevada State Journal*. Four well-known Renoites were brought into the new company, including Francis Newlands and M. D. Foley. The article declared that the articles of incorporation had already been filed with the Washoe County Clerk; however, the Nevada secretary of state's "Records of Incorporations" for the period make no mention of this entity having been registered prior to 1905, which leaves us with a puzzling contradiction. Finally, another newspaper article in early 1893 again excited Renoites when it announced, "Work on the new Riverside Hotel will be commenced in April." But still nothing happened, although it may have been financial concerns that caused Thompson's inactivity. The Comstock was in the midst of a twenty-year decline, and the nationwide financial panic, or depression, from 1893 to 1898 crippled much of the U. S. economy.[11]

It had also become apparent that Thompson's ardor as an innkeeper was cooling. His manager, W. R. Chamberlain, had retired a few years earlier due to failing health, and Thompson had since been operating the hotel himself. He had already been quite busy as a business executive, politician, and rancher, and perhaps the hotel was becoming too much for him. He had leased the hotel's successful livery stables to another man, and he had tried unsuccessfully to sell the hotel to a local business owner, M. D. Foley, but that deal fell through when there was a disagreement over how much of Thompson's adjacent property would be included in the sale. There were also other sales rumored in the newspapers, including one to noted East Coast actor, comedian, and vaudevillian Nat C. Goodwin, but nothing ever came of any of them.[12]

Finally, in early 1896 Thompson found buyers, and his plans for the palatial new Riverside Hotel were scuttled. The new buyers were Thompson's friends, C. C. Powning and Virginia City judge and later Reno resident C. E. Mack. For an additional $25,000, Thompson had also sold some adjoining land known as the Thompson Block to Powning and Mack. The new partners hired as their hotel manager thirty-nine-year-old Harry J. Gosse, who had owned and run the very successful Eureka House hotel in Silver City. Gosse was born on a ranch along the Sacramento River; his German-born parents had gone to California during the Gold Rush. When a flood devastated their property, the Gosse family moved to Silver City on the Comstock where the elder Gosse ran a boarding house. As a teenager young Harry tried his hand at mining, but when his father passed away in 1888 Harry took over the boarding house and eventually turned it into one of the most successful hotels on Mount Davidson. Over the years following Thompson's sale to Powning and Mack, the buyer was reported as having been Harry Gosse, but that was inaccurate. Newspaper stories of the day do make it clear, however, that Gosse had a free hand in the management of the property, being the experienced hotel manager that he was.[13]

Harry Gosse and his wife Josephine moved into the owner-manager apartment at the hotel where they would eventually raise two children, Harry and Marguerite. As a youngster Marguerite had a large playhouse in the backyard of the Riverside Hotel that was in fact a fully furnished and equipped miniature house. She would grow up to become the first woman native to Nevada to serve in the Nevada legislature, and she became an early and important feminist. Marguerite also became an expert horsewoman as she grew up, and her father built her a stable nearby.[14]

Gosse—Captain Gosse as he was often called for his role as commander of Company A, First Nevada National Guard—jumped right into Reno's business, social, and philanthropic communities. A jovial fellow with a loud laugh and a convivial personality, Gosse would be actively involved with the lodges of the Knights Templar, the Shriners, and the Elks that he personally organized in Reno.[15]

It didn't take the savvy Captain Gosse long to realize that this new hotel had great potential. Like Myron Lake and William Thompson before him, Gosse envisioned the property as primarily a comfortable family resort, but he also wanted to continue making the hotel a focal point in the community where local people would come in for meetings, political rallies, entertainment, and meals. Many years later, when Jessie Beck would reopen the hotel after it had been closed for years, Mona Kay Toogood, then ninety-four years

Pictured here is the Riverside Hotel's dining room that Mrs. Toogood spoke so highly of. It was a showplace in the city during the Gay Nineties and beyond. Courtesy of Jerry Fenwick.

old and once the wife of Myron Lake's son, Charles, would recall the Riverside Hotel of the 1890s under Thompson's and Gosse's management:

> It was a very nice hotel—it was a very gay hotel. It was the most important hotel in town. I used to think it was the friendliness that made that hotel. Everyone used to stay at the Riverside. I sort of remember a big veranda on the side of the river—there was dancing, and tables for supper. We did the waltz [and] the polka. Not this awful dancing we have today.
>
> They had quite a fine restaurant. I remember sitting at a table and being asked if I wanted frog legs. They had everything it was possible to have....
>
> [The] very first class kind of people came to the Riverside.... It used to take all day to drive up to it. I really liked the old days when Reno was a smaller place.[16]

Mrs. Toogood was a teenager during the period she was speaking about, and she lived in Virginia City. To get to the Riverside, she would either make a daylong horse and buggy ride or take the Virginia & Truckee Railroad, she recalled.[17]

On August 13, 1896, the *Reno Evening Gazette* published a perplexing item that likely had Renoites scratching their heads. Under the headline "Riverside Hotel Sold," the small article noted that owners Powning and Mack—most people still believed that Harry Gosse owned the hotel—had sold the hotel and the land it occupied to Anna Mudd Warren. Warren was a good friend of Mack's and a fellow Virginia City resident; she would go on to become one of Nevada's earliest female attorneys.[18]

Only seven months later, on March 10, 1897, Warren mysteriously deeded back to Mack an undivided two-thirds interest in the same properties, making the two the co-owners. Five years later, on a nearby lot purchased from Mack, Warren would move her Virginia City house—lock, stock, and barrel—to her new lot at 32 Island Avenue overlooking the river.[19]

Historical researcher Kim Henrick, who uncovered all of this heretofore unknown information on the Riverside's early ownership for an article in the Historic Reno Preservation Society's "Footprints" newsletter, opines that all these old Comstockers—Mack, Warren, and Gosse—may have carefully planned this entire takeover of the Riverside Hotel. Certainly stranger things have happened.

Despite the mysterious changes, the Riverside's business continued to flourish; so in late 1897 Gosse—still the manager of the enterprise—announced the addition of a second annex to the rear of the hotel. It included sixteen en suite (with toilets) rooms with electric lights, and baths with hot and cold water. The annex was built at the rear of the hotel facing the riverfront, and it was connected to the main hotel by a bridge on the second floor. The new annex was ready for occupancy before the end of the year. Gosse also continued the tradition of Myron Lake and William Thompson in providing a wagonette, or horse-drawn bus, that met every train at the depot for the convenience of those planning to stay at the Riverside.[20]

As the end of the nineteenth century approached, Reno—a twenty-nine-year-old township—finally came of age. Well, almost. On March 8, 1897, spurred by the enactment of special Nevada legislative charter #261, Reno was granted a city charter. A city council of "practical men" was hastily appointed to govern the West's newest city. "From now on the management of streets, alleys, sewers and city improvements will be handled by the proper committees," the *Nevada State Journal* boasted. The article continued: "The board is composed of practical men, all being property owners and in business and their knowledge of the needs of the community in the way of public improvements fit them especially for the responsible position for which they have been chosen."[21]

Unfortunately, it didn't quite turn out that way. Two years later, in 1899, city property owners petitioned to de-incorporate because, according to the *Weekly Reno Gazette and Stockman*, "Property owners of the city are paying for the luxury of incorporation without any of its benefits." Reasons cited for the action were promises broken, including improving the city's water supply and the condition of the streets, as well as being burdened with inept council members who were substituted for those "leading men" who it was promised would run the city. "Jugglery and tomfoolery," the newspaper called the attempt to de-incorporate.[22] The measure would pass, but four years later, in 1903, another vote would again incorporate the contentious little town into a city.

In spite of this political foofaraw, as the nineteenth century entered its twilight and the new century dawned, Renoites were counting their blessings. The *San Francisco Call* lauded the town–city–town–city, touting its natural attractions—its sheep, cattle, and agricultural bounty—and its bright prospects for the future. It also mentioned an infant industry the town was just beginning to discover, writing, "Reno has become known as Cupid's town; and that the Riverside Hotel has had to build an addition of twenty [actually sixteen] rooms lately is testimony that the marriage business, like other Reno enterprises, is booming."[23]

The new marriage business was an outgrowth of a recent California law straddling its divorced citizens with a one-year term limit before they could remarry, so many of them fled across the Sierra Nevada to Reno to tie the knot. But that was just for starters. At about the same time Reno was also beginning to venture into the divorce business, an enterprise that would eventually earn it a moniker as the "Divorce Capital of the Nation."

Historian, academic, and author William Rowley put the little city in perspective when discussing the ending of one century and the dawning of another, writing, "Reno still suffered from the general stagnation and dismantling of the mining economy…but in this arrested development…the city and the state would find much of their 20th-century identity."[24]

## NOTES

1. Quote from "The Fellow's History," *RWGS*, 09/24/1891; Trego, "When Ortiz Was Hanged from the Virginia Street Bridge," *NSJ*, 07/30/1950.

2. "The Fellow's History," *RWGS*, 09/24/1891.

3. All quotes from, "Ortiz Hung!," *RWGS*, 09/24/1891; additional information from Trego, "When Ortiz Was Hanged from the Virginia Street Bridge," *NSJ*, 07/30/1950.

4. "Quote from "Coroner's Inquest," *RWGS*, 09/24/1891; "Commissioners," *NSJ*, 10/20/1891; Johnson, "Two Reno Women Recall Old Times," *NSJ*, 11/11/1951.

5. "The Reno Guards," *NSJ*, 07/15/1882; "Company C," *REG*, 09/08/1882; "Admission Day," *NSJ*, 10/06/1891; quote from n.t., *NSJ*, 10/09/1891; Phillip Earl, Nevada historian, conversation with author, 10/23/2013.

6. Wren, *A History of Nevada*, 338.

7. Barber, *Reno's Big Gamble*, 32–33; Townley, *Tough Little Town*, 156–57.

8. Townley, *Tough Little Town*, 156–57; quote from "Nevada as a Sanitarium," *REG*, 12/24/1891, 12.

9. "Commissioners' Meeting," *RWGS*, 06/01/1894; quote from "Another Strike," *RWGS*, 07/10/1894.

10. "The Meeting Last Night," *NSJ*, 02/15/1891.

11. First quote from "The New Hotel," *NSJ*, 08/10/1892; "The New Riverside," *REG*, 08/09/1892; n.t., *RWGS*, 11/10/1892; n.t., *RWGS*, 12/08/1892; second quote from, n.t., *NSJ*, 02/28/1893; "Administrative Records of the Secretary of State, 1864–1995," p. 145.

12. n.t., *REG*, 11/26/1894; Adv. for "New Stable," *REG*, 12/23/1893; "Brevities," *NSJ*, 11/02/1893; "Talks About Nat Goodwin as Broker," *REG*, 08/19/1907; n.t., *RWGS*, 11/16/1893; "The New Riverside Hotel," *NSJ*, 12/02/1892; n.t., *NSJ*, 01/14/1896.

13. Henrick, "Anna Warren and the Riverside Hotel"; "Growth of the Riverside Shows Progress of Reno," *NSJ*, 05/27/1906; "A Change of Proprietors," *NSJ*, 02/01/1896; "A Live Man," *NSJ*, 01/17/1986. NOTE: In addition to many inaccurate reports of Gosse's ownership status in the Riverside Hotel in the local newspapers, two Nevada history books also contained the inaccurate material. They were Davis, *History of Nevada*, 2:1203–4; and Wren, *A History of Nevada*, 546.

14. Puddington, "A Biography of Marguerite Gosse," 3; "A Change of Proprietors," *NSJ*, 02/01/1896.

15. "A Man Who Kept His Promise," *REG*, 11/02/1912.

16. "It's 'Bye, Bye Blues' for the Riverside," *REG*, 03/31/1971.

17. "It's 'Bye, Bye Blues' for the Riverside," *REG*, 03/31/1971.

18. "Riverside Hotel Sold," *REG*, 08/13/1896; Henrick, "Anna Warren and the Riverside Hotel."

19. Henrick, "Anna Warren and the Riverside Hotel"; "Women's Biographies: Anna B. Mudd."

20. Hardesty, "The Site of Reno's Beginning," 22; "Riverside Annex," *NSJ*, 08/20/1897; "A Change of Proprietors," *NSJ*, 02/01/1896.

21. Statutes of Nevada 1897, ch. XLVIII, 50–61; "Reno Now a City," *NSJ*, 04/13/1897.

22. Quotes from "A Jumble," *RWGS*, 03/09/1899.

23. "The Metropolis of Nevada," *San Francisco Call*, 03/31/1898, 13.

24. Rowley, *Reno*, 31.

# CHAPTER 5

# BETWIXT HEAVEN
# AND THE HOT PLACE

FROM ITS BEGINNINGS, Reno's tough take-no-prisoners' attitude had doomed most older, more-established settlements that were located nearby. Washoe City, Franktown, Ophir, Galena, Crystal Peak, and Poeville, to name only a few of them, lost status, then population, to Reno's growing ambition. Even next-door neighbor Sparks—then called Glendale—had to be content with what-might-have-been when the fates of fortune wrested the Central Pacific Railroad away from the older, more-populated settlement at Stone & Gates Crossing. The opening decade of the twentieth century would continue the trend, and the tough, rowdy little frontier railroad town of Reno would finally come into its own as a city to be reckoned with. But the decade began on a low note. Nevada had lost a third of its residents in the twenty-year mining-induced depression from 1880 to 1900, the population falling from 62,266 to 42,335. One in five of these people lived in Washoe County, primarily in Reno. Things were so bad in the state in these last two decades of the nineteenth century that the *Chicago Tribune* encouraged Congress to withdraw Nevada's statehood. Despite these bleak figures, there were bright spots. Ranching, agriculture, lumbering, and even railroading were growing industries in Nevada; and new gold and silver discoveries in Tonopah and Goldfield early in the new century spurred another, albeit small, mining boom.[1]

An important change in Reno during the first decade of the new century was the construction and architecture of its public buildings and structures. Hundreds of buildings had been hurriedly put up since the town's founding, but none had been built for ornament or grace. But now wooden structures were on the decline, to be replaced by beautiful buildings of brick, steel, and stone. New during the decade, in addition to updated versions of the

Frederic DeLongchamps, a 1904 University of Nevada graduate, started an architectural practice in Reno in 1907. By 1926, when George Wingfield would select him to design the new Riverside Hotel, DeLongchamps had already designed a number of local buildings that would become landmarks in the city. Special Collections Department, University of Nevada, Reno Libraries.

Virginia Street Bridge and the Riverside Hotel, were a new Federal Building that also housed the Reno Post Office; a completely renovated Washoe County Courthouse; Reno Carnegie Public Library, on the river across Virginia Street from the Riverside, on land donated by the Lake family; a new Masonic Building; a $125,000 YMCA building; and a number of new schools, including four impressive elementary schools built in Mission Revival style that would become lovingly known as the four sisters. The emergence of the city's most famous architect during this decade, Frederic DeLongchamps, would change the look of many public buildings in the city forever.[2]

The *Nevada State Journal* printed a retrospective of the city in 1903, and quoted a traveler who had returned to Reno after a long absence: "I don't know the old town. Can this be the Reno that I left? I see great modern structures where were frame shanties or vacant lots. I see the smoke curling from the stacks of manufacturers. I see paved streets...but what I don't see are many familiar faces." This pioneer also recalled another tableau from his past: "A rough bridge spanned the stream and here the freight teams and prospectors' rigs passed on their way between Sierra Valley and the Comstock."[3]

By 1901 the iron Virginia Street Bridge had served the city well for one year shy of a quarter-century. The 1887 construction of a cattle bridge downriver had lengthened the life of the iron span, but the heavily trafficked structure was still showing its age. In September the bridge's roadbed—built initially of local pine rather than the stronger but more expensive Oregon pine—had to be replaced. Two-inch-thick planking was laid diagonally, then topped with four-inch timbers, and the braces on the bridge were all tightened to eliminate the frightening vibration of the iron structure that occurred whenever a heavy load passed over it.[4]

These repairs, however, did not quell the concern of many in the community that the city had outgrown the iron bridge. Of course there was an equally vociferous segment of the population who felt the bridge was just fine, thank you. The original builder had guaranteed the bridge for twenty years, but its lifespan had passed that mark by almost five years, and some citizens were concerned about its safety. City fathers, in their political wisdom, ordered that the bridge, which had been painted green and yellow for its entire lifetime, be painted black and white. This change, not surprisingly, did nothing to abate the citizens' concerns. One of the city's two newspapers asked the bridge superintendent of the Southern Pacific Railroad—the successor to the Central Pacific—his opinion of the bridge, and he replied that it was liable to go down at any time. The other newspaper asked well-known Reno architect M. J. Curtis the same question, and he replied that the iron bridge was absolutely safe for several more years. So there was no consensus, even among the experts.[5]

By 1903 city fathers finally began to show concern. The vibrations in the bridge were worsening, and rust was apparent in some critical junctures on the span. One published description of the old bridge stated, "It has been patched and painted, braced and bolstered, until it is like a crazy quilt with new and old material, and like the proverbial chain it is only as strong as its weakest link, and there are a number of them." Reno city engineer Thomas K. Stewart was given the job of planning for the next Virginia Street Bridge. Stewart's initial plan called for a structure that was a full eighty feet wide, the full width of Virginia Street at the time, and ninety feet long. The latest type of construction would be employed, Stewart proclaimed, but at the time he wasn't sure if that construction would be steel or concrete. In any case he promised it would be a substantial structure and an ornament for the city.[6]

Ironically, just as Thomas K. Hymers had been the public face of the 1877 iron bridge, Thomas K. Stewart would be the public face of the 1905 bridge. A Pennsylvania native of Scotch parents (like Hymers), Stewart was born in 1849 and came to Nevada as a young man. An engineer and surveyor, he worked for Washoe County and the Southern Pacific Railroad before joining the Reno city staff, and in his heyday he was recognized as one the finest engineers and surveyors in the state.[7] In an ironic twist, Hymers was not only still alive, but he was again serving as a Washoe County commissioner, and he jumped in with both feet when planning for the new bridge began.

As Stewart waffled on whether the new bridge should be steel or concrete, Hymers had no such indecision, saying publicly that he favored a three-arch cement or stone bridge, rather than another iron one.[8] The final decision, however, would belong to Stewart and to the city, which owned the bridge. A bridge expert from Cleveland was hired to come to Reno and determine if the old bridge was worth relocating. All the ingredients seemed to be in place for a city–county power struggle, but fortunately it never occurred. In its place, however, would be a major fiasco, the result of having two separate commissions performing overlapping functions.[9]

By late 1904 Stewart had also decided on a concrete bridge. "I mean to prepare plans and specifications for a cement bridge that will last for generations," Stewart boasted, likely not realizing how prescient his remark would be, continuing, "A bridge of this type will cost several thousand dollars more than a heavy steel bridge, but there is no comparison between their durability." Stewart also pointed out that the concrete bridge would require no unsightly overhead bridgework to mar its appearance. Still undecided, however, was whether it would be a single-arch bridge or a double-arch bridge, but after weeks of argument it was finally agreed that a double-arch bridge would be stronger.[10]

On March 15, 1905, the Nevada state legislature passed an act providing for the removal of the old iron bridge to another site if it was judged to be salvageable, the construction of a new concrete bridge at Virginia Street, construction and/or repair of other county bridges as necessary, and the issuance of $60,000 in 5 percent interest bonds to pay for all the work. The law also stipulated that two commissions be created. The first commission, which was unnamed, would comprise Washoe County commissioners and Reno City Council representatives, and they would jointly decide where to relocate the old iron bridge if it was deemed advisable to do so. The second commission, called the Bridge Commission, would oversee the actual work on the old and new Virginia Street bridges. The three members appointed to this commission were Reno mayor D. W. O'Connor and the two "T. K.s," T. K. Stewart who would be the supervising engineer, and T. K. Hymers who would chair the commission. For the now seventy-one-year-old Hymers, the appointment was déjà vu.[11]

The statute also specified details for the new bridge. It would be eighty feet wide with a sidewalk or walkway at least ten feet wide on each side, and two driveways for carriages, each driveway at least twenty-four feet in width. The bridge would also have to be long enough to span both the Sullivan-Kelly ditch that paralleled the river on the north bank and the Scott Ranch ditch that paralleled it on the south bank. These irrigation ditches dated back to the earliest settlement of the Truckee Meadows, and both were still uncovered at this time. Through the center of the bridge there would be a trackway twelve feet in width for the use of streetcars. It was later explained that the bridge would be very appealing to the eye, with a graceful sweep and a pleasing color due to the use of domestic Portland cement.[12]

Nonreinforced concrete provides great compressive strength as a building material, but it lacks tensile strength. Frenchman Joseph Lambot had solved that problem in 1849 when he designed a cement boat reinforced with wire mesh, and this new building material began to gain popularity. In the United States reinforced concrete found its greatest acceptance in northern California in the late 1870s, particularly in San Francisco, where it was first used to build sidewalks. The first application with a bridge was in 1889 on the Alvord Lake Bridge in Golden Gate Park. By the end of the century John B. Leonard had become California's foremost designer of concrete bridges, and in 1905 he was selected to design the Virginia Street Bridge. Leonard's final design would be in the then-fashionable Beaux Arts style, also called the American Renaissance style, that flourished from the late nineteenth century until the Great Depression. Following this style, there would be detailing in the form of decorative railings and lighting elements.[13]

With the project now officially under way, the first question many people asked was if the new bridge would eliminate the odd skew that had been built into the 1877 iron bridge in order to avoid having to cross Myron Lake's property. The answer appeared to be simple when Harry Gosse, acting for the owners of the Riverside Hotel, said he would allow the bridge to be built so its southern terminus fell on hotel property, thus eliminating the skew. It was a generous offer, but for some unknown reason it never happened. Thus the concrete bridge would be built with the skew of the old iron bridge and the wooden bridge before that.[14]

---

The consultant hired to determine the feasibility of moving the iron bridge to another location reported that the structure was indeed sound enough to save, as long as traffic over it would be lighter than it had experienced on Virginia Street. The cost of relocating it plus the cost of needed repairs, he estimated, would be $5,000. Since a brand new bridge of the same size and strength would cost only $7,000, the Bridge Committee decided they needed to ponder their decision. Meanwhile, the joint county–city committee whose responsibility it was to decide where to relocate the old iron bridge also pondered. The site where Rock Street meets the river, which was just west of the Virginia & Truckee Railroad Bridge, was considered. However, the land on both sides of the river at that point was privately owned, and arrangements would have to be made to purchase it. Also, there was a groundswell of public support to put the old iron bridge farther down the river at Second Street, which dead-ended at the river. Advocates of that plan said Second Street could then connect to North Street on the north side of the river. Still other Reno residents wanted the bridge at Chestnut (now Arlington) Street, and others wanted it at West Street. With these questions still undecided, the Bridge Commission began soliciting construction bids for the new reinforced concrete span.[15]

While all this political pondering was going on, the contract was let to build the temporary wooden bridge that would serve while the iron bridge was being removed and the new one built. A local firm, Delonchant & Curtis, won the contract that stipulated a $500 fee for the work with the condition that it must be completed within only eight days. There would be a penalty of $20 per day assessed for each day far past the specified time. The county was to pay for all the lumber, which would then be reused to build smaller bridges throughout Washoe County. In the firm of Delonchant & Curtis, Curtis was longtime Reno architect M. J. Curtis, while his partner was Reno carpenter and builder Felix Delonchant, the father of soon-to-be Reno architect Frederic DeLongchamps. The elder Delonchant was born in Montreal, Canada, in 1851, and came to Nevada as a boy in the 1860s, settling in Carson City with his parents. As an adult he became a builder and carpenter, and even spent a few years lumbering on the Nevada side of the Tahoe Basin during Comstock days. He eventually moved to Reno where he engaged in general construction and bridge building. In 1912 the elder Delonchant discovered that his Montreal ancestors had spelled their surname differently, and young Frederic immediately adopted the new spelling. Felix never embraced the old name, and died in 1926 with his named unchanged.[16]

The question of where to place the old iron bridge had still not been resolved by the joint county–city commission. Thus following the completion of the temporary wooden bridge by mid-August, and in order to keep the project moving forward, the iron bridge was dismantled and placed in an open field nearby to await its fate. While dismantling the iron bridge an exciting find was made: Some old log supports were unearthed beneath the streambed, and it was determined that they were remnants of C. W. Fuller's original 1860 bridge. The supports were in a poor state of preservation, but the discovery attracted a large crowd of onlookers, many of whom tore off splinters of the historic wood to take home as souvenirs. Later in the construction, another discovery was made when bridge workers uncovered an old-fashioned key-winding gold watch from the riverbed. The crowd of onlookers—the bridge site had become the city's chief entertainment venue—suggested two possibilities for the source of the watch. Many old-timers believed it was part of the loot thrown over the bridge by a robber as he was being led to jail several years earlier; but others speculated it was accidently lost in the river in 1891 by one of the vigilantes as they lynched the unfortunate Luis Ortiz. Along the same line, in 1900 Harry J. Gosse, manager of the Riverside Hotel, had also found a watch in the riverbed in front of the hotel. At the time the newspaper speculated that the watch was lost by the late M. C. Lake in 1859 while fording the river just below the site of the Virginia Street Bridge. It is possible that Lake may have been visiting C. W. Fuller at the time because in 1859 Fuller owned that property, not Lake. Regardless of the accuracy of any of these speculations, they once again spoke to the fascinating history of Reno and its iconic landmarks.[17]

On July 12 the Bridge Commission opened the bids for the contract on the new concrete bridge, and the lowest bidder at $37,737 was Cotton Brothers of Oakland, California. The California firm had barely squeaked in, only $163 below the next lowest bid. There was a flurry of excitement at the bid openings when one of the bids arrived just minutes past the noon deadline, the result of a late train arrival, and it was rejected by the commission. Opened later, the bid was the highest of the lot, so nothing was lost. Cotton Brothers' contract called for a completion date 100 days after the work began, and by August construction was under way. John B. Leonard, the bridge designer, came to Reno to evaluate how things were going. "Excellent progress is being made," he said. "When completed the Reno bridge will be the most handsome and durable structure west of the Rocky Mountains. The piers are being built on an excellent foundation, in fact the supporting soil has been found to be better than we had reason to expect."[18]

The construction would not be without problems, however. Right after Leonard's visit one of the temporary brick retaining walls that surrounded the abutments collapsed, causing a large section of an arch and masonry to cave in. Nearly three weeks later seven of the huge wooden arches, constituting the main part of the false structure of the bridge, caved in, setting progress back another day or so. And finally, one or two teams with their wagons fell into an excavation at the south end of the bridge. Fortunately, none of the accidents caused any injuries.[19]

By late October the decorative iron railings and the electric lamps were ready to be installed by the Nevada Power, Light, & Water Company. Decorative concrete walls, two feet high, ran along each side of the bridge, a feature that would prove to be a major flaw in the future. The iron railings, intended to keep pedestrians from toppling into the water, were affixed atop these walls. In the middle of the bridge, on each side, the walls were interrupted by a stone base sitting atop a pilaster that ran down the sides of the bridge and into the water, creating the illusion of a light tower once the electric lamps were mounted atop the stone bases. There would be six lamps in total, one on each corner of the bridge and one in the middle on each side, atop these bases. This layout, the designer said, would accentuate the arched structure of the bridge. Each lamp would consist of a quartet of white globes. Thomas Edison's incandescent lamps were only twenty-five years old at the time, and electricity had not made its way into most households, so the new lamps caused a great deal of excitement in Reno. A week later the contractor declared that the cement work was finished, and the first team of oxen carrying bridge-building supplies had plodded its way across the span with no problems. All that remained was to remove the wooden superstructure and pave the roadway, and by November 15 the new bridge opened for public travel. Immediately the temporary wooden bridge was taken down and the lumber hauled by wagon to Wadsworth to repair that bridge.[20]

The new bridge was an instant success. "The new structure pleases everyone.… It will be one of the best bridges on the coast," the newspaper boasted. As soon as it officially opened, long wagons pulled by teams, automobiles, and pedestrians boldly crossed it successfully, but the earth that filled the hollow concrete superstructure had not hardened yet, and bicyclists found themselves sinking deeply into the dirt.[21]

The John B. Leonard–designed bridge is described by the National Register of Historic Places, to which the bridge was elected in 1980: "Leonard's design employed concrete scored to resemble masonry. Other traditional characteristics of masonry construction include the classical arches and the pilasters rising to the level of the ornate iron railing. Above the arches, the bridge is a concrete shell, earth filled to the roadway and sidewalk level." The two arches were likewise scribed to resemble *voussoir*, wedge-shaped stones commonly used to construct stone arches. The finishing touch was a bronze plaque on the southeast post of the bridge that reads: "Virginia Street Bridge. Authorized by act of legislature approved March 15, 1905. T. K. Stewart, Engineer in Charge. Designer, John B. Leonard, San Francisco, California. Contractor, Cotton Brothers and Company, Oakland, California. Construction commenced, July 17, 1905. Opened for traffic, November 12, 1905." When finished, the bridge measured 146 feet end to end, and 80 feet wide. The structure had taken 2,150 cubic yards of concrete, and its total weight, including concrete, steel rods, and dirt filling was 12,830,000 pounds. The wooden frame box into which the concrete had been poured to form the bridge consisted of more than 200,000 feet of heavy timbers.[23]

------

The act passed by the state legislature in 1905 had mandated a trackway twelve feet wide down the center of the concrete bridge for streetcars, or trolleys. Reno's track record with trolley systems up to this time had been dismal. The first trolley franchise had been granted by the state legislature in 1889 to a group of local business owners, including C. C. Powning, to operate a system of horse- or mule-powered trolley cars that could travel no more than eight miles per hour. The trolleys, however, were not allowed to cross the river over the iron bridge, so this project never got off the ground. Five more unsuccessful trolley franchises followed. In 1904, when talk about the new bridge was just warming up, another local group, which included the Riverside Hotel's Harry Gosse, put forward a plan for an electric trolley system that local voters approved by an astoundingly wide margin, indicating how badly Reno citizens wanted a trolley system in their city. Charter in hand, the new group, Nevada Transit Company, immediately began laying track and purchasing streetcars, and by Thanksgiving Day of 1904 the system was on line and the first yellow trolley car began collecting dimes from eager riders.[24]

The track was planned to run from its terminus at the Southern Pacific Railroad yards in Sparks, west along Fourth Street to Sierra Street, south to Second Street, east to Virginia Street, then over the old iron bridge. According to the group's articles of incorporation, the trolley cars could be powered "by horse, cable, electric, steam, or any other power or means." Crossing the iron bridge greatly concerned Reno residents, who feared the old structure would collapse under the weight of a full car. It didn't. In 1906 a San Francisco company bought the system, renamed it the Reno Traction Company, and continued to extend the tracks. A second system started up about this time named the Moana Line. Some track was shared between the two companies, and both lines were allowed to use the tracks over the new concrete bridge. A passing switch was installed on Virginia Street just south of the bridge and in front of the Riverside Hotel to allow traffic to flow smoothly. By 1919, however, the gasoline combustion engine had won out over electrical systems and the Moana Line ceased operations soon after. The Reno Traction Company would continue to operate until 1927 when falling revenues finally forced its closure.[25]

------

In this 1905 photo of the Riverside Hotel, the tracks of the city's brand new electric trolley system are evident running down the middle of the road. Hotel front man and manager Harry Gosse was instrumental in getting voters to approve money for the system. It is obvious that work had already begun on the extravagant new Riverside Hotel, as can be seen in one of the brick towers looming at the end of the old wooden structure. Courtesy of Jerry Fenwick.

While most everything had gone smoothly with the construction of the new concrete bridge, it was just the opposite with the old iron bridge. By late 1905 two issues remained unresolved. First, whether the tired old bridge should actually be saved; and second, if it was saved, where it should be put. As scrap metal, the old bridge was worth little money, but there was a great deal of public sentiment—which county and city politicians hated to ignore—to save the old landmark. So the decision was finally made by the joint county–city commission to reassemble the bridge elsewhere. But where? The iron bridge couldn't be stretched or compressed, so a site had to be chosen where it would fit perfectly across the river. Only Rock Street met that criterion, despite the fact that the site was hardly suitable for a bridge because the streets on both sides were dead ends. Despite that, Rock Street was chosen.[26]

Having made their decision, members immediately disbanded their county–city commission. However, if Rock Street was selected, the commission had also been tasked with arranging the purchase of the private land on both sides of the river for rights-of-way, and they had completely forgotten about that task. But those in charge of reassembling the old bridge assumed the legal work had been done, and they reassembled it across the river at Rock Street as ordered. When the problem was discovered, the local newspapers assailed the Bridge Commissioners. "The Bridge that 'Tom' Built," the newspaper wrote with tongue-in-cheek. "The old iron bridge that formerly spanned the Truckee on Virginia Street is…suspended betwixt heaven and the hot place." Additionally, Stewart, the supervising engineer, came under even more public censure because the bridge had been improperly reassembled. Fortunately for everybody concerned, the right-of-way problems were eventually resolved amicably. One of the privately held parcels of land the bridge had poached on belonged to Felix Delonchant, and he graciously donated it to the city; the other parcel was sold to the city for $1,500. Additionally, the necessary repairs were made to the bridge, and the citizenry was finally mollified. Perhaps most importantly, the old iron bridge lived on to serve Reno and Sparks for another half-century, finally succumbing to a flood in 1950.[27]

An article appeared in the *Nevada State Journal* in 1905 during the construction of the new bridge that contained a prescient comment by the reporter, and it serves as an appropriate homage for the iron and concrete Virginia Street bridges: "Within a couple of days the old bridge, which has stood through winter's storms and summer's rains, will be a thing of the past and a new edifice to last a hundred years will rear itself on the place of the old bridge." Today, 116 years later, we can honestly say that truer words were never written.[28]

Stepping back in time a bit, in 1903 when discussions had first begun about replacing the old iron bridge, another important local event had occurred that ensured that the old span would go out with a flourish rather than a whimper. In July of that year thirteen hardened convicts had escaped from Folsom Prison, about twenty miles northeast of Sacramento. During the prison break one of the escapees, Joseph Murphy, killed a guard, and an all-out Western style manhunt was immediately launched. As soon as the escapees were clear of the immediate area, they decided to split up. Five of the men headed for Nevada, stopping in Lake Valley at the south end of Lake Tahoe to grab some lunch. Then three of these five convicts headed for Carson City while the other two—named Murphy and Woods—decided to head for Reno. A posse had been only a few miles behind the men, but the deputies were forced to split up when the convicts had done so, and they fell farther behind. At about 5:00 PM, the two Reno-bound escapees boarded a train at Steamboat Springs south of Reno near the Geiger Grade, but their luck was beginning to run out. They had been spotted, and a phone call alerted Reno sheriff's deputies that the two men were headed for the city, and to be on the lookout for the armed convicts. A second call three hours later said the two had just been spotted passing the Southside Tavern on South Virginia Street. It was then that Deputies Sharkey and Maxwell took positions on the north end of the old iron bridge, lying in hiding for their quarry to arrive. When the convicts entered the bridge and reached the mid-point, Sharkey and Maxwell sprang from their hiding place and charged the two men. Other deputies moved in from the south end of the bridge, cutting the escapees off. Trapped on both sides by the old iron railings, convict Murphy pulled a revolver. Both deputies immediately jumped Murphy, disarmed him, and wrestled him to the ground where they hogtied him, then dragged him to the jail. Woods escaped in the melee but he would be captured later. In July 1905, just about the time the old iron bridge was being removed, Joseph Murphy was hanged at Folsom Prison for the murder of the prison guard. It was a fitting end for the old iron structure that had once been the site of a far less heroic hanging.[29]

The 1891 hanging and the 1903 capture of an escaped convict were not the only death or near-death experiences that would transpire on the Virginia Street Bridge over its long lifetime. Over the years a number of people fell, jumped, or were pushed into the roiling waters of the Truckee River from the five versions of the bridge. In 1910 a "demented" Swiss visitor, fleeing from imaginary demons, hurled himself off the bridge to escape. Through good fortune and quick action on the part of a nearby night watchman, the delusional fellow was pulled from the water 250 feet downstream, although the newspaper reported that "he set up a fearful howling" when pulled from the river. In the next decade a young Italian immigrant named Ernesto Pincolini, whose family had a small vineyard in Verdi, was riding his bicycle across the bridge when a team of horses ran over him. Many other young men over the years, while testing their manhood, have jumped from the bridge. (In these earlier days, before the river was tampered with, it was deeper.) A few of these men died, and most of the others soon regretted the foolish prank.[30]

Just a few years after the new bridge was completed, on February 26, 1909, T. K. Hymers passed away in his seventy-fifth year at his home in Reno. No man past or present had done as much for his town, his city, and his county as Hymers. He was one of the rare individuals who bore witness to more than a half-century of Reno's prehistory and early history. In his lifetime he laid eyes on every Virginia Street Bridge but one, seeing even the rope-hauled ferry that preceded them all; the only bridge he missed seeing was the new bridge built in the twenty-first century. With his own eyes he saw C. W. Fuller's 1859–60 ferry and his 1860 bridge, and Myron Lake's two wooden bridges at Lake's Crossing, and he was instrumental in building both Reno's iron bridge and finally the beautiful new concrete bridge. A few years later, reminiscing about early Reno, a newspaper neatly summed up Hymers's contributions to his city: "T. K. Hymers…had to do with nearly everything touching Reno's improvement and its upbuilding."[31]

Just as his good works outlived his lifetime, so too did his name. Lew Hymers, T. K.'s grandson born in 1892, was an accomplished artist and caricaturist who entertained Renoites with his creative genius in the local newspapers for many decades.[32]

## NOTES

1. Trego, "Glendale Once Came Close to Being What Reno Is Now," *NSJ*, 10/08/1950; Zhang, "Nevada Outpost."

2. Rowley, *Reno*, 40; Barber, *Reno's Big Gamble*, 78.

3. "A Retrospective View of This City," *NSJ*, 05/19/1903.

4. "Traffic Blocked by Bridge Work," *NSJ*, 09/04/1901.

5. "Life of an Iron Bridge," *REG*, 09/27/1901; "A Study in Colors," *NSJ*, 11/24/1901; "Discusses the Bridge," *NSJ*, 09/29/1901.

6. Quote from "New Bridge Is Absolute Need," *NSJ*, 01/07/1905; "Bridge Over the Truckee," *NSJ*, 12/01/1903.

7. "Thomas K. Stewart Dies," *NSJ*, 07/13/1923.

8. "Favors Modern Cement Bridge," *REG*, 04/06/1905.

9. "Favors Modern Cement Bridge," *REG*, 04/06/1905.

10. Quote from "Cement Bridge for the River," *REG*, 12/19/1904; "Beauty of Scene on Truckee River," *NSJ*, 10/03/1905.

11. "Plan and Specifications for New Bridge," legal adv., *NSJ*, 05/24/1904; "Talk and Act About Bridge," *NSJ*, 05/06/1905.

12. Statutes of Nevada 1905, ch. LXXXII, 155–58; "Virginia St. Bridge Starter 40 Years Ago," *REG*, 07/04/1945; Miramon, "Reno's Heritage Bridge Is in Jeopardy," 2–3.

13. Snyder and Mikesell, "The Consulting Engineer and Early Concrete Bridges in California," 38–41.

14. "New Bridge Is Absolute Need," *NSJ*, 01/07/1905.

15. "Will Cost $5,000 to Remove the Virginia Street Bridge," *REG*, 05/13/1905; "City Attorney Says Old Bridge," *REG*, 11/06/1905; "Will Brook No Delay in Building Bridge," *NSJ*, 05/19/1905; "Bridge Plans Are Adopted," *NSJ*, 06/06/1905; "New Bridge to Be of Concrete," *NSJ*, 05/18/1905; "Proper Place for Old Bridge," *NSJ*, 05/23/1905.

16. "Material Has Been Ordered," *NSJ*, 06/24/1905; "Oakland Firm Gets Contract," *NSJ*, 07/13/1905; "Retired Nevadan Expires on Coast," *NSJ*, 05/27/1926; Online Nevada Encyclopedia, "Frederic DeLongchamps"; Mella Harmon, correspondence with the author, 04/22/2013.

17. "Virginia St. Bridge Started 40 Years Ago," *REG*, 07/04/1945; Prouty, "The Development of Reno," 24; "It Long Since Stopped Running," *RWGS*, 08/02/1900.

18. "Oakland Firm Gets Contract," *NSJ*, 07/13/1905; quote from "Mr. Leonard Talks Bridge," *NSJ*, 08/19/1905; "Virginia St. Bridge Started 40 Years Ago," *REG*, 07/04/1945.

19. "Virginia St. Bridge Started 40 Years Ago," *REG*, 07/04/1945; "False Work on New Bridge Fell," *REG*, 09/07/1905.

20. "Lights for New Bridge," *NSJ*, 10/24/1905; "Cement Work Is Finished," *NSJ*, 10/30/1905; "Bridge Opens in the Morning," *REG*, 11/14/1905.

21. Quote from "Will Erect New Building," *REG*, 11/15/1905.

23. Quote from "National Register of Historic Places Inventory—Nomination Form: Virginia Street Bridge"; "Beauty of Scene on Truckee River," *NSJ*, 10/03/1905.

24. Cahlan, "Trolley Town," 107–9.

25. Cahlan, "Trolley Town," 107–9; "Articles of Incorporation of the Nevada Transit Company."

26. "Not Much Use for Old Bridge," *NSJ*, 10/19/1949.

27. "Now Up to the Lawyers," *NSJ*, 01/03/1905; "Erects Bridge and Failed to Get Road Right," *NSJ*, 09/29/1906; quote from "The Bridge That 'Tom' Built," *NSJ*, 10/12/1906; "$1500 Asked for Bridge Landing," *REG*, 11/155/1905.

28. Quote from "Old Bridge Disappearing," *NSJ*, 08/11/1905.

29. "Excellent Work Done by Local Officers," *NSJ*, 08/25/1903; "Convict Murphy Was Hanged This Morning," *REG*, 07/14/1905.

30. Quote from "Demented Swiss Jumps into Icy Waters of the Truckee," *NSJ*, 03/28/1910; Vacchina, "The Italian-America Experience in Northwestern Nevada."

31. Quote from "When Virginia Street Was a Lane," *REG*, 10/30/1914; "Eventful Life of Pioneer Has Closed," *NSJ*, 02/27/1909.

32. Online Nevada Encyclopedia, "Lew Hymers."

# CHAPTER 6

# A MODERN CARAVANSARY

DURING THE FIRST DECADE of the twentieth century, while city and county officials wrestled with the problem of replacing the old iron bridge with a modern, concrete span, other important changes were also occurring in Reno, changes that would alter the economic fabric of the region for the next five decades.

On November 5, 1859, in Genoa, Carson County, at that time part of Utah Territory—at about the same time C. W. Fuller was venturing into the Truckee Meadows—a woman named Rebecca Bristol charged her husband with desertion, and was granted what is believed to be the first divorce decree in what would soon become Nevada Territory. Two years later, when territorial status was proclaimed, visionary lawmakers, in considering the transitory nature of their population, decreed that six-month continuous residency was all that was required to obtain a divorce in the territory. The same law would carry over when Nevada gained its statehood. Every other state and territory at the time required at least a year of continuous residency to qualify for a divorce. On top of that, while most states allowed very few grounds for divorce, Nevada recognized seven, a few of which were open to broad interpretation. Despite these advantageous laws, there would be few divorces in the territory or the state for the remainder of the nineteenth century; but the divorce business, such as it was, had been kick-started.[1]

By the first decade of the twentieth century these things would begin to change in Nevada. In the year 1900 a British earl, Earl Russell, or John Francis Stanley Russell—he would later become known as the "wicked earl" in Edwardian society after a 1901 bigamy conviction—arrived in Glenbrook on Lake Tahoe to establish residency to divorce his first wife and marry his second, a mere commoner. The divorce took place in Genoa, in Douglas County, Nevada, and the marriage occurred at the Riverside Hotel in Reno.

The publicity on the Earl's scandalous activities first drew national and international attention to Nevada's lenient divorce laws. That attention was accelerated when the spotlight was placed directly on Reno in late 1905 when New York socialite Laura Corey, the wife of millionaire William Corey, president of United States Steel Company, arrived in Reno and arranged a six-month lease on an expensive local residence. She brought with her a retinue of maids and servants, and what the newspaper described as a powerful automobile. In July of the following year, she was granted her highly publicized divorce and full custody of the couple's son. This was the first many easterners would know of Reno and its lenient divorce laws. The next year a prominent New York City divorce lawyer, William Schnitzer, moved to Reno and opened a law office to take advantage of what he saw as a growing trend. He published a pamphlet describing how the suffering wife or husband could find relief in Reno, and promoted it in newspaper ads throughout the East. "Cupid's town," as the *San Francisco Call* had dubbed Reno a decade earlier because of its marriage business, was now on the way to earning a more lasting and profitable reputation as the divorce capital of the nation.[2]

And so they came, mostly women—they were called "divorcees" in Reno even before the divorce process began—but also some men. They had six months of idleness before them, but most did not languish in their bedrooms shedding tears. As *Collier's* magazine wrote in 1911, "They are always in the landscape—marketing; at the post-office; about the nice little hotel by the river [the Riverside]; in Reno's favorite restaurants—a curiously exotic note, with their unmistakable air of having come from somewhere else." They rented a house, a cottage, a hotel suite, or an apartment, or they stayed in a nearby guest ranch; and they hired a local attorney. Then they sashayed about the streets of Reno, visiting its gambling houses, its restaurants and cafés, its fashionable clothing shops, its theatres, and its health resorts. The city's commercial center moved with this well-heeled crowd, from Commercial Row several blocks south to the more fashionable riverfront area where Harry Gosse and the Riverside Hotel stood ready to serve them.[3]

The Riverside Hotel would become one of the primary beneficiaries of the newly minted divorce business. Harry Gosse had already branched out, and the hotel had become much more than merely a place to hang one's hat overnight. The upscale dining room was always packed, often with local diners, the bar was a favored gathering place, and the stables were always full. The Eagles, the Elks, various university groups, and other men's and women's organizations had their meetings and their banquets at the hotel. The convention business, although primarily regional, briskly picked up as

The registration desk at the Riverside Hotel, shown here early in the new century, attracted the local trade as well as business and vacation travelers and convention-eers. The bar was directly behind the registration desk, evidenced by the whiskey sign on the wall. Courtesy of Neal Cobb.

well. In addition to overnight guests, divorce seekers, and some permanent local residents, the hotel rooms were a primary place for visiting merchants to set up shop for a day or two as well. Ads in the local newspapers regularly carried announcements of vendors selling all types of wares: men's suits, carpets, saddle horses, dress goods, lace curtains, cigars, patent medicines, and millinery, to mention only a few of the items available on a regular basis at the Riverside. Gosse had built a multifaceted business at the Riverside Hotel, and the hotelier couldn't have been happier.

In September 1901 Harry Gosse began announcing plans for a new River-side Hotel. Even without the heavy demands of the divorce business, which was just beginning to surface, Gosse was forced to arrange rooms for some of his guests at local homes because he was constantly running at 100 percent occupancy. As a longtime hotel operator, he knew it was time to act. With the approval of the ultra-private owners, construction started soon after when excavation of the cellar began, and in February 1902 the first description of the planned hostelry appeared in the newspaper:

> Reno will shortly be possessed of the most palatial hotel in the west, outside of the larger cities.... The great building, which will be really five stories in height including the basement, will be provided throughout with hot and cold water and electric lights.
>
> Every apartment will be heated by low pressure steam. It will contain seventeen suites with baths and one hundred separate rooms with public baths. The conservatory will be one of the attractions of the place. Two rapid passenger elevators will make the top floor as desirable as any, especially as the structure will be fire and earthquake proof.
>
> The dining room will be a marvel of beauty. It will be frescoed and paneled in the most artistic manner.
>
> Every comfort and convenience will be provided in the office and reading room. Liveried bellboys will anticipate every wish of the patrons of the house. The contemplated street car line will pass the doors of the hotel.
>
> Important changes will be made to the grounds which will be greatly beautified. The surrounding outbuildings, including the original Lake house, the first building erected in Reno, will be razed to improve the landscape.[4]

The hotel was to be built entirely of brick with stone accents, in an H-shaped configuration. Many local residents immediately saw the resemblance between Gosse's plans and the one put forth by William Thompson a decade earlier. The south wing and north wing would be the legs of the H with a smaller wing connecting the two. The south wing and the connecting wing were to be built first, and then the old wooden frame hotel on the riverfront would be torn down and replaced by the north wing. Both of the main wings would feature broad balconies. At no time during the construction period, Gosse promised, would the hotel be closed. Well-known Reno architect and contractor M. J. Curtis had been selected as the architect, and he would oversee all construction as well. Gosse's construction schedule was aggressive: he planned to have the new hotel open by spring of 1902, ready to entertain his guests. However, his plan would hit numerous snags along the way: strikes, construction delays, mistakes in the architectural drawings, and eventually a realization that the planned hotel had to be even bigger and grander than first anticipated in order to meet the accelerating demands of the marketplace.[5]

Gosse decided to personally oversee the excavation for the foundations and the cellar; so he hired some men and set to work. The south wing was to be 130 feet × 40 feet, and the connecting wing 40 feet × 50 feet, and both would be three stories high, not including the basement. By November Gosse's work was complete, and Curtis was ready to begin the stonework. The north wing, which was to be built last, would be identical in size to the south wing according to the initial plans. Along the river near the hotel there was a deep, abandoned trench called the Cochran Ditch that had once run south from the river into what is today south Reno. The Cochran was one of a number of irrigation ditches, or canals, that had been dug years earlier in the western portion of the Truckee Meadows for crop irrigation. Gosse had the trench filled with the dirt from the excavation, and had a decorative brick archway built over it to enhance the hotel grounds. By the end of 1901 the foundation for the south wing was almost complete, and Gosse said that construction on the building would begin in early spring.[6]

During the excavation there had been a flurry of excitement when it was believed that gold had been discovered in the diggings. Longtime Renoite H. H. Beck had ventured down into the excavation with a prospector's pan and shovel, and begun to test some of the coarse red sand that surrounded the underground boulders. According to the newspaper, Beck obtained "a lovely prospect—quite a string of colors." To local residents this was reminiscent of the situation that had occurred the previous year following a small gold find near the courthouse, and the entire neighborhood had been taken up with placer claims. Local folks called it a "post-hole boom." The following week after finding his string of colors, Beck sent a letter to the editor of the newspaper clarifying his find: "[I] took what I estimated as six pounds of dirt or pay gravel. This I washed down until I had a clear trace of gold and black sand, which when dry weighted fifty-one grains. This residue I assayed and found it was worth $492.50 per ton." Apparently this translated to a very small sum, so there was never a stampede to Gosse's excavation.[7]

During the winter months Gosse had a large crew jacking up the old wooden Lake House hotel and installing sturdy timbers, or "stilts" as the newspaper called them, under the old structure. The plan was to somehow slide it farther back from the river in order to create space for the north wing to be built in its place. Gosse did not want to tear down the old building and forfeit the revenue it generated until the last possible moment. By this time Gosse had begun to fudge a little on his timetable, announcing that the completed hotel would be ready for occupancy in the fall, not in spring as earlier estimated. Meanwhile the front of the south wing was being trimmed with granite from quarries in Rocklin, California, a stone that was reputed to take a beautiful polish. However, Gosse received more bad news in early April when he was told that the brickwork would have to be suspended because of a fire at the Reno Press Brick Company. This was particularly disappointing because Gosse had planned to have the first floor looking good and ready for inspection for visitors by Carnival Week in early July, the city's biggest annual event. Fortunately, however, by early May the brick factory was back on schedule and bricklaying was restarted.[8]

In June, with work almost completed on the south wing, a costly mistake came to light. The circular towers at each corner of the south wing were topped by a dome that would serve as an observation deck for guests, and windows had been installed in the front of the domes facing south. Neither Curtis nor Gosse, however, had noticed that no windows had been installed facing north across the river and into the business district. It was a careless error, and it took time and money to correct.[9]

By the end of June the excitement level in the city was running high; Carnival Week would begin the next day, July 1. "The town looked like a fairyland," the newspaper reported. "The iron bridge was decorated and lighted with hundreds of colored incandescent lights. Virginia Street [is] 'a blaze of glory' from the [race]track to the Riverside Hotel." The brickwork and the granite work had been completed on the south wing, and fourteen carpenters were busy putting on finishing touches. Gosse would have his wish; there would be some rooms ready for public inspection during the festivities, but occupancy was still a way off. But by the time of the city's next big event in late August, the annual convention of the Silver Party, held at the Riverside, a portion of the south wing was ready for occupancy and every available room was booked. The old wooden hotel had been moved to its new location by Carnival Week, and it would be completely occupied for both the Carnival and the Silver Party convention.[10]

Finally, by late 1902 the south wing was completed. A newspaper article observed, "The rooms are very elaborately furnished throughout. The carpets of each room are entirely different, the coloring of each corresponding with the decorations of the room." The new dining room too was finished. It was large and airy in the summer, but for the comfort of the diners it was kept warm in the winter by a large new steam heater. For hotel guests, dining was American style, with three meals a day included in the cost. An electric elevator, the first in Nevada, was operational, and each room had an electric call button to page a bellhop. Some rooms had been set aside for the commercial trade, and a number of the new rooms were already occupied by businessmen, divorcees, and local families.[11]

With the south wing now open, and the old wooden hotel still accepting guests, local residents, traveling executives, and vacationing families were anxiously awaiting the construction of the north wing. However, despite occasional news items that Gosse's plans were on schedule, no construction was visible on the new wing. In September 1903 he did tell the *Nevada State Journal* that the new wing should have been completed by summer, but, he said, "It seemed impossible to secure the character of material desired." However, he insisted, construction would begin again in the following spring. But 1904 and the first half of 1905 came and went with no work on the north wing, leading many to wonder if the secretive owners had changed their minds or had simply run out of money.[12]

Strangely, throughout this entire period, Gosse's name was the only one ever mentioned in the newspapers in relation to the new hotel; the names of the owners, C. E. Mack and Anna Warren, were never mentioned. How many of the major decisions on building the new hotel were Gosse's own, and how many were handed down to him by the owners, is not known.

In mid-1905 speculation was seemingly put to rest when some of the city's leading moneyed men came together to issue bonds that would carry the building project forward. The Riverside Hotel Company's articles of incorporation, notarized on January 15, 1905, and officially recorded on May 2, 1905, stated that the purpose of the new company was "to acquire, own and operate...the 'Riverside Hotel,'" as well as to deal in other real estate and property opportunities that might present themselves. There were three principals in the corporation, all identified as Reno residents. They were H. E. Reid, George H. Taylor, and S. H. Wheeler, in equal shares. Harry Gosse's name appeared nowhere in the legal document. The key words in these incorporation papers were that the new group's purpose was "to acquire...the Riverside Hotel," but, in fact, that did not happen; the group never succeeded in purchasing the hotel. Despite this group's failure, however, the sale of the hotel was imminent.[13]

In December 1905 and January 1906 local newspapers published stories that the Riverside Hotel was now in different hands, and that new incorporation papers had been filed under the names of H. J. Gosse, Josephine Gosse,

and present owners C. E. Mack and A. M. Warren. What financial maneu-
vering had taken place in the meantime is not clear, but both newspapers
were jubilant that work would finally progress on the north wing of the new
hotel. "To Complete the Riverside, Construction of North Wing…Said to Be
Contemplated," reported the *Reno Evening Gazette*, while the *Nevada State
Journal* wrote, "In Readiness to Complete the Riverside, Corporation Headed
by H. J. Gosse…Orders That Work Begin at Once."[14]

Nearly a full decade after first associating with the state's leading hotel,
and having been inaccurately described as the "owner" or the "proprietor"
of the famed hostelry for that entire time, Harry Gosse had finally realized
his dream of ownership.

The hotelier had been able to put his financial worries behind him and
enjoy one brief interlude in September 1905 when famous but controversial
poet Cincinnatus Heine Miller, whose pen name was Joaquin Miller, had
paid a visit to the Riverside Hotel. Miller, often called the poet of the Sierras,
had come to Reno to speak at the Methodist church where more than 400
people enjoyed his hour-and-a-half lecture, "The Days of Old, the Days of
Gold—the Days of Forty-Nine." Miller had gone to California during the
Gold Rush, where he found a job as a camp cook. When he came down with
scurvy from eating only the food he cooked, however, he decided it was time
to seek other work. Among his following occupations were stints as a judge,
a newspaper writer, and a horse thief, none of which he excelled at. It was in
Britain, however, where he found success as a poet, although his work was
always controversial. When he returned to the U.S. West he had developed
a small but faithful following.[15]

During his stay at the Riverside Miller met his host, Harry Gosse, and
told him, "You have a picturesque city here and a truly fine hotel." Then in
typically brusque Miller style, he added, "You don't look like you have any
sense, but I must say you are conducting one of the best hotels I have ever
stopped at." The unflappable Gosse later told a newspaper reporter, "[H]e's
the first man candid enough to tell [me] how I look."[16]

In January 1906, the new owners announced that the old wooden Lake
House would be sold and moved away, and construction begun on the north
wing, "as soon as weather permits." True to the owners' word, within the
next two weeks a classified ad began appearing in the local papers: "FOR
SALE—The old Riverside Hotel building. Purchaser to tear down and move
from premises. Inquire of H. J. Gosse, Riverside hotel." If nothing else, Gosse
had become an expert in keeping the hotel's name in front of the public.
Almost weekly there were announcements of one sort or another in the

The new Riverside Hotel, managed by Harry Gosse and completed in 1907, was recognized as one of the finest hostelries in the West. A covered veranda facing the river was on the north side of the building (on the right in this photo). Courtesy of Neal Cobb.

newspapers about the planned caravansary: a new clerk was hired, another contract was awarded, a different peek at M. J. Curtis's architectural drawings was available. But still nothing happened.[17]

Finally, in May 1906 the Riverside Hotel Company began tearing down the old Lake House when they were unable to find a buyer for the lumber. A brief flurry of excitement occurred during the razing when an unidentified Reno pioneer told carpenters there was $40,000 in gold coins—a princely fortune at the time—hidden somewhere in the hotel. According to the folklore, Myron Lake had had some business setbacks at one time, and, fearful that his money would be attached, he withdrew it from the bank and concealed it somewhere in the old building. True or not, the story did focus the carpenters' attention, hastened their work, and added to the care with which they handled the razing of the building. Unfortunately, nothing of value was ever found.[18]

The work of dismantling the old wooden hotel went quickly. Soon the excavation was under way for the north wing, and by late 1907—six years after Harry Gosse first announced his plans—the new Riverside Hotel was completed and fully open for business. The south wing was three stories high while the north wing was four, discounting the basement under each wing. In the center of the north wing was a large veranda, covered by a roof and facing the Truckee River as it tumbled merrily by. There were now 130 rooms, all with private telephones and many with private baths. The turrets on the northeast and southeast corners had been converted into private, in-the-round guest rooms.[19]

The Riverside's main dining room, which had been located in the south wing, was closed and the space converted to nine more rooms and four communal baths, and the new dining room was opened in the veranda in the north wing. It was described as "the best of its kind anywhere from San Francisco to Denver." The room was glassed in and faced the river. It had twenty-four tables, all built of old oak seasoned until they were almost black, which presented a beautiful contrast to the stark white table linens. Brand new china, each piece featuring the Riverside Hotel crest in green and white, was paired with expensive new silver and glassware. In the kitchen Gosse had all the walls and flat surfaces painted white so every speck of dirt or grease could be easily spotted and cleaned. The kitchen was completely outfitted with new appliances, including large steam tables to keep food and dishware warm. In addition to the main dining room there was a porch café on the open second level, also facing the river, that was heated by steam in the winter but completely open to the elements during warm weather. The room would eventually be named the Lanai, and in addition to café fare it would be used for banquets and to host tango parties, which were all the rage at the time.[20]

Harry Gosse had finally fulfilled his promise to Reno and the traveling public. He and his architect, however, had made one blunder that they seemed to have gotten away with. Unpaved Island Avenue ran right along the river, stopping short of Virginia Street by some distance. When the north wing of the hotel was built, part of it fudged onto Island Avenue, which was owned by the city. Anyone who knew of this breach remained silent until 1908 when the city was building a large stone retaining wall along the river-bank. At that time the city attorney discovered the breach and demanded that either the hotel pay the city for the land and then pay for a portion of the retaining wall, or give up the land altogether. The Riverside was one of the city's largest taxpayers, and its Captain Gosse one of its outstanding citizens. Perhaps for that reason, no further action was ever taken on the matter, unless it was done privately.[21]

The Riverside was well known for the level of service it provided its guests. Joseph McDonald, who would later spend forty-two years on the staff of the *Reno Evening Gazette*, rising to the top as publisher, told a story about the Riverside's service while he was a student at Reno's University of

Nevada around 1908: "And I remember—the Riverside Hotel, of course, was the big hotel in Reno then.... And there was a colored porter used to drive that [Riverside Hotel] bus, and he'd come over to the depot and he'd pick up passengers.... His name was McDonald, and he was an Englishman.... I used to love to talk to the guy because he talked with a British accent [and] he was more or less of a fixture around the depot there."[22]

In 1909 the Riverside would host two special guests. One was a visitor to the city and the other was a well-known and important local citizen. The visitor was the famous adventurer Alice Ramsey, a twenty-two-year-old Vassar graduate, New Jersey housewife, and mother. She had set off from Hell Gate in Manhattan in an attempt to become the first woman to drive an automobile across the country. In a 1908 Maxwell Model K Gentleman's Roadster (perhaps the name should have been changed?) she and three other women began their 3,800-mile journey. About fifty-six or fifty-seven days later, and after only 152 miles of the entire trip on paved roads, the women reached Sparks, Nevada at night and first saw the skyline of Reno. "I shall never forget the surprise of the vista busting upon us in the darkness. Here was a hollow in which lay a community brilliantly lighted with electricity!... Suddenly we had returned to civilization!" she remarked in her 1961 book, *Veil, Duster, and Tire Iron*. The four dust-covered ladies drove on until they found the elegant Riverside Hotel, where they joyfully bathed, dined, and slept peacefully before resuming their historic drive to the Golden Gate the next morning.[23]

The local resident who graced the hotel was philanthropist Clarence Mackay, the son of wealthy Comstock miner John Mackay, the father of the Big Bonanza of Nevada silver mining fame. Just the previous year, Clarence and his mother, in John Mackay's name, had financed the building of the Mackay School of Mines building on the University of Nevada campus. The story of Clarence's visit went something like this:

Silas Ross, who would later become a prominent funeral director and business leader in Reno, was president of the university's student body at the time. It was football weekend, and Mr. Mackay, who had also financed the building of the football field, was due to be honored at a big reception at the university president's home the next evening for his financial support. Most of the city's influential citizens would be there to honor Mackay. When the football team won their big game, Silas Ross and his fraternity brothers decided it would be fun to "kidnap" Mr. Mackay from the president's reception the next night and take him "out on the town with the boys" to celebrate the victory. Somehow Mackay heard about the scheme beforehand, and being a good sport he decided to play along. The fraternity boys arrived at the reception and hid in the bushes, while word was sent inside that someone wished to see Mr. Mackay on the front porch. He whispered to his wife that he would be gone for a while, and leaving all the good citizens who had shown up to honor him, he and the fraternity boys spent the whole night carousing. Early the next morning—at Mr. Mackay's expense—the whole fraternity joined the multimillionaire for ham and eggs at the Riverside's outdoors Lanai restaurant.[24]

Although the building of the new Virginia Street Bridge and the Riverside Hotel were two of the most notable projects in the Truckee Meadows during the first decade of the twentieth century, there were other important things going on in the city as well. Early in the century a wooden walkway was built along the river just below the Riverside Hotel. It was called the River Walk. Although it didn't last too many years because of the constantly rising water, still it served as the forerunner of the permanent Riverwalk that would be built nearly a century later.

On March 19, 1907, the Truckee River reached its highest point since records began. Although no lives were lost, there was extensive damage from Sparks to the base of the foothills when the river breached its banks. Downtown Reno was fortunate, suffering some damage but escaping the worst of the flood. The Verdi and Mayberry Bridges were washed out, others were damaged severely, and the water reached the top of the arches of the new Virginia Street Bridge. There was no damage to the concrete bridge, and it became the only safe crossing in the Truckee Meadows for days. However, city officials were concerned for the structure, and posted firefighters on the bridge to patrol it and deter as many crossers as possible. The bottleneck in the river where floating debris backed up against the new bridge's large concrete arches would be a harbinger for the future, and this dangerous condition would haunt the Virginia Street Bridge during every severe flood for the next century.[25]

## NOTES

1. Summerfield, "On the Way to Reno," 113; Barber, *Reno's Big Gamble*, 54.

2. Riley, *Divorce, An American Tradition*, 135–36; "Mrs. Corey Will Leave Reno Tonight," *REG*, 12/06/1905; "Mrs. W. Ellis Corey Granted a Divorce," *NSJ*, 07/31/1906; Bartlett, *Is Marriage Necessary*, 5–6.

3. Quote from Ruhl, "Reno, and the Rush for Divorce."

4. "Little Bits of Items," *NSJ*, 09/28/1901; "Work Will Soon Be Commenced," *NSJ*, 10/12/1901; "The New Riverside," *NSJ*, 10/10/1901; "Terse and to the Point," *NSJ*, 11/09/1901; quote from "A Palatial Hotel Being Built in Reno," *NSJ*, 02/09/1902.

5. "Terse and to the Point," *NSJ*, 09/28/1901; "Building Reno's New Modern Hostelry," *NSJ*, 10/24/1901; "Work Will Soon Be Commenced," *NSJ*, 10/12/1901.

6. "The New Riverside," *NSJ*, 10/19/1901; n.t., *NSJ*, 11/09/1901; "A Great Improvement," *NSJ*, 11/20/1901; n.t., *NSJ*, 12/04/1901; Miramon, "Reno's Heritage Bridge Is in Jeopardy," 2.

7. First quote from "H. H. Beck Finds a Color," *NSJ*, 10/29/1901; second and third quotes from "Chance to Earn a Dollar," *NSJ*, 11/01/1901.

8. "Got on Stilts," *REG*, 04/11/1902; "Trimmed with Stone," *NSJ*, 04/11/1902; "Hurrying the Hotels," *NSJ*, 04/11/1902; n.t., *NSJ*, 06/06/1902.

9. "Changing the Building," *REG*, 06/24/1902.

10. Quote from "Fairyland," *REG*, 06/30/1902; n.t., *NSJ*, 06/30/1902; "Nearing Completion," *NSJ*, 08/03/1902; "All Sorts of Little Jots," *NSJ*, 08/22/1902.

11. Quote from, "New Riverside Hotel," *NSJ*, 01/23/1903; Riverside Hotel adv., *NSJ*, 01/23/1903; Bond, *Six Months in Reno*.

12. Quote from "Building Boom Is Not at End," *NSJ*, 09/15/1903.

13. "Riverside Hotel Costing $125,000 To Be Built Soon," *NSJ*, 06/14/1905; both quotes from "Articles of Incorporation of the Riverside Hotel Company," p. 1.

14. First quote from "To Complete the Riverside," *REG*, 12/23/1905; second quote from "In Readiness to Complete the Riverside," *NSJ*, 01/16/1906; Warren C. A. & Co. "Miscellaneous Index of Filings: Vol. 1, 1875–1912" (NOTE: The actual incorporation papers filed with the secretary of state have been misplaced or lost at the Nevada State Library and Archives, Carson City. Thus the only official proof of this filing is its inclusion in this index.)

15. Cafferata, "Poet Joaquin Miller Visited Reno," *RGJ*, 07/14/2013; Miller, "Classic Cowboy Poetry, Joaquin Miller."

16. Quotes taken from Cafferata, "Poet Joaquin Miller Visited Reno," *RGJ*, 07/14/2013.

17. First quote from "In Readiness to Complete the Riverside," *NSJ*, 01/16/1906; second quote from "FOR SALE," *REG*, 02/04/1906.

18. "May Discover Hidden Gold," *REG*, 06/02/1906.

19. Quote from "Landmark Is Disappearing," *REG*, 06/02/1906; Barber, *Reno's Big Gamble*, 65; Hardesty, "The Site of Reno's Beginning," 12.

20. Quote from "Riverside's Dining Room Is Now a Gem," *NSJ*, 09/20/1907; "Sun Parlor to Be the Lanai," *REG*, 06/12/1914.

21. "City Attorney King Makes Some Pointed Statements," *REG*, 05/16/1908.

22. McDonald, "The Life of a Newsboy in Nevada," 22–23.

23. Foster, "A Distinguished Drive"; Ramsey, *Veil, Duster, and Tire Iron*.

24. Ross, "Recollections of Life at Glendale," 157–58.

25. Miramon, "Reno's Heritage Bridge," 1; "River Reaches Highest Recorded Point," *NSJ*, 03/19/1907; "Verdi Steel Bridge Gone," *REG*, 03/18/1907; "The 25th Anniversary of Big Truckee Flood Recalled Today," *REG*, 03/17/1932.

This 1868 photo, the oldest known photo that shows any part of the second Virginia Street Bridge, captures the look and feel of the brand new town of Reno. The man on the right, at the end of the bridge, is most likely Daniel Pine who Myron Lake had hired the preceding year to be his toll collector. The view is facing the south end of Virginia Street, where the downtown area looks much like any other nineteenth-century western town. Courtesy of Jerry Fenwick.

Another version of Cyrenius McClellan's oil painting entitled *Reno Twenty Years Ago* is shown here. The bridge, and likely the hotel and tavern, had just been rebuilt following a major ("300-year") storm and flood the preceding winter. Nevada Historical Society.

North Virginia Street in the mid-1890s, looking from the end of the iron Virginia Street Bridge, was still composed primarily of wooden structures, although buildings of brick, steel, and stone were beginning to replace the old planked buildings. The Truckee Livery, Feed, and Stables building at the end of the bridge on the left belonged to longtime politician and businessman Thomas K. Hymers, who was instrumental in building both the iron and the concrete Virginia Street bridges. Courtesy of Jerry Fenwick.

The old iron bridge is nearly three decades old and failing in this 1899–1900 photo. Note the planked river walk that predated the city's present Riverwalk by almost a century. The idea for a promenade along the river had originally been advanced by Francis G. Newlands as early as 1889. The white building with the tall steeple was the Nevada State Fair Building. Courtesy of Jerry Fenwick.

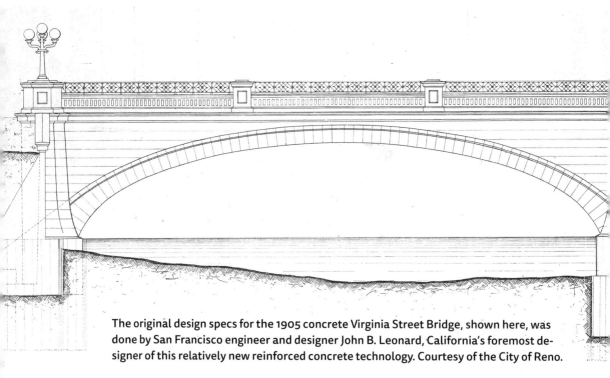

The original design specs for the 1905 concrete Virginia Street Bridge, shown here, was done by San Francisco engineer and designer John B. Leonard, California's foremost designer of this relatively new reinforced concrete technology. Courtesy of the City of Reno.

New Court House and Riverside Hotel Reno, Nev.

In this 1910 photo, the concrete Virginia Street Bridge, the grand new Riverside Hotel, and the Washoe County Court House (behind the Riverside) would become inexorably linked in fact and fable as the burgeoning divorce business changed the face of the small city. Courtesy of Jerry Fenwick.

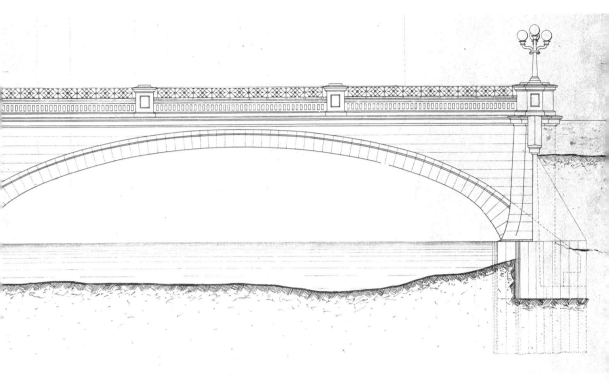

BANQUET TENDERED POST C ~ T.P.A. ~
~ BY CAPT. H.J.GOSSE ~ RIVERSIDE HOTEL ~
~ RENO, NEV APR 5, 1913 ~

The Riverside Hotel's large banquet room was a favorite meeting venue for men's business and fraternal organizations, women's charitable banquets and gatherings, and regional conventions. Here, in 1913, Captain Harry Gosse hosted members of an unidentified gentlemen's business or fraternal organization. Nevada Historical Society.

The magnificent Riverside Hotel, only fifteen years old at the time, was completely consumed by fire in this 1922 blaze that started in the basement. Miraculously, nobody died in the fire, but it took valiant efforts by hotel workers, passers-by, and city firefighters to prevent a human tragedy. Courtesy of Jerry Fenwick.

IVERSIDE HOTEL
J DELONGCHAMPS          RENO NE
ARCHT

By 1926 the Riverside Hotel, now under the new ownership of George Wingfield, was well under construction next to the Truckee River. Wingfield's huge chateau-esque hotel was designed by Frederic DeLongchamps to take full advantage of the burgeoning divorce trade. Courtesy of Neal Cobb.

The twelve-story Mapes Hotel opened in downtown Reno in 1947, diagonally across the Truckee River from the Riverside. It was the first major hotel to be built in the United States following World War II. Locally owned by the Mapes family, the hotel would give the aging Riverside Hotel the first real competition in its eighty-eight-year history. Special Collections Department, University of Nevada, Reno Libraries.

The demolition of the 105-year-old concrete Virginia Street Bridge was scheduled for June and July 2015. Like every step in the complex process, the demolition went off right on schedule. This photo, from June 23, 2015, shows the remains of the north span as the debris waits to be toted away. Courtesy of the City of Reno.

# CHAPTER 7

# THE DELMONICO OF RENO

"THE WORLD WAS STARTING to notice Reno—a wild, raucous town in a beautiful mountain setting where divorce seekers, cowboys, free-flowing liquor, and boxing fans mingled openly in a wide-open society," Nevada historian William D. Rowley observed about Reno at the beginning of the second decade of the twentieth century. The city's population had grown to 10,867 by 1910, certainly big for Nevada, but not big enough to warrant the national—occasionally even international—publicity the city had begun to attract.[1]

Barely into the new decade, the six-year-old Virginia Street Bridge became the site of local controversy. The winter of 1910–11 was a severe one. Although it was not a record-breaker in terms of snowfall, still there was enough to make Renoites nervous, especially with the flood of 1907 fresh in their minds. By early March heavy snowfall had destroyed or damaged many of the Southern Pacific Railroad's snow sheds in the Sierra Nevada, and more snow was forecast. With a month or so still to go before the winter runoff would begin cascading down the Truckee River, people began making preparations. Under the headline, "If Floods Threaten," the *Reno Evening Gazette* ran an editorial excoriating the new bridge; and Mayor E. E. Roberts and other city council members put forth an extreme solution for fixing the problem. "It is true that a grave error was made in certain details in the planning of the new bridge," the newspaper wrote. The problem, the editor charged, were the twenty-four-inch-high concrete walls that ran along each side of the bridge, supporting the decorative iron railings. These parapets turned the bridge into a sluice when raging waters reached that level, and floodwaters would be diverted to either or both ends of the bridge, and then would cut channels into the ground that could do heavy damage to the buildings on the riverfront. Those buildings at most risk were the Riverside Hotel, the Carnegie Public Library, the Masonic Building, and the new

Circus Day on the Virginia Street Bridge, 1915. The solid, two-foot-high parapets along both sides of the concrete Virginia Street Bridge, built a decade earlier and evident here, acted like a sluice for floodwaters, threatening the Washoe County Courthouse (*left*) and the Masonic Temple (*right*), as well as the Riverside Hotel and Carnegie Public Library. The bridge would remain the nexus for city celebrations such as this one for more than a century. Nevada Historical Society.

U.S. Post Office building, some of the most historic and expensive buildings in the city. The editor called for the immediate removal of the walls and a different type of railing substituted, one that would allow floodwaters to drain over the sides of the bridge, as they had done with the old iron bridge. Apparently the city council discussed actually blowing up the bridge if a dangerous flood threatened, a possibility even the complaining newspaper editor called "a very foolish idea."[2]

Ultimately the snowmelt did lead to the collapse of the Hobart Creek Reservoir on Mount Davidson, east of Reno (often called Sun Mountain by Nevadans), which killed two people, but the Truckee Meadows remained relatively unscathed by the winter runoff. As for the ideas put forward by the city council and the newspaper editor, neither idea ever came to pass.

As years went by the bridge did become a very popular fishing spot, and almost any hour of day or night men and boys could be seen casting their lines over the parapet. At Christmastime during the same era, it was fashionable to place brightly lit candelabras on the parapets as a popular part of the downtown holiday decorations.[3]

In late 1912 a longtime staff member of the Riverside Hotel—and certainly a favorite of the traveling public who regularly lodged at the hotel—passed away quietly of old age. He was important enough that the newspapers regularly published tidbits about his activities, including one when he became ill and another two days later when he passed away. The staffer was Cleo the dog, the hotel's official mascot and beloved pet of fifteen-year-old Harry Gosse Jr. Harry had picked up the sickly stray pup at the Southern Pacific Railroad Depot eleven years earlier, and the pooch had lived at the hotel ever since. The newspaper wrote, "Cleo...known by every traveling man from Salt Lake to San Francisco...and known to pretty nearly everyone in Reno, has passed away." Every guest could count on being greeted by Cleo when he or she entered the hotel, and the dog was always happy to share a trick with any visitor who showed the least interest. When Cleo became ill, many hotel visitors even took the time to visit him at the vet hospital. His passing was mourned by many.[4]

One of the most popular attractions for divorcees staying at the Riverside was Captain Gosse's bountiful dining room, which also attracted many of the city's most prominent citizens, particularly on special occasions like Thanksgiving. The menu for that day in 1912 was enough to make even the most sophisticated palates drool with anticipation. Appetizers included Blue Point oysters and mock turtle quenelles, while desserts like English plum pudding with brandy sauce, tutti-frutti ice cream, and hot mince or Nevada pumpkin pie were all offered. For the main course, diners could select from planked halibut à la meunière, sweetbread cutlets Béarnaise, salmi of duck à la chasseur or, naturally, roast turkey from nearby Fallon, with chestnut dressing. Dining at the Riverside was always a special treat. The hotel's sumptuous banquet room also hosted a number of local and regional meetings.[5]

Anything that promised to bring more tourists to Nevada would certainly benefit the magnificent new Riverside Hotel. The biggest obstacle to attracting the rapidly growing motorist trade, however, was the abysmal condition of Washoe County's roads. It was widely known by the populous of Northern Nevada that once you entered Washoe County, from that time on, the roads were nothing but ruts and chuckholes, and in many places the roads were nothing but irrigation ditches.[6]

An unlikely impetus would eventually kick-start state, county, and city officials to take road building and repair seriously. In mid-1913 it was announced that an Indianapolis man, Carl Fisher, had proposed a plan to construct a "Coast-to-Coast Rock [i.e. gravel] Highway" that would run from New York City to San Francisco. The plan was not to build a new highway, but to cobble together and improve existing local and state roads, and then to promote it as one unified thoroughfare. It was an audacious plan, and an expensive one, but Fisher theorized it would be funded by the fledging automotive and auto parts industries. The road was to be named the Lincoln Highway after the nation's sixteenth president, a wise choice as people in the industrial North, where most of the hoped-for sponsors lived, still revered the memory of the fallen president. Reno city officials, like those at every other city and town along the proposed route, were informed that a group from the Indiana Automobile Manufacturers Association would be in the city in late July to discuss the matter. The tour group's letter to the city requested advice on the best place to dine and lodge, and informed that their group would be about 100 men, "among who will be found many of national prominence." As the city's leading hotel, the Riverside was chosen to feed and house the team during their stay.[7]

City officials, Renoites, and Captain Gosse were disappointed when the group changed their proposed touring route and bypassed Reno altogether, traveling through the state instead on a southern route.[8] By October, however, after many organizational changes and a great deal of politicking, Reno was back on the Lincoln Highway map. The Lincoln Highway Committee and Reno city fathers decided to stage a giant Highway Day Parade of automobiles through town to celebrate the occasion. "Long Line of Machines Drive Through Streets of City in Parade; Many Fine Floats Shown," newspaper headlines boasted the day after the big celebration.[9]

For all intents and purposes, the highway was completed by the early 1920s, but some segments would not be surfaced with gravel or asphalt until the following decade. In Nevada, the Lincoln Highway primarily followed what are now State Highways 50 and 40, Prater Way through Sparks, and Fourth Street through the city of Reno. The first Lincoln Highway sign in Reno—and perhaps in all of Nevada—was posted on the northeast corner of the Washoe County Bank building at the corner of Virginia and Second Streets on April 7, 1914. The red, white, and blue horizontal stripes on the sign bore a large "L" in the middle and the smaller words "Lincoln" and "Highway" at the top and bottom of the sign. Similar signs would follow all along the route of the highway. As Gosse and other Reno merchants had hoped, the Lincoln Highway would ultimately bring thousands of new visitors to the city.[10]

As a professional hotelier, Gosse was always full of ideas to keep both visitors and locals coming to the Riverside. In the summer of 1915 he arranged to have a maple-floor roller rink built in the rear of the hotel, under a large open-air tent. It was open daily except Sunday from 10 AM to noon for beginners, and from 2:30 PM to 5:30 PM and 7:30 PM to 10:30 PM for all skaters. Admission was ten cents, with ladies admitted free, and skates rented for a quarter. An orchestrion, a mechanical instrument that sounded like a full orchestra, provided the music. Gosse also kept an eye open for new ways to pamper his divorcee-to-be guests. In the late teens he rented a couple of rooms to a lady mysteriously called Madame Grimm, a huge woman who was also a talented masseuse. Madame Grimm had previously employed her talents at the Hotel Mizpah in Tonopah, but when she married she relocated to Reno and shifted her operation to the Riverside.[11]

Early in the new century many Reno residents saw the city's wide-open gambling as a black mark that brought in undesirables, robbed the hardworking poor of their wages, and created an overall shoddy reputation for their beloved city. Reformer groups like the Anti-Saloon League and the Women's Christian Temperance Union did all they could to fuel those sentiments against gambling, which had been legal in Nevada since 1869. This pressure helped propel state legislators into passing a statute, to be effective in 1910, outlawing gambling throughout Nevada. Then in 1919— a year before national prohibition—state legislators also outlawed the sale of nonmedicinal alcohol throughout Nevada. Both vices had been primarily practiced in the state's saloons; there were 795 of them in Nevada when the liquor ban took place. In Reno the saloons were mostly huddled along the railroad tracks on Commercial Row, which was anchored by the large Palace Hotel where gambling and liquor were the chief attractions. Gambling was not a major draw at the Riverside Hotel, although there was a small gambling area available, but the loss of the liquor business—an important part of catering to the traveling business trade—would be a costly loss for Gosse.[12] But for Nevada's saloons—a historic part of the state's Old West heritage—the double whammy was enough to put many of them out of business. Others, however, slunk back into the shadows where they quietly and unlawfully continued their operations.

Although Reno's vociferous do-gooder faction would successfully deal with the demons of gambling and alcohol during the decade, it would not enjoy the same success when it took on the powerful divorce interests. Cries for reform in the lenient divorce trade reached a fever pitch in 1913 when an entire trainload of antidivorce militants boarded the Virginia & Truckee Railroad to Carson City, and occupied the state capitol building. There they forced a change in the six-month residency requirement, extending it to one year. Governor Tasker Oddie signed the measure, but he and many of the legislators paid the price when they were defeated at the polls the following year. Under intense pressure by hotel keepers like Harry Gosse, lawyers, and business persons, in 1915 the residency requirement was quietly changed back to six months, although women's groups, the clergy, and another delegation from Reno protested mightily. During the same legislative session, the popular Nevada State Fair was officially moved from Reno to nearby Fallon, a significant loss for the Biggest Little City.[13]

During the decade the publicity the city received because of the divorce trade was far-reaching. Occasionally it was positive, but normally it was negative, and much of it was written with tongue in cheek. The simple fact that most eastern writers wrote disparagingly about Reno's divorce-seekers ignored the fact that most of these men and women were, in fact, easterners themselves.

The *New York Times* featured two almost full-page stories on Reno's divorce trade, and the well-respected *Collier's* magazine ran a two-page spread that included this pretentious observation:

> As we were at dinner, our first evening in Reno, at the Riverside—which resembled a summer hotel whose summer girls were all about ten years older than they usually are—they would come sailing into the dining-room in twos and threes, chatelaines jangling, in a curious pseudo-girlish camaraderie. A London correspondent at my table... confided to me, as he surveyed the room, that he assumed all the women he saw in Reno were trying to get unmarried—'although I dare say I'm doing many of these estimable ladies an injustice.'... Mr. Thomas's [Gosse's restaurant manager] restaurant, [is] sometimes called the 'Delmonico's of Reno.'...Here you will find a menu almost as large as those of the city hotels, and even on quiet mid-week evenings enjoy the exquisite excitement of seeing waiters flit to and fro with ice-buckets of real champagne.[14]

It was during this decade that one of the city's preeminent judges would become nationally known for his divorce work. George A. Bartlett was accepted to the Nevada bar late in the nineteenth century, after graduating from Georgetown University Law School. Following stints as a county district attorney, a member of the U.S. Congress, and a practicing attorney in Reno, Bartlett became a judge in the Nevada court system in 1918. Over the next thirteen years Judge Bartlett would officiate at over 20,000 Reno divorces before returning to the local bar in 1931. A romanticist at heart, Bartlett preferred working things out to divorce; he wrote a number of books on the subject, becoming somewhat of a "Dr. Phil" McGraw for his generation.[15]

The popularity of boxing matches in Reno was another draw for the visitor trade. In 1910 Reno hosted the biggest fight in the new century when the world's heavyweight champion, Jack Johnson, fought and soundly defeated James Jeffries in what was touted as "The Fight of the Century." The fight had initially been scheduled for San Francisco, but California's governor cancelled it following an outpouring of public indignation, and Reno was happy to step in. Johnson, a black man, had won the title in 1908, and leading sportswriters, led by the renown Jack London, called for a Great White Hope to reclaim the title for the white race. Jeffries, however, would not be that man. Despite that, the Riverside was sold out for weeks thanks to the international prefight publicity the fight generated. Fight promoter George Lewis "Tex" Rickard and his staff were all headquartered at Captain Gosse's hostelry. Between 20,0000 and 30,000 fans poured into Reno for the bout on July 4, and although the majority of fans were disappointed in the outcome, Gosse and his fellow Reno businessmen were elated.[16]

The Johnson–Jeffries fight didn't turn Reno into the Boxing Capital of the West, as the city had hoped—the next big-time bout would not be staged in Reno until 1931—but the city did play host to many second- and third-tier fights over the next two decades, providing another source of guests for Gosse's restaurants and rooms.[17]

## NOTES

1. Rowley, *Reno*, 37.

2. "Big Storm Is in Progress All Along Coast," REG, 03/08/1911; first and second quotes from "If Floods Threaten," *REG*, 03/09/1911.

3. "Body of Mrs. Campbell Recovered," *NSJ*, 04/22/1911; Online Nevada Encyclopedia, "Virginia Street Bridge."

4. "Dog of Many Friends Sick," *REG*, 11/20/1912; "Cleo, Noted Dog Is Dead," *REG*, 11/22/1912.

5. Riverside Hotel, "Thanksgiving Dinner Menu," 1912.

6. McDonald, *History of Washoe County*, "The 1910's."

7. First quote from Franzwa and Petersen, *The Lincoln Highway*, ix; second quote from "To Choose Auto Road in Nevada," *REG*, 05/21/1913.

8. "Lessons from the Tour," *REG*, 07/28/1913.

9. Quote from "Motorists Out to Dedicate Lincoln Highway," *NSJ*, 11/01/1913.

10. Skorupa, "The Mighty Lincoln Highway," *RGJ*, 06/23/2013; "First Lincoln Sign in Place," *REG*, 04/08/1914.

11. "Tonight's the Night for Roller Skaters," *NSJ*, 05/01/1915; Blair, "Days Remembered of Folsom and Placerville, California," 46.

12. Barber, *Reno's Big Gamble*, 50–51; Statutes of the State of Nevada Passed at the Twenty-fourth Session of the Legislature, 1909, 307–9; Statutes of the State of Nevada Passed at the Twenty-ninth Session, 1919, 1–13; "John Barleycorn's Career in Nevada Is to End at Midnight," *REG*, 12/15/1918.

13. Blake, *The Road to Reno*, 155–56; Riley, *Divorce, An American Tradition*, 136.

14. Ruhl, "Reno and the Rush for Divorce," 19.

15. Bartlett, "George A. Bartlett Papers," biography; Bartlett, *Is Marriage Necessary*, passim.

16. "Fight Excites Local Interest," *NSJ*, 06/18/1910; Rowley, *Reno*, 37.

17. Guy Clifton, boxing expert, private communication with the author, 05/24/2013.

# CHAPTER 8

# DEATH AND REBIRTH

BY THE BEGINNING OF THE 1920S, World War I was over and a period of economic growth had begun. It was the Roaring Twenties, with flappers, bathtub gin, and speakeasies. Although most of these icons of the era belonged to the nation's largest cities, some smaller places including Reno were also getting their share of the good times. A traveling salesman from New York put it in perspective, saying, "Reno is one of the most cosmopolitan cities in the country." Another observer of Reno in the early 1920s wrote, "Do you know that Reno has a theatre equal in beauty to the Lyric or Knickerbocker in New York? Stroll over some evening and examine the audience. What other town of twelve thousand souls can exhibit such a wonderful aggregation of well-dressed people? Metropolitan and cosmopolitan in appearance and in fact, a greater number appear in evening costume than one sees at a Gotham first night. Bored in Reno? Absurd!" Reno's 1920 population was 12,016, up almost 11 percent from a decade earlier.[1]

Since rebuilding the Riverside Hotel for its owners on the bank overlooking the Truckee River in 1902, Captain Gosse had maintained the enviable position the Riverside Hotel had held since the earliest days of the town when the Lake House reigned supreme. In those earlier days, the hotel was the choice for most travelers who passed through Reno; but it was also the social focal point for the entire community. With the dawning of the 1920s, the Riverside was still the leading hotel in Reno for both visitors and locals. In mid-1920 city officials took a tourist count with statistics garnered from all the city's hotel registers. There had been approximately 25,000 visitors to Reno in the first five months of the year. The Riverside, with 8,050 guests, had hosted one in three of all travelers to the city. The Overland and Golden Hotels ranked a distant second and third, respectively, and all the others trailed far behind. Travelers, the study found, came from all walks of life:

those in sales, mining, farming, along with federal officials, aviators, tourists, wool buyers, and cattle buyers. The Riverside didn't just lead numerically—it also captured the crème de la crème of all travelers from the tourist trade, the divorce trade, and the business trade. A New York writer penned a small booklet, *Six Months in Reno*, in the early 1920s for those considering a Reno divorce. The booklet noted, "There is one hotel running on the American plan suitable for men, women and children.... The Riverside Hotel, well situated just out of the business district and overlooking the Truckee River, is the hotel to which many people go upon their arrival."[2]

The Riverside Hotel remained the focal point for the local community, too. It was the hotel of choice for every important social occasion and business event: women's luncheons, afternoon teas, dances, group dinners, school commencements, banquets, weddings, receptions, business lunches, and special occasion dinners. As a career hotelier, Harry Gosse had proven that he was at the top of his game.

At 2:00 AM on Wednesday, March 15, 1922, C. J. Scott and a few other Riverside Hotel guests were playing cards in the elegant smoking room on the ground floor. Suddenly Scott noticed smoke coming out of the elevator shaft. He hurriedly left the room and reported the problem to desk clerk Norman Dawson. Dawson rushed to the basement to check, but he was engulfed by heavy smoke, although he could see no flames. He rushed back upstairs, and following protocol he switched on the fire alarm, warning guests of the potential danger, and alerting the fire and police departments. Captain Gosse, whose family lived in an apartment on one of the upper floors, awoke immediately, threw on some clothes, and dashed into the basement, but, he remarked, "The smoke was so dense I could not get very far." He rushed back upstairs to see that his family and the hotel's guests were alerted and ushered outside. Quickly he recruited bellhops and taxi drivers, and they all began going door to door throughout the hotel rousing sleeping guests, while the smoke intensified throughout the entire building, making breathing nearly impossible.[3]

By 3:00 AM the flames finally broke through into the center of the building and onto the roof, while fire fighters futilely tried to halt its progress. Flames were said to be shooting 150 feet into the air. It wasn't until fire fighters broke into the basement at the rear of the H-shaped building, under the barbershop, that they discovered the source of the fire. However, the cause of the fire was never established, although Gosse guessed it was caused by either spontaneous combustion or crossed electrical wiring. By 4:00 AM the entire building was engaged in what was described as a roaring furnace. An ammonia tank in the south-side basement suddenly exploded, breaking every window in the cellar. By this time the fire was so intense that fire fighters had to back away, and they began hosing down surrounding buildings to save them from flying embers.

By 5:00 AM several sections of the south wall of the building had fallen in, when a second explosion—this time an oil burner—rocked the entire area, scattering bystanders with sparks and flying bricks. It would be 9:00 AM before the fire was completely out, and fire fighters began pulling down the walls fronting Virginia Street so they would not topple on unwary pedestrians. By early afternoon, the newspaper wrote, "The once proud hostelry was only a mass of smoldering ruins."[4]

Miraculously, all the guests and hotel employees had made it out of the hotel safely. Many in the upper floors escaped by fire department ladders, the fire escape, or ropes made from bed sheets, as the smoke was so thick in the hallways people could not escape by that route. Fortunately, since the fire had occurred in the early morning, and midweek, the hotel had not been crowded; there were only seventy people in the entire building at the time of the fire, including guests and employees. A number of men were recognized for their heroism in clearing the building. Desk clerk Dawson and police officer Capps each rescued a child, and taxi driver Sam Freeman carried a woman who had collapsed from the smoke out to safety from the third floor. Freeman returned and carried two more women down the fire escape from the third floor on his back. These, however, were just a few of the many employees, bystanders, police, and fire fighters who performed heroically to save lives during the disaster.

The Gosse family's losses were huge. By this time, according to a statement by Harry Gosse in the *Reno Evening Gazette*, "Mr. and Mrs. Gosse own all the stock in the Riverside Hotel Company. They have bought up all the outstanding stock during the past few years and the entire property belongs to them." The building and its furnishings were valued at $250,000, but only $100,000 of that was covered by insurance, so Harry and Josephine were now forced to shoulder much of the financial burden on their own. To make matters worse, the family had also lost all of their personal possessions, including a large collection of priceless relics from the Comstock era. A local family, the Sebelines, were friends of the Gosses and allowed them the use of a vacant home they owned in the city, so at least the family would have a roof over their heads.[5]

At 2:00 AM on March 15, 1922, a fire started in the basement of the Riverside Hotel. By the next morning, shown here, the huge structure had been reduced to smoking rubble, with only the brick walls still standing. Despite numerous promises to the public, Gosse was never able to raise the funds to rebuild, and in November 1924 he sold the property to George Wingfield. Courtesy of Jerry Fenwick.

The morning after the fire, as Gosse stood looking over the smoking, steaming ruins of his once grand hotel, a newspaper reporter approached him and asked what his plans were. "As soon as it is possible to do so, I will have plans drawn for a new hotel which will be modern in every respect and which will be four or five stories high," he said. Then perhaps realizing the question many would be asking, he added, "I have assurances of plenty of money to finance the building of the structure and expect to begin clearing of the grounds within a few days."[6]

The ground the hotel had occupied had a Virginia Street frontage of 246 feet, and was 310 feet deep, all the latter being river frontage, according to the *Reno Evening Gazette*. However, the official Washoe County Riverview Survey tract maps indicate that the newspaper was in error. These records show that the Virginia Street frontage was 210 feet and the river frontage boundary was 265 feet. Regardless of this discrepancy, Gosse valued the land alone at $100,000. The hotel's rear walls were still standing, and they would not be knocked down until a crew had a chance to comb the wreckage for hotel guests' lost valuables, said to be worth over $75,000 and including a number of expensive diamonds. The huge stone chimney, however, was knocked down that afternoon.[7]

Perhaps it was an omen, or maybe a shrouded warning to the Gosses, but exactly a week after the devastating fire, fellow Renoite George Wingfield announced in the newspaper that he planned to build a $220,000, five-story commercial hotel on downtown property currently occupied by the Russ House, the Golden Hotel, and the Golden Annex that he owned. Wingfield was one of the state's most important business and political figures, having risen from a humble job as a cattle drover to being the richest and most powerful man in Nevada. In describing his first visit to Reno some three decades earlier, Wingfield proved he wasn't above spinning a little yarn. He was, he said, a fourteen-year-old cowboy when he stepped off the train at the Reno depot. One of the first things he saw as he started walking down Virginia Street were two Indians hanging from the Virginia Street Bridge, an event that is not verified anywhere, including in both local newspapers. Wingfield said he immediately knew Reno was too tough a town for him, and he hurried back to the depot vowing never to return to Reno again. By 1922 he had made a fortune mining in Tonopah and Goldfield, and had become heavily involved with banking and hotel keeping, and he returned to Reno. Whether his plan for a grand new hotel was a threat to Harry Gosse or not, we cannot know, but it certainly would have given Gosse something to ponder.[8]

For the next two and a half years, articles would appear in the newspapers from time to time announcing Gosse's new plan for rebuilding the Riverside: a San Francisco architect had been hired, a general contractor was retained, financing from the East had been arranged, or a magnificent new $500,000 Riverside Hotel was on the horizon. One financing plan called for part of the stock in a new company to be offered to Reno residents as an investment. On August 16, 1924, a small story even declared that work was to begin that very day, and the hotel would be completed within seven months. Although there was a small amount of excavating done a few months later, that was the extent of the work done on the site, which had been completely enclosed within a green plank fence. Thus it was a surprise to almost everyone when in mid-November stories appeared in both newspapers announcing that George Wingfield, through his Reno Securities Company, had purchased the Riverside property for $70,000 and would reveal his plans for the property the following spring. By the time of the sale Harry and Josephine had also granted stock in the company to their daughter Marguerite and her husband, Richard Stoddard. All of Harry's hard work to keep the hotel in the family had been for naught, as all of the financing plans he had worked on had gone up in smoke, much like the chateau-esque Riverside Hotel itself.[9]

Harry J. Gosse, "Captain" or "Pops" to his many friends and admirers, had been an excellent steward for the historic site during the nearly three decades it was under his management or ownership. He made a comfortable

© 1928 BY H E JOHNSON.

Fifty-two-year-old George Wingfield, pictured here in 1928, was Nevada's most powerful business and political figure when he purchased Harry Gosse's riverfront land where the Riverside Hotel had stood before the disastrous 1922 fire. Wingfield had accumulated a significant fortune, mostly through shrewd mining investments and banking. Special Collections Department, University of Nevada, Reno Libraries.

living for himself and his family, and he had become a prominent and well-respected member of the Reno business community. Following the sale of the riverfront property to George Wingfield, Harry Gosse retired from business, but he remained active in civic and fraternal affairs in Reno until his death at the age of eighty-seven in 1944.[10]

Initially George Wingfield was unsure of what he should do with his new property, according to his biographer, Elizabeth Raymond. The riverfront site was an excellent location, but it was quite a few blocks removed from the business axis of the city on Center Street at Commercial Row, where the successful Hotel Golden he had purchased in 1914 was located. One thought was to build short-term apartments on the site, catering to the divorce trade, but Wingfield took considerable criticism from competing apartment owners over that idea. He also considered parceling out the property to the city, county, and state, all of which had eyes on various pieces of the prestigious land. Eventually he did sell off two small parcels. For $3,500 he sold a parcel to the city so it could enlarge and extend Island Avenue along the river until it met Virginia Street. Island Avenue bordered Wingfield Park—once known as Belle Isle, and home to an amusement park—which its namesake had donated to the city. He also sold a $24,000 parcel to Washoe County so the county could add outdoor spaces to the adjoining county courthouse.[11]

By late June 1926, over a year and a half after he had purchased the property, Wingfield had made his decision, and he announced his plans in the newspaper. He would rebuild the Riverside Hotel, he said. The plans were grand; Wingfield estimated the cost at $750,000, an enormous price tag for the times. The first phase, occupying the east half of the property fronting Virginia Street, would be a concrete and brick structure six stories high, with a basement. There would a total of 140 guest rooms, plus an additional 100 bathrooms. Forty corner suites, primarily for the divorce trade, would combine a living room, a bedroom, a kitchenette, a dinette, three closets, and a bathroom with tub, basin, and toilet into cozy but elegant apartments. The other sixty rooms would be standard, though upgraded, hotel rooms. Each individual room would have a temperature regulator, an unusual amenity for the day.

The first phase of the project would be a T-shaped building, with the top of the T facing Virginia Street. The lobby would initially be in the leg of the T, but it would be moved to the Virginia Street side when the second phase was built. The ground floor of the Virginia Street frontage would consist of the hotel entrance, retail stores, and a bank—to be owned by Wingfield—positioned on the northeast corner. Behind the stores would be a spacious dining room that could be converted into a ballroom or banquet hall when needed. The other five floors would be devoted to the hotel rooms and apartments. The second phase of the project, on the west half of the property, would be added later when demand dictated, Wingfield said, although that would not happen for more than a quarter century. It was apparent that Wingfield's plans, although certainly not ignoring the vacation market and the locals market, was aimed primarily at taking advantage of the burgeoning divorce trade.[12]

When Wingfield announced his plans, architects from several cities sent him letters of solicitation. One of those letters came from Renoite Frederic DeLongchamps, who wrote, "If you decide to go ahead with this building, it would give me great pleasure to do the architectural work. I am equipped better than I ever have been before to turn out your work in the best possible manner." Unknown to DeLongchamps, Wingfield had already decided to use a local architect, and in short order the two men had sealed the deal. The contractor for the job would be P. J. Walker Company of San Francisco.[13]

Frederic DeLongchamps was born in 1882, educated in Reno, and graduated from the University of Nevada with a degree in mining engineering in 1904. Following the 1906 San Francisco earthquake, young Frederic spent a year there helping to rebuild the city while serving as an apprentice to a Bay Area architect. He returned to Reno in 1907 to begin his own practice, and achieved his first notoriety when his architectural plans were selected for the design of the Washoe County Courthouse in 1909. During the course of his career, DeLongchamps would become Reno's most celebrated and prolific twentieth-century architect, designing over 500 public buildings, commercial structures, and homes. Some said the Riverside marked a departure from the formal, neoclassical design he favored for most of his major public and commercial structures. However, preservation and architectural historian Mella Harmon disagrees. By the time he designed the Riverside, Harmon says, he had already demonstrated his ability with a wide range of styles, including Classical, Mediterranean, and Prairie styles. "For an untrained architect, he was versatile and willing to explore his abilities," she writes. Throughout his career the architect also favored stone, brick, and terra cotta as building materials, and this is easily seen in his work on the Riverside.[14]

The Riverside Hotel's basic architectural design is described in its nomination papers for inclusion in the National Register of Historic Places: "The

Construction was completed on George Wingfield's Riverside Hotel in May 1927. Thirty-six years later a new wing would be added, then later demolished, but the exterior of the main structure as pictured here would remain much the same for at least the next nine decades. Courtesy Jerry Fenwick.

Riverside Hotel is a large and imposing six-storied, red brick, Period Revival structure with terra cotta decoration in the Gothic style.... The original portion of the building was T-shaped. A major casino/restaurant/theater wing was added to the west side in 1950." Another, more in-depth study of the hotel's distinctive architecture noted: "Details [are] in cream terra-cotta, such as pointed-arched windows on the sixth floor, traceried parapets, and stacked bay windows embellished with panels and quoins."[15]

Wingfield biographer Raymond described the reasoning behind the Riverside: "The new hotel...would be something distinctive in Reno.... The Riverside was planned as a luxury establishment intended to cater to travelers who sought amenities that the commercial hotels didn't offer.... The upper floors mixed standard hotel rooms with apartment suites designed for the longer sojourns that divorce-seekers were forced to make.... The building positioned George Wingfield to take advantage of Reno's burgeoning divorce trade, especially its upper echelons, where men and women were willing and able to pay for gracious surroundings while they put in their time."[16]

One ground floor apartment certainly proved Raymond's latter point about the upper echelons. It contained two bedrooms and two baths, a living room, dining room, kitchen, storage room, and two maids' quarters. Over the years this apartment would be leased to über-wealthy divorcees when it wasn't being used as a home by the hotel's owners. The remaining apartments were more modest in size, but just as elegant in their appointments.[17]

There were forty suites in all. Most had a combination living room and bedroom, with a dining room, kitchen, and bathroom, but some also had a second bedroom. These second bedrooms had their own bathrooms, and were connected to the main corridors. They could be shut off from the remainder of the apartment and rented as single rooms.[18]

Excavation work for the pouring of the foundation on the first phase of the new Riverside Hotel began less than a month later, and it was planned that by November all the concrete and brick work would be completed, the roof would be in place, and the oil-burning steam furnaces would have been installed in the basement.[19] By mid-May 1927 the hotel was ready to open, and it was as modern and elegant as promised, according to the *Reno Evening Gazette*:

Gothic style of architecture has been used in the design in the exterior and the interior. Bay windows were built on some of the living room[s] to give maximum sunlight and view, and at the same time add to the architectural effect.... Living rooms have paneled walls with stippled paint finish. Bed-rooms have papered walls and painted wood-work. The floor of the lounge is "Gagas" mahogany random width planks, the wainscoat is of "tanguile" mahogany and the walls are of textured plaster. All wood-work in the lobbies and corridors, including the doors, is of mahogany.

The hotel part of the main floor is divided into a business lobby and lounge. The floor of the lobby is of Tennessee marble in three colors and the walls are of Travertine stone.

The building is piped for [a] circulating hot water system which insures the immediate delivery of hot water on the opening of the faucets. The equipment also includes a water filter.... A complete refrigerating plant...has been installed...[and] each apartment is fitted with a specially designed cork-insulated and tile-lined refrigerator.... Each of these small refrigerators is also fitted with trays for making ice cubes for table use in the different apartments. Each apartment is also equipped with an electric range.

A kitchen located in the basement has been equipped especially to provide service into private dining rooms.

All rooms and apartments are provided with telephones connected to the switchboard from which four trunk lines are connected to the Reno central office.[20]

The building had cost $600,000 and the elaborate furnishings another $150,000. Early visitors claimed it was worth every penny. Two weeks later the stores facing Virginia Street began to open. There was a beauty parlor, a florist and art store, and a cigar store, while a barber shop and valeting (tailor) shop would occupy rooms in the basement, along with storage rooms and employees' dining room and lockers. A massive, secure vault was also housed in the basement. Wingfield selected Charles J. Sadleir, who had managed his Hotel Golden for many years, to operate the new hostelry.[21]

On May 14, the day of the grand opening, there was a festive air. As the front door was opened, Wingfield and his chief engineer, Estey Julian, each decided he wanted to be the first to register, and both men raced for the registration desk. It was fitting that Wingfield won the contest, and he was officially the first guest to register in his own hotel. By noon thirty-four other guests had registered, and when added to the advance registrations, the hotel was completely booked for its first night. Public tours began at 2:00 PM in the lounging area and the first two floors of rooms and apartments, and everyone was wowed by what they saw. The newspaper announced that 5,000 people had attended the opening, and "[the attendees] pronounced everything perfect."[22]

One of the early local couples to enjoy all the magnificent amenities of the Riverside Hotel was newly married William and Dorothy (Gray) Royle. The young couple was married on June 5 at a home on Chestnut (today Arlington) Street, and had decided to honeymoon in the brand new hotel. As their baggage was whisked away by a liveried bellhop, William registered, and then bride and groom headed up to their room. Upon entering, William was astounded to discover that they had been given a room with twin beds, not the ideal setup for newlyweds. He hurried back down to the reception desk and demanded another room, which was immediately provided. Hotel manager Charles Sadleir would have been shocked had he been made aware of the careless breach.[23]

Concurrent with the opening of the hotel had been the opening of Wingfield's new Riverside Bank, which occupied a prime location on Virginia Street in the hotel's northeast corner store. This would be the investor's tenth bank in Nevada, but he was confident of its success. "The banking business in this state is the best it has been in its history. This is a good town and has grown considerably the past year," he told a business acquaintance. Years later an employee of the new bank explained to Wingfield's biographer that the banker had established the Riverside Bank mainly to ensure capturing the business of long-term hotel residents and keeping them away from the rival First National Bank just down the street.[24]

Once George Wingfield had decided to rebuild the Riverside Hotel, he knew how important Reno's burgeoning divorce trade would be to his future plans. The divorce business was good, but Wingfield and a number of other prominent business leaders and politicians believed it could be better. Using shady tactics, the group got a new law passed in March 1927 lowering the residency for divorce in the state from six months to three, a law that would certainly propel the divorce trade to even greater heights in "The Biggest Little City in the World," as Reno would dub itself on its famous Virginia Street sign two years later. It has been estimated that the divorce business in Reno accounted for more than $5 million annually at the time (equivalent to $66 million today), and George Wingfield wanted to get the lion's share of it. With a grand new hotel and a looser divorce law in place, he was well on his way to attracting the high-end clientele. In 1929, for instance, early suffragette and writer Clare Boothe, later to be Clare Boothe Luce, American diplomat and the wife of Henry Luce, publisher of *Time*, *Life*, and *Fortune* magazines, arrived at the Riverside Hotel to establish her residency for divorce from her first husband. She would be just one of many wealthy women and men who would seek the comforts of the Riverside Hotel for their three-month stays.[25]

The Riverside also regained its popularity with the locals' trade as soon as it reopened. Renoites had missed their favorite special occasion spot in the five years the hotel had been absent, and once more the local newspapers were brimming with reports of banquets, anniversary dinners, meetings, weddings, and other special occasion events. Wingfield hired well-known restaurateur R. Scott Weaver to oversee the hotel's dining room. When Weaver left the hotel five years later, his work was described in laudatory terms as "appeasing the gastronomic pleasures of Reno's '400,'" which indicated the hotel's commitment to the business, social, and political elite of the city.[26]

Early in 1929, a scant two years after opening phase one of his grand new hostelry, Wingfield announced his plans for phase two. "The Super Riverside of Tomorrow," the newspaper declared under a picture of the architectural rendering of the entire structure once it was completed. An additional

$1.25 million would be spent to turn the hotel into the "Tourists Mecca of [the] Far West," doubling the size of the current structure.[27]

Unfortunately, however, the decade that had begun with so much promise ended with a thud. On October 29, 1929—forever after known as Black Tuesday—the most catastrophic stock market crash in the history of the United States occurred, putting an end to Wingfield's ambitious plans. The Roaring Twenties would be replaced by the Great Depression, and for millions of Americans, including George Wingfield, nothing would ever be the same again.

## NOTES

1. First quote from "Reno Entertains Many Guests in Five Months," *REG*, 06/04/1920; second quote from Curtis, *Reno Reveries*, 24. Population data from Harmon, "Divorce and Economic Opportunity in Reno," 75.

2. "Reno Entertains Many Guests in Five Months," *REG*, 06/04/1920; quote from Bond, *Six Months in Reno*, 24.

3. All details of the Riverside Hotel fire are from "Riverside Hotel Ravaged by Fire; Guests in Danger," *NSJ*, 03/15/1922; quote from "Jagged Remnants of Walls and Gaunt Chimneys Where Revelry Long Has Reigned," *NSJ*, 03/16/1922; "None Missing Among Guests," *NSJ*, 03/16/1922; "Many Brave Deeds Are Enacted When Hotel Burns Down," *NSJ*, 03/16/1922.

4. Quote from "Jagged Remnants of Walls and Chimneys Where Joy Reigned," *NSJ*, 03/16/1922.

5. "Riverside Hotel Ravaged by Fire; Guests in Danger," *NSJ*, 03/15/1922; "Jagged Remnants of Walls and Gaunt Chimneys Where Revelry Long Has Reigned," *NSJ*, 03/16/1922; "None Missing Among Guests," *NSJ*, 03/16/1922; "Many Brave Deeds Are Enacted When Hotel Burns Down," *NSJ*, 03/16/1922; quote from "New Building Plan Being Considered by Manager of Hostelry," *REG*, 03/16/1922.

6. Quotes from "New Building Plan Being Considered by Manager of Hostelry," *REG*, 03/16/1922.

7. "New Building Plan Being Considered by Manager of Hostelry," *REG*, 03/16/1922; "Riverside Hotel to Be Rebuilt at Once States Harry Gosse," *NSJ*, 03/17/1922; Washoe County Recorder's Office, "Riverview Survey Tract Map T-105."

8. "Geo. Wingfield Plans Large Modern Hotel," *NSJ*, 03/22/1922; Raymond, *George Wingfield*, 1, 10, 114; "Born 100 Years Ago: Controversial Wingfield Built a Nevada Empire," *NSJ*, 08/15/1976.

9. "Final Hotel Plans Made by Architect," *NSJ*, 09/05/1924; "Circular Tells of New Hotel Plans," *NSJ*, 08/31/1923; "Riverside Contract Let by Promoters," *NSJ*, 08/12/1924; "Work on Riverside Hotel Starts Today," *NSJ*, 08/16/1924; "Wingfield Buys Site of Hotel," *NSJ*, 11/13/1924; "Holding Company's Plan Is to Build on Lot Soon Is Stated," *REG*, 11/12/1924; Henrick, "Anna Warren and the Riverside Hotel."

10. "Harry Gosse, Prominent Reno Resident, Civic and Fraternal Leader Is Dead," *NSJ*, 12/19/1944.

11. Raymond, *George Wingfield*, 126–27, 304, fn24; "Riverside Hotel to Be Started Shortly," *REG*, 04/07/1926.

12. "Plans for New Riverside Announced by Wingfield on Return to Reno Today," *NSJ*, 06/30/1926; Raymond, *George Wingfield*, 127; Hardesty, "The Site of Reno's Beginning," 3–4,

14; DeLongchamps, "Frederic J. DeLongchamps Architecture Records, 1899–1962," Box 3, Folder 175.

13. Quote from DeLongchamps, "Frederic J. DeLongchamps Architecture Records, 1899–1962," Box 3, Folder 175; Harmon, "The Extraordinary Career of Frederic J. DeLongchamps," 201.

14. Quote from Harmon, "The Extraordinary Career of Frederic J. DeLongchamps," 201; "National Register of Historic Places Inventory—Nomination Form: Riverside Hotel"; Mella Harmon, correspondence with the author, 07/09/1913.

15. First quote from "National Register of Historic Places Inventory—Nomination Form: Riverside Hotel"; second quote from Nicoletta, *Buildings of Nevada*, 70.

16. Quote from Raymond, *George Wingfield*, 127.

17. Raymond, *George Wingfield*, 127; Wingfield, "George Wingfield Papers," box #032, Riverside Hotel Apartments architectural drawings, first floor plan, 1926.

18. *Nevada Newsletter: Reno Nevada, Its Resources*, n.p.

19. "Riverside Hotel Work to Begin Tomorrow," *REG*, 07/26/1926.

20. "New Structure Completed and Ready," *REG*, 05/13/1927.

21. "New Structure Completed and Ready," *REG*, 05/13/1927; "New Riverside Shops to Open," *REG*, 05/30/1927; "Sadler to Have Charge of Hotel," *NSJ*, 03/18/1927; DeLongchamps, "Frederic J. DeLongchamps Architecture Records, 1899–1962," Riverside Hotel, NC1215/175.

22. "Riverside Hotel Opens Doors to Public," *REG*, 05/14/1927; quote from "5,000 View Riverside in Opening," *NSJ*, 05/16/1927.

23. Reno resident Marilyn (Royle) Melton, 10/24/2013, interview with the author.

24. Adv. for the Riverside Hotel, *REG*, 05/09/1927; quote from Raymond, *George Wingfield*, 138, 307 fn48.

25. Raymond, *George Wingfield*, 130–31; Barber, *Reno's Big Gamble*, 114; Hardesty, "The Site of Reno's Beginning," 16; "National Register of Historic Places Inventory—Nomination Form: Riverside Hotel," 2.

26. "Resigns Hotel Post; R. Scott Weaver," *NSJ*, 02/02/1932. "Reno's 400" refers to the city's leading citizens, business people, politicians, and so on.

27. "New $1,250,000 Riverside Hotel Announced by George Wingfield," *NSJ*, 03/30/1929.

# CHAPTER 9

# THE GREAT DEPRESSION

In 1931 Nevada's legislature passed into law two of the most far-reaching pieces of legislation that would ever come out of the Carson City capitol building. While Nevada was certainly not depression-proof, its unusual mix of industries did serve to keep the wolf from the door for at least a short time, and legislators were willing to try to extend these good times a little longer with these two new laws.

The first law passed called for an even more liberal divorce law. The 1927 law had lowered the residency period from six months to three, and that had produced a spurt in the divorce business in Reno. The new law shortened the residency requirement to only six weeks, and it erased the existing language that divorce seekers had to stay put in the same county for the entire period. The new law also decreed that divorce cases would be private, and property settlements sealed. These measures would prove to be a boon for Reno, already touted as the "Divorce Capital of the Nation," and it would thwart the plans of Idaho and Arkansas, which had recently passed their own three-month residency requirements for divorces.[1]

But it was the second law passed in 1931 that would have the longest-lasting and most dramatic impact on the state: the nation's first legalization of wide-open casino gambling. It included games like faro, monte, roulette, keno, fan-tan, twenty-one, black jack, seven-and-a-half, big injun, klondyke, craps, stud poker, draw poker, "or any banking or percentage game played with cards, dice or any mechanical device or machine." Each live game would require a $50 monthly licensing fee, with 50 percent going to the city where the license was located and 25 percent each to the county and the state. For paying slot machines, the monthly fee would be $10, with the same revenue split. Minors under the age of twenty-one were not allowed to play or even frequent the gambling parlors and casinos. The new law became effective immediately upon the governor signing it, which he did within three days.[2]

In Nevada—and particularly in Reno—the floodgates were about to open. As it would turn out, the two new laws would not stave off the Great Depression in the state, but they would certainly ease it considerably, especially for those involved either directly or tangentially with the divorce and gambling industries.

George Wingfield, now at the peak of his career as a businessman and political influencer, was ready for both new laws. In fact, he confided to his personal bankers at San Francisco–based Crocker First National Bank that he had been "busy with Legislative activities…[and] we got everything we wanted, and killed everything we did not want." This left no doubt that the state's most influential string-puller had used his considerable political clout to see that both laws would pass. He immediately applied for and received his full casino gaming license at the Riverside Hotel. So that he wouldn't upset the sedate atmosphere of the place, he used caution and installed only a few slot machines at first.[3]

An inveterate traveler from St. Louis, Mary Davis Winn, spent the late 1920s and early 1930s enjoying a 10,000-mile motor coach journey around the United States to see what the burgeoning motoring craze was all about. Upon returning home she penned a delightful little book entitled *The Macadam Trail: Ten Thousand Miles by Motor Coach*. In it she delivered perhaps the most understated and genteel praise George Wingfield's grand hostelry would ever receive: "The soap in the Riverside Hotel in Reno was more highly perfumed than that in any other hotel I stayed in during ten thousand miles of traveling," she wrote. Of her stay at the Riverside, she added, "[It] is a sophisticated hostelry patronized almost one hundred percent by divorce-seekers." She had captured the very essence of George Wingfield's plans for the Riverside. As for the city itself, she said it had more sex appeal than any other town between New York and Hollywood, and it was the liveliest little city in the United States.[4]

When Mary Winn had arrived on the scene in the early 1930s, she had been greeted by a new set of signs Wingfield had installed on the hotel to attract visitors like her. Two huge lighted signs featuring the hotel's name were placed atop the building, one facing north and the other south. Letters eight feet high alternately flashed red, blue, and purple on one of the largest signs in the West. This change in the Riverside's normally sedate and understated marketing efforts was simply another effort by Wingfield to juice up his business during the hard times.[5]

In May 1932 the Riverside celebrated its fifth anniversary in its magnificent new building. In observance of the milestone, the newspaper listed some of the prominent men and women who had called the hotel home since its 1927 opening. Some were there to establish their six-week residencies, while others were simply vacationing or passing through. The list was a virtual "Who's Who" of national and international men and women of the arts, business, sports, and royalty. Topping the list were Charles A. Lindbergh, Amelia Earhart, and Cornelius Vanderbilt. Famous people in the arts included actors Will Rogers, Edward G. Robinson, and Wallace Beery; composers Oscar Hammerstein II and Nacio Herb Brown ("Holiday Review of 1929," "Babes in Arms," and others); author Bart Green; cartoonist Peter Arno; and screen director George W. Hill. Sports figures included boxers Jack Dempsey and Max Baer, while people of royalty included countesses, princesses, and ladies of the world's courts. The world of commerce was represented by such legendary names as Hoover, Gillette, Dodge, Hearst, Baldwin, Mars, Macy, Wanamaker, Strauss, and DuPont. The Riverside Hotel had indeed become world famous.[6]

The constant comings and goings of such luminaries was of great interest to the nation's press. A "Reno" dateline in a newspaper story ranked only behind datelines from Hollywood and Washington in terms of reader interest. All the major wire services had bureaus in Reno, and full-time Reno correspondents from major newspapers were commonplace. The *New York Daily News* had a tough photographer named Lola Bell stationed in Reno. Because the Riverside Hotel was where the rich and famous—and the infamous, too—hung out, Bell would station herself outside the front door in her car with a little Leica camera in hand. She shot clandestine photos of everybody who came and went, then sent the rolls of film back to the *Daily News* where they would print them, blow them up, and study each one carefully to see if it featured anyone worth publishing. Reno journalist John Sanford said, "By God, that's the way she caught up with a lot of 'em, too.... They'd come out, [and Lola'd think,] 'This gal looks like she's got real class.' Bang! Lola had her!"[7]

Legal gambling in Reno, on the other hand, had a slow start. After the first full year, 1932, Washoe County had taken in only $116,775 for its share of the licensing revenues. Reno's figures were double that, but still not as much as many had anticipated. As a matter of fact, licensing revenues peaked in July of 1931 and decreased from then until early 1932. More than half of the 600 or more games that had been in operation in Washoe County in June

1931 had been discontinued by March 1932. This was primarily due to the closure of unprofitable gambling joints during the early years following the new law. Once those had been winnowed out, pioneer Reno gambling boss Silvio Petricciani noted about the remaining casinos: "They all made money during the Depression—they *all* made money" (emphasis in original). Despite Petricciani's glowing analysis, however, everything was not peaches-and-cream in Reno, particularly for Nevada's number one citizen.[8]

Despite his grand new Riverside Hotel and its prestigious list of lodgers, and the divorce and gambling industries, George Wingfield's financial empire was beginning to crumble. Nevada had experienced a series of dry winters, and the state's cattle and sheep ranchers were losing stock at an alarming rate due to the shortage of edible fodder for their livestock. To carry them through, the ranchers had been taking increasingly large loans from Wingfield's string of small-town banks. On top of that, the demand for the cattle and sheep that did survive plummeted as the Great Depression worsened. To cover his banks' loans, Wingfield borrowed heavily from Crocker Bank and from the U.S. Government's newly created Reconstruction Finance Corporation. Instead of calling the ranchers' loans, he extended them in a goodwill gesture that would cost him dearly. Finally, in November 1932 all of Wingfield's banks were closed, and most of them—including the hotel's Riverside Bank—were forced into receivership. At about the same time, Wingfield's two hotels—the Riverside and the Golden, which were also mortgaged to Crocker Bank as collateral for his outstanding loans—were foreclosed. Wingfield was a personal friend of bank owner William Crocker, and the banker allowed Wingfield the opportunity to manage the Riverside and Golden Hotels as a salaried employee. Wingfield was paid $500 a month to manage the two properties. Three years later he would be forced into personal bankruptcy as well. All in all, it was quite a comedown for the prideful man who had once been referred to as a Sagebrush Caesar, and had enjoyed a net worth of over $25 million.[9]

In the midst of these personal problems, and to generate some much-needed cash flow, Wingfield decided to lease out the Riverside Hotel's gaming concession. Apparently, the Crocker National Bank allowed him a free hand to run the hotel as he saw fit. Nathan "Nick" Abelman and Wingfield had been acquaintances since shortly after 1906 when both men had arrived in Goldfield, Nevada. Both men were later involved in mining and gambling in Tonopah, Nevada. By 1932 Abelman had relocated to Reno and opened the ornate Ship and Bottle Club with partners Steve Pavlovich and Bert Riddick;

Abelman had also purchased the Riverside Hotel's cigar store in late 1933. When Wingfield decided to lease out the gambling concession in 1934, he turned to the Ship and Bottle's three partners, and they began operating the Riverside's gambling interests. Wingfield, or more likely the bank, was to receive a substantial portion—up to 25 percent, according to one source—of the profits from the leased gambling space, an arrangement Wingfield had used at a number of his other clubs before gambling was legalized. He had also obtained licenses under his own name for a few slot machines scattered around the public areas of the hotel.[10]

The gambling concessionaires' first task was to remodel and expand the gaming and entertainment areas of the hotel. They took over the large ground-floor corner store that had previously housed the now-defunct Riverside Bank, removed the bank's large vault, and tied both spaces into the huge area that had previously served as the hotel's social hall. They gutted the space and spent $20,000 remodeling and refurnishing it, then named the entire area the Riverside Buffet. Despite the word "buffet" in the name, it did not serve food in the beginning; the hotel's existing restaurants continued to fulfill that important function. A large circular bar was installed with the most modern equipment available, and a large lounge area featured easy chairs and settees for seating, along with low tables for drinks and ashtrays. The décor featured hand-painted murals highlighting an Old West theme, showing cowboys and cowgirls, dudes and Indians, "cavorting about the walls with a gay and carefree air." The three partners also built a casino area in the buffet and installed a roulette table, a twenty-one game, a dice game called hazard, and a number of slot machines. The Riverside Buffet opened on July 7, 1934, and the newspaper reported that the bar would cater strictly to a drinking clientele, serving no food and having no dance floor. Music and dancing, however, were available in the separate lounge restaurant. In 1936 musician and singer George Hart would become a regular entertainer at the Buffet. The popular Hart had previously played at the swank Willows nightclub, partially owned by Reno gangsters Bill Graham and James McKay, but it had burned to the foundations in 1933. After a time playing at the Riverside, Hart had built such a loyal following that he kept a telephone on the piano so former patrons could call in a song request to him. He'd sing the requested song into the telephone while delighted audience members cheered him on. By the late 1930s that portion of the Buffet that had once occupied the old Riverside Bank building would affectionately be called the corner bar by Renoites, and it became a favorite watering hole for locals, business people, and politicians for the next quarter century.[11]

A few years earlier, when the corner bar space had still been occupied by the Riverside Bank, the bank, and by association the Riverside Hotel, had been involved in the greatest crime mystery in the history of the city. It had all begun back in 1929 when the aforementioned Bill Graham and James McKay set up a nationwide bunco scheme to dupe unwary individuals out of their money. The complicated scheme worked something like this: Con artists would befriend individuals with substantial financial resources. Those individuals would "find" a wallet discreetly placed by the con artist that contained either a winning betting stub from a horseracing track or a hot stock market tip. Whichever one the wallet contained guaranteed the finder a huge sum of money when it was cashed in. However, the payment would only be made when "good faith" money was put up. The victims were instructed to bring their securities or other assets to Reno where they could be exchanged at the Riverside Bank for cash to make the good faith payment. Once the bank had the money, a "complication" ensued and the individuals were instructed to return home and wait for their money. Naturally, the money never arrived. Graham and McKay facilitated the exchanges, even going so far as to give the Riverside Bank their personal funds when the bank did not have enough cash on hand to complete a transaction. For this they received 15 percent of the transaction. A man named Roy J. Frisch was the bank's cashier, and he became aware of Graham's and McKay's shenanigans, but he kept mum on the subject, probably because he was fearful that his boss, George Wingfield, was also in on the scheme. When the bank failed in 1932 Frisch began working as an assistant to the federal receiver for Wingfield's failed banks.[12]

Meanwhile, the federal government began investigating Graham and McKay, and in early 1933 the duo was indicted for mail fraud. Frisch had testified before the grand jury investigating the case, and he was due to be the government's key witness when the trial began in April 1934. About ten days before the trial was to begin, Frisch left the home he shared with his mother and sisters on Court Street, and walked downtown to attend a movie. He has never been seen or heard from since, and his disappearance has become the stuff of local legend. It has always been assumed that George "Baby Face" Nelson and his accomplice, John Paul Chase, who were frequent Reno visitors, killed Frisch and hid his body, at Graham's and McKay's bidding, but to this day, now more than eighty years later, the case is still unsolved and Frisch's body has never been found. Despite Frisch's absence, Graham and McKay were convicted on the charges, although it took three trials to do so. Each man spent only six years in prison and was fined $11,000.[13]

Early in 1935 the Riverside's main dining room was closed for renovation. By this time Abelman and his two partners had also taken over the dining and entertainment for the hotel. In May the dining room reopened as the Riverside Café. Entertainment for the opening was provided by nationally known pianist Horace Heidt and his big band, the Californians. The opening night dining menu was sumptuous, with lobster supreme, filet of brook trout, and breast of guinea hen offered as a few of the choices. On Christmas Eve of that year, supper dancing was inaugurated as a regular weekly feature. Tommy Gillette's six-piece orchestra played for the supper dances, with drinks provided by the Riverside Buffet. The El Cortez Hotel, which had opened in 1931, had been the first one in Reno to offer entertainment in their Trocadero Club, and the Café was the Riverside's response. The El Cortez, like the Riverside, was considered a first-class hotel, but it was small at only sixty rooms and without the Riverside's international reputation, so it offered limited competition. The Riverside had originally been run on the American plan—all meals included in the price—which seemed to be favored by the type of café society guests it attracted. By the mid-1930s, however, as a result of the rigors of the Great Depression, the hotel had switched to the European plan, where meals were charged separately. Many of the area's dude ranches, or "divorce ranches" as they were called locally, were forced to close during this period, and they were replaced by a number of new, moderately priced boarding houses in the city.[14]

Norman Biltz was another of those larger-than-life characters that Nevada has always spawned. A Depression-era real estate agent and land investor in Lake Tahoe and northern Nevada, it was Biltz's skilled marketing hand that had guided the state of Nevada in its mid-Depression "One Sound State" campaign to attract millionaires to relocate to tax-haven Nevada. Despite his business genius, Biltz had a weakness: he was a prodigious gambler. In the 1920s he owned the Cal Neva Lodge at Lake Tahoe, and he had sold it to the notorious Reno gangsters Graham and McKay. Biltz had accepted their $58,000 IOU for the purchase. That same night, to celebrate the sale, he got drunk and gambled at the Lodge. The next morning, he later wrote, "I got up about noon and went in to see Jim McKay." Despite Biltz's heavy drinking and gambling on credit the previous night, MacKay told him he didn't owe anything. "Thank God for that," Biltz said. Then McKay said, "I got news for you: we don't owe you anything, either." Biltz had lost the entire $58,000 IOU at the gambling tables.[15]

By the mid-1930s Biltz had yet to mend his ways, and he had gotten in debt to the Riverside where he was living at the time. He asked manager

Charles Sadleir to take him to see Wingfield, whom he had never met. "So he really took me apart," Biltz recalled later, "but he...had sort of a twinkle in his eye. He said, 'You're going to move out of [the] Riverside and you're going to move over to the Golden. Rooms are much cheaper.'" After some time Biltz had gotten the debt down to about $1,600—"Not very much but it's a lot if you don't have it," he said—when he convinced Wingfield to take a ride with him to Lake Tahoe. He showed Wingfield a piece of property and asked for a $50,000 loan to buy it, promising that he'd make enough off the land to settle his original debt. "You must be out of your mind," Wingfield told him. "Give you $50,000 to get $1,600 back?"[16]

Wingfield eventually relented, however, and that was how Norman Biltz ended up with the Crystal Bay Development Company, one of Lake Tahoe's most successful land developers.

By 1937 Wingfield had reduced his obligations to Crocker First National Bank significantly, and his personal financial circumstances had greatly improved. The bank allowed him to mortgage the Riverside and Golden Hotels for $700,000 over ten years, and Wingfield along with his son and daughter became the owners of the two hotels he had been managing for the bank. From this point forward, Wingfield would begin to rebuild his personal fortune, although he would never recapture the political influence he had once enjoyed.[17]

As the decade came to an end for the famed hostelry, Wingfield's very capable hotel manager, Charles Sadleir, resigned his post. Wingfield hired thirty-one-year-old Owen Winslow Nicholls, previously with a large hotel in Miami, to replace Sadleir.[18]

The decade of the 1930s had seen dozens of hotel–casinos and slot joints come and go in the downtown area, but most served the middle classes and did not offer much direct competition to the Riverside. The most memorable of those was Harolds Club, which operated from 1935 to 1995.

---

While Nevada's reentry into legalized gambling in March 1931 may have begun slowly, that was not true of its more liberal divorce laws. Once the new divorce requirements went into effect on May 31, potential divorcees arrived in Reno in droves.

During the summer of 1931 so many people arrived to establish their six weeks' residency that accommodations filled up almost overnight. Tent cities popped up along Virginia Street, and crude campsites appeared all along the banks of the Truckee River. Enterprising Truckee Meadows

A 1930s postcard comically illustrates a common occurrence in downtown Reno as a woman emerges from the Courthouse with her divorce decree in her hand and a jubilant smile on her face. According to the folklore, she would then have kissed one of the columns on the Courthouse, and proceeded to the Virginia Street Bridge where she would throw her wedding ring into the Truckee River. Special Collections Department, University of Nevada, Reno Libraries.

ranchers turned working ranches into divorce settlement or dude ranches, promising a healthy outdoor experience for divorce seekers, while many homeowners moved in with relatives and rented their furnished houses at exorbitant fees. In 1931 alone there were 5,260 Nevada divorces, primarily in Reno, which was the highest number in the entire decade. Each divorce action, it must be remembered, included a plaintiff; a defendant, unless the divorce was uncontested; other family members; witnesses; often friends and supporters; and in the case of wealthy divorce-seekers, maids and servants. It was a huge influx of people—many with money to spend—for "The Divorce Capitol of the Nation," and the rush would go on throughout the Great Depression, easing the effect of the financial trauma on Reno.[19]

In Reno, the Virginia Street Bridge, the Washoe County Courthouse, and the institution of divorce are as inexorably linked in fact and fiction as the three legs of a tripod. Fable has it that as a regular custom, the divorcees, upon coming out of the courthouse after their successful trial, kissed one of the courthouse pillars and then went immediately to the center of the bridge and hurled their wedding ring into the swirling waters of the Truckee

River. The myth most likely started in the late 1920s as a promotional stunt, and through the years it was nurtured in books, magazines, newspapers, movies, postcards, and by word of mouth until it became embedded in the public consciousness. Once the myth grew, it spurred some divorcees to actually perform the ritual, although it was never as common a practice as the myth implies. However, Reno journalist Paul Leonard had been a witness to just such a ritual as a teenager in the 1920s: "One time, I recall...some of my friends and I became friends with one young lady who was here for a divorce. She'd get in the car and drink bootleg whiskey with us, all this sort of thing.... And when she got her divorce...she called us and said she'd gotten it...and we all gathered and went out and got drunk. She pulled her ring off and threw it in the river, according to the old tradition in Reno, except that she threw it over the bridge at Booth Street, instead of the Virginia Street Bridge."[20]

A 1938 article in the local paper reported on two Pennsylvania tourists who, believing the legend, searched the river bottom below the bridge for some valuable booty. Skeptical Renoites watching from the bridge were amazed when the duo actually recovered a ring set with seven diamonds. A 1973 newspaper article told of a Sparks, Nevada, gentleman who used a gold dredge near the bridge to search for valuables. He found three rings, 270 pennies, a half-dollar, and several quarters, dimes, and nickels. But the biggest wedding ring haul belongs to three Reno amateur prospectors who, over three summers in the late 1970s, are said to have dredged up more than 400 rings. Their most ironic find was a gold ring set with a garnet and carrying this inscription etched on the inside of the wedding band: "Love Is Stronger Than Death, 1890." Nevada State law NRS 503.425, which dates back to the late 1960s, does allow for prospectors to dredge in Nevada rivers after paying for a permit, and under certain restrictions, so these stories certainly appear to hold up.[21]

One enterprising fellow charged with promoting the city saw the wedding ring story as an opportunity to enhance the city's reputation and its divorce business. Thomas Cave Wilson ran an advertising agency in Reno and, as a member of the chamber of commerce in the 1950s and 1960s, he donated his services to that organization. Wilson explained,

> While I was doing their stuff for free, I used to go over to the Woolworth's store on a dull day and buy a few dollars worth of dime store wedding rings, and then when nobody was lookin', toss 'em in the river off the bridge. And this meant that kids lookin' for crawdads

in the summer months would occasionally come up with a ring, and they'd always stand up and hold the ring up and yell with all their friends who were doing the same thing. This would attract the tourists on the bridge, and [they'd yell] "Here's a wedding ring that had been thrown off the bridge!' And so it proved that it was a true legend."[22]

Wilson also admitted to another public relations stunt. "Divorcees kissing the pillars of the courthouse was supposedly an old tradition, and occasionally [with] a little [K]leenex, I could [put] a little pink smear on the courthouse pillar…and this encouraged a number of people to [kiss the pillar]."[23]

So fact or fiction, Reno's myths and legends did help spread the fame of the Virginia Street Bridge, and tag it with a number of sobriquets, including the Bridge of Sighs, like the famed bridge in Venice, Italy; the Wedding Ring Bridge; and the Bridge of Meditation, among them.

Just as the Riverside Hotel had become the social center for special events in Reno, despite its emphasis on the divorce trade, the Virginia Street Bridge had become the gathering site for public ceremonial events. Veterans' memorials, parades, public songfests, Scouting programs, and the like usually assembled at the bridge, and often caused it to close to local traffic. Memorial Day was perhaps the most celebrated of these occasions. Every year songs, prayers, and eloquent patriotic speeches kicked off the event, followed by throwing flowers and wreaths from the bridge into the river to honor those service members who had died at sea. This was followed by a grand parade from the bridge to the Hillside Cemetery—Reno's oldest, located near the university campus—where a second program followed. Another such event occurred in 1930 when the Nevada chapter of the Daughters of the American Revolution presented a bronze plaque to the city to commemorate the early pioneers who crossed the Truckee River where the bridge is located. The plaque was placed on a pillar on the southeast corner of the bridge, where it remained until the new bridge was built in 2015–16.[24]

In 1933 it was necessary to repair the bridge for the first time in its twenty-eight-year life span. The center pier was resurfaced because it had been badly eroded by the action of normal water passage, and by the damaging effects of high water and debris carried downriver during heavy rains and annual mountain snowmelt. There was also talk of reshaping the lower part of the pier so it would not offer as much resistance to the current and the flotsam that always accompanied flood conditions, but this was never accomplished and the cycle of erosion and repair continued. Also in the early

1930s—perhaps in concert with the aforementioned repairs—an elegant concrete wall was built atop the retaining wall running along the southeast side of the river from Virginia Street to Center Street. In 1933–34 the Frederic DeLongchamps–designed U.S. Post Office was built just behind the new concrete wall on the site previously occupied by the Carnegie Library. The beautiful, zigzag Moderne–style post office building, part of the art deco and art Moderne movements that took hold during the decade, would serve as the community's main post office until 2013 when the building was privatized. The building would be placed on the National Register of Historic Places in 1990, thus the privatization into shops, restaurants, and offices retained its historic art deco character.[25]

By the second half of the 1930s there were seven vehicular and pedestrian bridges spanning the Truckee River within the city limits of Reno. The Virginia Street Bridge carried the majority of traffic, as it connected the primary commercial and business sections of the city. In 1937, at a cost of nearly $750,000, three new bridges across the Truckee were approved to relieve the congestion on the Virginia Street Bridge. One would be at Sierra Street, west of Virginia Street, the second one to the east at Lake Street, and the third one farther east at Alameda Street. All of the bridges would be arch types, of concrete and reinforced steel, but the Sierra Street Bridge was also supported by heavy steel beams because of its greater length. All three were scheduled to open in late 1937. Anyone who expected Renoites to officially open three new bridges without the appropriate fanfare, however, simply did not understand the psyche of the fun-loving city.[26]

Some sharp-eyed historian noticed that 1937 would be the seventy-fifth anniversary of the first bridge across the Truckee River, now the Virginia Street Bridge, in what would eventually become Reno. Never mind that he was two years off—1935 would have been correct—that was a minor detail. So a giant two-day festival was planned for September 10 and 11. Events included a dedication and appropriate speeches at each of the three sites by Governor Richard Kirman; past governor of Nevada, member of the U.S. House of Representatives, and U.S. senator James Scrugham; and U.S. attorney for Nevada and future governor Ed Carville. More-enjoyable events included a golf tournament, a hip-boot derby race down the river, junior and senior events at the first annual Nevada State Swimming Meet, an Italian music pageant that included serenading from a gondola as it traveled up and down the river, a Reno City Band concert, a boxing card at the State Fairgrounds, the Sierra Nevada baseball championship at Threlkel Park, a huge parade, and, naturally, a fireworks show.[27]

The hip-boot derby featured fourteen four-man relay teams. Each team had but one pair of hip boots, and had to pass the boots along from one runner to the next in midstream. The parade—dubbed the longest parade in the history of Reno—featured fifty floats plus numerous bands and marching groups. The crowd favorite was the second section of the parade, the Evolution of Transportation. A pair of Native Americans on foot led the march, followed by prospectors, trappers, pioneers, and then various forms of wheeled vehicles, including teams of oxen, covered wagons, stagecoaches, high-wheeled bicycles, ancient automobiles, and finally a modern, streamlined 1937 sedan.[28]

Reno citizens and visitors who today enjoy special events like Artown, Hot August Nights, and Street Vibrations owe much to these 1937 Renoites who staged what was perhaps the first huge public gala in the city's history.

The decade of the 1930s ended with a great deal of public attention being paid to the old iron bridge that had once crossed the river at Virginia Street, and was the pride of the whole town in its heyday. The iron bridge had been moved to Rock Street when the current concrete bridge was built in 1905, but by this time, at the ripe old age of sixty-two, the old bridge was showing its age. It was constantly being referred to as noisy, ugly, unsafe, and a public menace by many people in the community. At some point the idea surfaced—it started as a letter to the editor in the newspaper by a person calling himself simply "A Renoite"—to convert the iron bridge into a European style bridge of flowers. Soon the idea had taken on a life of its own, and it was being discussed in the newspapers and in the corridors of power within the city. Under the plan, the bridge would be replanked—something that was sorely needed, flowers or no flowers—and dirt-filled troughs would run the length of the span on each side, planted with beautiful climbing flowers and vines that would eventually cover the ironwork.[29]

Within weeks the initial idea also spawned another great idea from the public. At the time there was a crude dirt road on both sides of the river running a couple of blocks both east and west of the Virginia Street Bridge. A newspaper reader suggested the dirt paths could easily be converted into promenades with outdoor cafés and smart shops. "You can dine in sidewalk cafes of New York, Paris—many cities—but here, in this marvelous climate—with superb view of mountains and river—those of us who live in hotels must take our meals indoors!"[30]

Unfortunately, the bridge-of-flowers idea never moved past the discussion stage, while the promenade idea, first put forth in the nineteenth century, would take six decades more until it became a reality.

## NOTES

1. "Bars Down in Nevada," *Los Angeles Times*, 03/20/1931, 1.

2. "Gambling Bill Passes Nevada Senate," *REG*, 03/17/1931, including quote.

3. Raymond, *George Wingfield*, 137, 195; Kling, *Biggest Little City*, 140.

4. Winn, *The Macadam Trail*, 71–72.

5. "Riverside Sign Now Operating," *REG*, 05/27/1932.

6. "Fifth Anniversary of New Hotel Riverside Celebrated: Famous Men and Women Enjoy Its Hospitality," *NSJ*, 05/15/1932.

7. Sanford, "Printer's Ink in My Blood," 47.

8. "County Collects $116,775 in Year from Gambling," *REG*, 04/05/1932; Raymond, *George Wingfield*, 223–32; quote from Petricciani, "The Evolution of Gaming in Nevada," 20.

9. Kling, *Biggest Little City*, 1, 140; Raymond, *George Wingfield*, 200–6, 217, 219; Moody, "The Early Years of Casino Gambling," 227; n.t., *Sacramento Bee*, 01/07/1934, 3.

10. Kling, *Biggest Little City*, 1, 149–50; Michael Fischer, grandnephew of Nick Abelman and Nevada history scholar, correspondence with the author; also source of statement on 25 percent of profits being returned to Wingfield.

11. "Riverside Bank Quarters to House Bar," *REG*, 06/20/1934; first quote from "Riverside Buffet Will Open Today; Bar Is Circular," *NSJ*, 07/07/1934; Kling, *Biggest Little City*, 142; Sawyer, *Reno, Where the Gamblers Go*, 31–32.

12. Earl, "Disappearance of Roy Frisch," *Nevada*, 20–22, 78–79; Michael Fischer, independent Nevada history scholar, conversation with author.

13. Michael Fischer, independent Nevada history scholar, conversation with author.

14. Riverside Hotel, "Riverside Hotel Menu," May 11, 1935; Sawyer, *Reno, Where the Gamblers Go*, 31–32; "Supper Dancing Soon to Start at the Riverside," *NSJ*, 12/14/1935; "The Biggest Little City in the World," *Keeler's Pacific Hotel Review* 30 (35), 08/28/1937, 9; Kling, *Biggest Little City*, 45; Harmon, "Divorce and Economic Opportunity in Reno," 92.

15. Biltz, "Memoirs of 'The Duke of Nevada,'" 45–46, 49–50.

16. Biltz, "Memoirs of 'The Duke of Nevada,'" 50–51.

17. Raymond, *George Wingfield*, 244; "Wingfield Interests Repurchase Hotel," *NSJ*, 09/02/1937.

18. "Sadleir Resigns Hotel Position," *REG*, 04/20/1939.

19. Harmon, "Divorce and Economic Opportunity in Reno," 1–2; Blake, *Road to Reno*, 158.

20. Rocha, "Myth #68—Getting 'Reno-Vated'"; quote from Leonard, "Tales of Northern Nevada," 22–23.

21. "More Rings Are Sought in River by 2 Visitors," *NSJ*, 09/01/1938; "Truckee River Dredgers Find Divorce 'Glory Hole,'" *REG*, 07/07/1973; Walton-Buchanan, "Reno-Vated"; correspondence from Maureen Hullinger, License Office Supervisor, Nevada Department of Wildlife, Reno, 12/18/2013.

22. Wilson, "Reminiscences of a Nevada Advertising Man," 105–6.

23. Wilson, "Reminiscences of a Nevada Advertising Man," 105–6.

24. "Plans Completed for Memorial Day Service in Reno," *REG*, 05/27/1933; "Pioneer Plate to Be Placed on Bridge Here," *REG*, 05/27/1933.

25. "Virginia Bridge to Be Repaired," *REG*, 09/28/1933; Walton-Buchanan, *Historic Houses and Buildings of Reno*, 9.

26. "Reno Constructs Two New Bridges," *Nevada Highways and Parks* [magazine], March 1937, 13–16; "Two-Day Program Packed to Limit with Features," *NSJ*, 09/10/1937.

27. "Two-Day Program Packed to Limit with Features," *NSJ*, 09/10/1937.

28. "Two-Day Program Packed to Limit with Features," *NSJ*, 09/10/1937.

29. "Good Morning," *NSJ*, 06/23/1939; "Letters to the Editor," *NSJ*, 08/03/1939; "Reno Review," *NSJ*, 08/05/1939; "Past and Present," *NSJ*, 09/27/1939.

30. Quote from "Reno Review," *NSJ*, 08/05/1939.

CHAPTER 10

# TOP HATS AND
# TEN-GALLON SOMBREROS

THE 1940 CENSUS SHOWED 21,317 residents in Reno living in 7,309 dwelling units. Nearly 20% of the dwelling units were identified as "tenant occupied," indicating the ongoing presence of divorce seekers still flocking to the Biggest Little City. In 1940 Nevada's divorce rate—which reflected the comings and goings of all the temporary divorce residencies—was forty-nine divorces per one thousand residents, by far the largest in the nation. The annual number of divorces in the state had risen steadily throughout the 1930s, following a huge upward blip in 1931 when the new, more-liberal law had gone into effect. From the middle of the 1930s until the end of the decade the number was hovering around 4,700 to 4,800 divorces per fiscal year, which the state had switched to in 1932. Just as World War I and the Great Depression had not stifled the nation's divorce seekers, neither would World War II, as the numbers continued to escalate in the early 1940s. By the war's end in fiscal year 1944–45 there were 13,547 divorces. The number would climb for one more year, then begin a slow decline back to 9,342 in 1949–50. Obviously all this activity continued to ensure that the Riverside Hotel thrived throughout the war and postwar years along with the rest of the city.[1]

The opening year of the new decade would see the Virginia Street Bridge make headlines, while the Riverside Hotel would become part of the most macabre folklore legend in Nevada history.

Reno had been selected by MGM Pictures to stage the world premiere of their newest film, *Virginia City*, on March 17, 1940. The movie starred a long list of Hollywood's top stars: Errol Flynn, Miriam Hopkins, Randolph Scott, Humphrey Bogart, Alan Hale, Ward Bond, and dozens of other fan favorites. The premiere and its attendant festivities promised to be one of the grandest events ever held in the city. Two days before the movie premiere, which would be showing in Reno's top three theaters, a special eighteen-car train carrying 250 actors, MGM executives, and writers arrived in Reno to an enthusiastic greeting estimated at over 10,000 people. In addition to the movie's cast, other notable actors including Tom Mix, Gilbert Roland, Bruce Cabot, Leo Carrillo, and dozens of others were also on the train. Reno—already known for its over-the-top celebrations—had never witnessed the likes of this party in its seventy-two-year history.[2]

For two days the Hollywood stars roamed the streets of Reno in Old West costumes, talking to residents and visitors and signing autographs. They also attended the costume balls, the movie's premiere, and the parade that was staged in honor of the film. The top-level stars and executives were housed at the Riverside Hotel, and the lobby was "thronged with autograph seekers or those waiting to catch a glimpse of the celebrities," the newspaper noted.[3]

The parade kicked off the festivities on the morning of the premiere. Tom Mix, America's favorite silent-movie-era cowboy, was selected to drive the two-horse team pulling the city's Western wagon float. All went well in the beginning, with fans waving and shouting greetings to Mix as his wagon made its way down Virginia Street. However, as soon as the team stepped onto the Virginia Street Bridge they stopped abruptly and refused to go on. "Tom Mix, Hollywood cowboy and master of horses, couldn't make his team behave," the newspaper reported. For five minutes, the second half of the parade waited patiently while Mix unsuccessfully cajoled his team to move. Finally, the remaining part of the procession continued around the stalled float, and city officials who were occupants of the wagon jumped off and boarded other floats. For a full half hour, while Mix fumed, the horses refused to move. After this 30-minute wait, a substitute team was hooked up to the wagon and Mix was on his way again. Tragically, Tom Mix, who had been starring in Western movies since 1909, would be killed later that year in an automobile accident.[4]

The macabre incident at the Riverside Hotel would occur seven months later, in November. Nevada's popular Democratic U.S. senator, Key Pittman, died on November 10, just five days after winning reelection for another four-year term. However, soon after his death rumors began circulating throughout the state that he had actually died one day before the election, and that his Democratic cohorts had kept the news of his death quiet to ensure the party's victory. They had literally kept his body on ice in a bathtub in the Riverside Hotel in the interim, according to the rumor. The reason for the deception was that if it became known that Pittman passed away before the election, his Republican opponent would surely have been elected. But by claiming Pittman had died after his reelection, Democratic governor Ted Carville would be able to name another Democrat to fill the Senate seat. If the rumor turned out to be true, Nevada's citizens had made history by electing the first dead man to the U.S. Senate; and to this day, nearly three-quarters of a century later, the rumor, which has now risen to the status of folklore, is still believed by some old time Nevadans.[5]

Like all rumors, there was a grain of truth to it. Four days before his actual November 10 death, and one day before the election, the hard-drinking Senator Pittman had gone on a drinking binge in his Riverside Hotel suite. When he passed out drunk, an aide called his doctor who arrived and discovered that Pittman had also had a massive heart attack. He was secretly whisked away to a hospital, and a specialist called in to examine him declared that the senator was in a terminal condition. Governor Carville and his Democratic cronies decided not to tell the press that Pittman was terminally ill, so as not to jeopardize the reelection. So the election went on as if nothing was wrong with the candidate, and he won handily. When he died three days later, Governor Carville appointed Democrat Berkeley Bunker from Las Vegas as his replacement. Thus, Nevadans hadn't actually elected a dead person to the Senate, only a terminally ill one. The full story did not come out until 1996 when Nevada state archivist Guy Rocha investigated the matter and wrote about it in *Nevada* magazine. But as Rocha pointed out in his article, "Once a story gains a place in the public mind, it takes on a life of its own."[6]

The early to mid-1940s were relatively uneventful years at the Riverside, although they would be noteworthy years for George Wingfield personally. The George Wingfields, senior and junior, hired a new general manager for the property in 1940. Arthur Allen, who would remain with the Riverside for many years, would be instrumental in the expansion and renovation that would take place later in the decade. The divorce trade continued to grow, Reno's postwar economy was soaring thanks in part to the growing respectability of casino gambling, and George Wingfield's hotel profits were solid. Robbins Cahill, a longtime state government employee and the first chairman of the Nevada Gaming Control Board in 1955, described the essence of the Reno casino scene during this period: "Gaming in Reno, practically, could be defined as the Riverside Hotel, Harolds Club, the Bank Club, and the Palace Club," he said. "There were...[many other] places that had one or

two games...and, of course, some areas on Commercial Row. The Riverside...
was *the* place to go [emphasis in original]. Old-timers in Reno still remember the Riverside fondly for its reputation, and as the place where everyone
wanted to go," Cahill said. Harry Atkinson, an attorney from Tonopah who
often came to Reno, agreed: "The old Riverside Hotel...had a nice outdoor
porch that faced the river...and they had a bar right there on the corner....
That's where Mrs. Atkinson and I stopped on the day we got married.... [The
hotel] had a nice dining room and dancing, and they had a fellow playing
the piano."[7]

The Riverside also continued to be an active marketplace for local shop-
pers and small retailers, as many traveling sales agents made the hotel their
Reno headquarters as they had done for more than a half-century. Clients of
early Reno advertising executive Thomas Cave Wilson's ad agency included
a large appliance distributor. "They'd have their dealers come in from little
appliance stores all over Nevada, eastern California and Oregon. [They'd]
take a suite at the Riverside Hotel, and the retail dealers would look at the
new merchandise, the new models for the coming year," Wilson said.[8]

In 1940 George Wingfield sounded out his bankers at Crocker Bank about
the possibility of a $250,000 loan to build the postponed second phase of the
Riverside. This addition, he boldly predicted, "should discourage any competition for years to come." After considering the idea, however, he decided to
postpone the expansion again, this time due to concern over the widening
war in Europe.[9]

By 1944, thanks mainly to his profitable mining interests, Wingfield
finally paid off all his debts to Crocker First National Bank and his other
creditors. Mixing metaphors, he wrote to his friend, William Crocker's son
Billy: "Since March 31, 1937, I have dug myself completely out of the foxhole
which has been a long row to hoe." With all his debts paid, he again began
to give thought to resurrecting his 1929 plans for phase two of the Riverside.
To raise funds toward that end, in late 1946 he sold the aging Hotel Golden
for $1.5 million to a group of investors that included his onetime protégé,
Norman Biltz. To a friend, he confided in a letter, "We are almost forced to
put an extension on the Riverside Hotel...and make it the 'headquarters' for
Nevada. There is a tremendous shortage of rooms here." He contracted the
Reno architectural firm of DeLongchamps and O'Brien to draw up architectural plans for a massive addition to the existing structure, an addition that
would have again made the Riverside one of the largest hotels in the West.[10]

Another strong motivation for the Riverside's long-awaited expansion had come earlier with the announcement, on November 22, 1945, that
Mrs. Charles Mapes and her son Charles Jr. planned to build a ten-story,

In the mid-1940s the Riverside Hotel was doing very well with the divorce trade, the convention trade, and the even the locals trade. Many Renoites loved stopping off at the hotel's soda fountain for a cherry coke or an ice cream cone. Pictured here (forefront) is longtime Renoite Ruth Cantrell, who passed away in 2015, and an unidentified coworker. Courtesy of Neal Cobb.

class-A hotel on the site of the old U.S. Post Office building, diagonally across the Truckee River from the Riverside. The Mapes family planned to spend $1 million on the project, which would include 250 rooms, some of which would be apartments; a cocktail lounge; a casino; and extensive banquet facilities. It was immediately obvious to many Renoites—including George Wingfield—that the Riverside Hotel would soon face the first real competition in its eighty-seven-year history.[11]

Ground was broken for the Mapes Hotel on December 1, 1945, and it opened two years later. It was even larger than initially proposed; the hotel was twelve stories high with three hundred rooms and suites; it featured one of the earliest nightclubs inside a Reno hotel, the elegant Sky Room atop the building. George Mapes leased the gambling concession to a group headed by Lou Wertheimer, a Michigan man who, along with his three brothers, had previously operated illegal casinos in Detroit, Palm Springs, and in a few cities in Florida. The group was licensed to operate three craps games, three roulette wheels, six twenty-one games, and sixty-six slot machines. The Mapes Hotel opened to rave reviews. Reno casino historian Dwayne Kling wrote, "The Mapes Hotel and the Sky Room [were] by far the most exciting attractions in Reno…. The Mapes immediately became the showplace of Reno and a venue for the most famous entertainers in show business."[12]

Any doubt anyone may have harbored about the strength of this new competition for the Riverside Hotel quickly evaporated. Other significant properties also opened in the 1940s, but provided little direct competition for the Riverside's high-end market. Those included Harrah's (1946 to the present), Club Cal Neva (1948 to the present), and the Nevada Club (1946 to 1997). Despite all that, however, George Wingfield continued to waffle on his expansion plans for the Riverside.[13]

By early 1949, however, Wingfield was finally ready to proceed with his Riverside expansion plans. His planned changes were significant, although they had been scaled back from his original 1929 Phase 2 expansion plans. He promised the public that construction would not interfere with hotel occupancy or meeting space, but there would be an interruption of service in the dining room. Before construction began, however, another big change occurred. The Abelman group, which had operated the gaming concession at the hotel for seventeen years, announced they were giving up their Riverside lease. Nick Abelman and his two partners had had a great run at the Riverside, but they weren't interested in taking on the larger challenge of the expanded property. Abelman went on to purchase a controlling interest in the smaller Waldorf Club, which he headed until his death in 1951. Wingfield quickly turned to Mert Wertheimer, whose brother Lou ran the gaming at the Mapes, to take over the lease with two other men, Raymond "Ruby" Mathis and Elmer G. "Baldy" West. Wertheimer immediately began to obtain the necessary gaming licenses and establish his residency at the Riverside.[14]

For George Wingfield and other Reno hotel–casino owners, the upcoming Fourth of July celebration in the Biggest Little City promised to be a big payday. The annual Reno Rodeo, plus other Independence Day celebrations, was expected to bring 15,000 to 20,000 visitors to the city, and every hotel, restaurant, bar, and casino was gearing up for the crowds. But just prior to the festivities, the largest labor dispute in the city's history reared its ugly head, promising to wipe out any profits business owners were anticipating. City leaders, the chamber of commerce—of which George Wingfield was president—and the Employers' Council had been frantically and semi-secretly bargaining with representatives of the bartenders and culinary workers' unions for three months to forgo a strike until after the Fourth of July weekend, but to no avail. At the heart of the dispute was the unions' demand that the hotels allow their other service workers—housekeepers, maids, bellhops, elevator operators, cashiers, and others—to organize into an allied union. There were also lesser demands for better wages, improved working conditions, and shorter hours, but organizing the hotels' nonunion workers was the primary issue.[15]

The nonunion bargaining organizations called for Reno citizens to make spare rooms in their homes available for the large crowd expected to descend on the city: "Many visitors will be forced to sleep in their cars," the newspaper lamented, unless residents volunteered space. Union pickets had also begun to appear in front of the city's largest hotels: the Riverside, Mapes, Golden, and El Cortez. The one-year-old Cal Neva had signed with the unions and was spared. As many as fifty-five non-hotel bars and forty-two restaurants were also being targeted as the dispute grew and union employees walked off their jobs, to be replaced by average citizens with no experience who stepped in to help.[16]

Finally, on July 10—the big Fourth of July weekend now a dim memory for most—the strike officially ended, and bartenders and culinary workers returned to work. The unions had gained some concessions on the secondary issues; but the hotels had held fast to their refusal to allow collective bargaining for the remainder of their workforce. Although no figures were released on the amount of lost revenue to hotels, bars, and restaurants during the ten-day walkout, Reno's worst labor dispute ever undoubtedly cost everyone serious money.[17]

On the brighter side, two months before the strike in May 1949, George Wingfield submitted his first set of building plans for his hotel to the city inspector, but over the next six months those would be followed by a number of changes, additions, and alterations because Wingfield seemed unable to settle on exactly what he wanted to do with the hotel. There were even rumors floating around town that he was trying to sell the Riverside, rumors that Wingfield strongly denied: "Bunk!" he said; "That's just conversation." He put California architect Frank W. Green in charge of the project's design, with Reno-based Frederic DeLongchamps's firm assisting.[18]

Wingfield, his son, and general manager Arthur Allen finally agreed on a $1.5 million plan that would triple the Riverside's ground floor area, increase guest accommodations by 33 percent, and boost food service capacity by 350 percent. A hotel trade publication explained the rationale behind the final decision: "The Riverside Hotel in Reno, Nevada, was a conservative residential hotel.... Like any hotel of 'middle age,' the Riverside had become a little old fashioned, and needed several modernizing features.... [Wingfield] wanted to convert the Riverside from a quiet residential hotel to a lively downtown resort-type hotel."[19]

The expansion and remodeling of the bar, cocktail lounge, dining room, and casino area—the space known as the Buffet since 1934—was completed first. The existing space was more than doubled by adding the Virginia Street frontage space previously occupied by a cigar store, newsstand, and gift shop, plus some additional interior space. On July 1, 1950, Mert Wertheimer welcomed state and city officials and invited guests to the official opening of the new area. The huge Riverside Theatre Restaurant, as it would be called, combined dining space for 250 guests with a theater to host world-class entertainers; it was the focal point of the new area. It was open for dinner daily, and hosted women's lunches, fashion shows, and other events during the midday hours. A large glass wall allowed diners to look out over a new swimming pool area. The theater stage was a modern marvel, constructed so it could be moved forward or backward, up or down, at the touch of a button, and could also serve as a dance floor. The new room was decorated in Western style, with native Nevada flagstone, redwood accents, and green plants scattered about. For the opening night crowd, Wertheimer had booked veteran entertainer Ted Lewis to entertain the guests from the theater stage. The casino area was also enlarged and renovated, and another new restaurant—the Chuck Wagon, seating sixty people—was added behind the casino. A large curved bar looked out over the Theatre Restaurant, which in turn overlooked the swimming pool. On the other side of the pool was the new banquet facility called the Redwood Room, which would seat more than four hundred people, or could be subdivided to accommodate a number of smaller groups simultaneously. A large service bar provided speedy service to all parties and banquets. The new kitchen was 20,000 square feet larger than before and featured all modern, stainless steel equipment. With the addition of the Redwood Room, the Riverside Hotel was now able to host the city's largest conventions.[20]

An exclusive and expensive club for men only, the Prospectors' Club, had recently organized in Reno, and the group was provided with its own bar, dining room, and casino on the second floor above the Redwood Room overlooking the outdoor pool. The group, made up of the most influential men in the city, had initially met at the Mapes Sky Room, but Wingfield wooed them to the Riverside with the exclusive private club facilities. The Prospectors' Club formally opened on September 27, 1950, with cocktails, dinner, and dancing for members and their guests only.[21]

When the hotel renovation and expansion was completed in August, it had also added a new three-story wing that ran east and west along the south side of the present structure, a two-story addition facing Sierra Street, and a colonnade-type structure along Island Avenue. All existing hotel rooms and suites had also been remodeled. The new wings formed an outdoor courtyard where a large kidney-shaped swimming pool and outdoor entertainment facilities were located. Eighty-four rooms were added to the hotel by the new wings, each facing the river with its own sun balcony; these were called the Lanai apartments. Ground-floor shops were also added to replace the ones given over to the remodeling. Air conditioning was added to the entire structure. Both the swimming pool and the air conditioning were firsts for Reno hotels.[22]

Architect Frank Green had designed the hotel so it would reflect an easygoing resort atmosphere, combining luxurious comfort with Old West informality, a deviation from the more formal environment of the past. The *Pacific Coast Record*, a western hotel trade magazine, wrote, "In the execution of his commission to create an atmosphere that is both informal and luxurious, Architect Frank Green plays the West's natural stone, leather, redwood, green plants and spacious vistas against the modern luxuries of fine carpets, rich wallpapers, copper fixtures, high ceilings and the sparkle and brilliance of metals and glass.... Western motif [is] calculated to invite and enchant persons in white ties and top hats as well as those in spurs and 10 gallon sombreros. It will give a new name to a new style of hotel—'Western sophisticate.'"[23]

George Wingfield was justifiably proud of what he had accomplished with the Riverside Hotel. He wrote to his good friend Bernard Baruch, financier, diplomat, and political consultant, inviting him to visit: "Things have changed materially around the village, especially at the Riverside.... We have quite an institution there now.... It is a beautiful place." Although the Riverside was never the linchpin of his business empire—mining was his chief interest—Wingfield had always taken a personal interest in the hotel. Like Harry Gosse before him, he had been an excellent caretaker of the historic property. He walked daily to his office downtown, and always stopped at the hotel to check in with the manager. He knew the big picture well, but he also kept his eye on the small details, like the appearance of the stores in the lobby area, the placement of the taxi stand, and such. He personally saw to it that the Riverside retained its position as one of the West's preeminent hotels.[24]

Wingfield had also nurtured his staff so they would provide the level of service that had always marked the Riverside. At the reopening, the hotel had 260 employees, and their average length of service was ten years.[25]

As the decade of the 1940s came to a close, the Virginia Street Bridge again became the focal point of the city. Reno artists—a previously disorganized group of individual artists who had always been somewhat subdued in a city with so much else going on—joined together to plan the city's first outdoor public art exhibit, a two-day event to be staged on the Virginia Street Bridge. In a meeting with the chamber of commerce, a committee of artists explained that outside exhibits were commonplace in Greenwich Village and other art colonies, and they believed Reno was ready to become such a place. The morning of the event, however, threatened winds and perhaps even rain, and the *Nevada State Journal* pleaded, "Rest, o Winds!" in support of the event.[26]

Fortunately, it turned out to be a perfect day. Twenty-one artists had created seventy-five paintings for the exhibit. Paintings were hung on the rails on the west side of the bridge, under large, brightly colored umbrellas, and artists were on hand to paint scenes and portraits for attendees. The artwork ran the gamut from "the understandable to the impressionistic," and a steady crowd of locals and visitors strolled the bridge admiring and buying the art. The event was the forerunner of similar events that would one day morph into Reno's extraordinary, month-long Artown.[27]

## Notes

1. Harmon, "Divorce and Economic Opportunity in Reno," 90; Watson, "Tarnished Silver," 57; Riley, *Divorce, An American Tradition*, 138. Population data from U.S. Census Bureau 1940.

2. "Players, Writers to Arrive Here Saturday for Festivities," *REG*, 03/15/1940; "Costume Ball, Pageants Conclude 'Virginia City' Film Event Here," *NSJ*, 03/17/1940.

3. "Costume Ball, Pageants Conclude 'Virginia City' Film Event Here," *NSJ*, 03/17/1940.

4. "Premiere Highlights," *NSJ*, 03/17/1940; IMDb, "Tom Mix."

5. Rocha, "The Mysterious Demise of Key Pittman," 80–83.

6. Rocha, "The Mysterious Demise of Key Pittman," 80–83.

7. "Typically American, Peculiarly Nevadan," *Pacific Coast Record*, January 1951, 21; first quote from Cahill, "Recollections of Work in State Politics," 211; second quote from Atkinson, "Tonopah and Reno Memories," 34.

8. Wilson, "Reminiscences of a Nevada Advertising Man," 105–6.

9. Raymond, *George Wingfield*; quote on p. 262.

10. Raymond, *George Wingfield*; first quote on p. 251, second quote on pp. 262–63.

11. "Hotel to Replace Old Post Office," *NSJ*, 11/22/1945; Raymond, *George Wingfield*, 262.

12. Kling, *Biggest Little City*, 101–2.

13. Kling, *Biggest Little City*, 23, 73, 114.

14. DeLongchamps, "Frederic J. DeLongchamps Architecture Records, 1899–1962," Riverside Hotel, NAA1/175/51; Kling, *Biggest Little City*, 105. Regarding Abelman's cancellation of the Riverside gambling lease, Michael Fischer, grandnephew of Nick Abelman, conversation with the author, 07/31/2013; "Wertheimer Seeks Permit for Riverside," *REG*, 04/04/1949.

15. "Please List Those Rooms," *NSJ*, 07/01/1949; "A Call to The People of Reno" adv., *NSJ*, 04/02/1949.

16. Quote from "Please List Those Rooms," *NSJ*, 07/01/1949; "Labor Dispute Widens; City Crisis Grows," *NSJ*, 07/03/1949.

17. "Strike Is Settled and Reno Is Happy," *NSJ*, 07/10/1949.

18. Quote from "Riverside Hotel Addition Plans Drawn by Firm," *NSJ*, 05/05/1949; "Expansion Planned at Riverside Hotel," *NSJ*, 08/10/1949.

19. "Expansion Planned at Riverside Hotel," *NSJ*, 08/10/1949; quote from "Reno Has a Downtown Resort Hotel," *Hotel Monthly*, February 1952, 23–25.

20. "Remodeling of Bar, Casino at Riverside Hotel Underway," *REG*, 04/12/1949; "New Riverside Hotel Casino, Show Opened," *REG*, 07/03/1950.

21. "Reno Has a Downtown Resort Hotel," *Hotel Monthly*, February 1952, 23–29; "Exclusive Prospectors' Club Fills Quota; Waiting List Established," *NSJ*, 11/04/1947; "Prospectors Are Moving to the Riverside," *NSJ*, 07/06/1950; "Prospectors' Club Opens New Rooms," *REG*, 09/27/1950.

22. "Riverside Hotel Addition Plans Drawn by Firm," *REG*, 05/05/1949; "Expansion Planned at Riverside Hotel," *REG*, 08/10/1949; "River Hotel Eventually Will Have Swimming Pool," *NSJ*, 05/20/1949; "Riverside Hotel Project Delayed," *NSJ*, 06/28/1949; Kling, *Biggest Little City*, 140.

23. "Typically American, Peculiarly Nevadan," *Pacific Coast Record*; quote on pp. 21–22.

24. Raymond, *George Wingfield*; quote on pp. 263–64.

25. "Typically American, Peculiarly Nevadan," *Pacific Coast Record*, 21–22.

26. "Art Exhibit Set by Local Group," *REG*, 05/27/1949; quote from "Breezes Could Play Hob Here Today," *NSJ*, 06/04/1949.

27. "Breezes Could Play Hob Here Today," *NSJ*, 06/04/1949; quote from "First Reno Art Show Held Success," *REG*, 06/06/1949.

# CHAPTER 11

# IT WAS THE BEST OF TIMES

## THE 1950s

ONE HISTORIAN DESCRIBED the decade of the 1950s as "Nevada's Turbulent '50s," writing that the decade was Nevada's entry into the modern era. As for Reno, Clint Hamilton, a weathered old cowboy in one of Reno writer Robert Laxalt's short stories, was growling about how much Reno had grown and changed by the 1950s. "Getting more like a big city every day.... Goddam city, eating its way right into ranching country," he observed wryly. Although it's a fictional account, most Renoites would have agreed with the old cow-puncher's analysis of the city on the Truckee River.[1]

Although many of the decade's changes were national, or even international, in scope—the dawning of the space age, the introduction of television into daily lives, the civil rights movement—Reno was swept up in most of them. Tourism, which had once centered on the divorce trade, was growing in the outdoor recreation and gaming sectors as well. Still, the divorce business remained robust, with annual divorces granted in the state during the decade averaging 9,500 a year, although Las Vegas was getting an increasingly large share of that trade. Warehousing Western goods was also becoming big business in Reno. Early in the decade, Las Vegas would surpass Reno as the largest city in the state, and would overtake it in gaming revenue, thanks to the growth of the Las Vegas Strip.[2]

Natural forces would also play havoc in Reno in the turbulent 1950s. In late November 1950 five straight days of heavy rain inundated the Truckee Meadows, Carson Valley, and surrounding areas, resulting in what became known as the Thanksgiving Day Flood of 1950.

"Reno was a divided city for almost 12 hours," the *Reno Evening Gazette* reported on November 21. "None of the bridges was usable from midnight until noon, and it was impossible to cross the river." Bridges over many rural and secondary state routes were washed out, but Reno and Sparks Bridges

stood fast against the flooding waters, save one. Reno's oldest and most historic bridge, the iron span across Rock Boulevard that had once served as the
Virginia Street Bridge, collapsed and disappeared down the Truckee River
during the flood. Just the prior year, city engineers had surveyed the seventy-
three-year-old bridge—it had been guaranteed by the original builder to last
only twenty years—and decided it was beyond repair for vehicular traffic. It
was no wonder; the old span had been built in 1877, a decade before German
inventor Carl Benz had even envisioned the first motorcar. So the iron bridge
had been converted to pedestrian traffic only, and served out its remaining
year in that fashion. The last vestige of the old bridge was a piece of its
decking seen hung up downstream on the Wells Street Bridge, just before it
shook loose and disappeared down the river.[3]

The concrete Virginia Street Bridge fared much better than the iron
bridge it had replaced. The floodwaters reached the top of the twin arches
then rushed over the two-foot-high concrete parapet, depositing dirt, sand,
tree branches, and other flotsam across the roadway. When the water subsided, it continued to pile debris up against the center pier, creating a bottleneck, but without causing the bridge any structural damage.[4]

The Riverside Hotel was not saved from the storm's wrath as both it and
the neighboring Mapes Hotel were directly in the path of the surging floodwaters. Most downtown businesses and stores were forced to close for days,
but not the city's two top hotels. One reporter noted that he watched a man
peacefully playing a slot machine at the Mapes while standing in two feet
of water. Meanwhile, across the raging river at the Riverside, the hotel went
totally dark on Tuesday morning when the basement flooded, shorting out
all the electrical circuits.[5]

One newspaper report summed up the Riverside's dilemma:

> The Riverside, the hardest hit [of downtown buildings] is a scene of
> chaotic confusion with plush furniture swept every which way in a
> rage of mud and water.
>
> The luxurious open-air swimming pool is a slippery sea of brown
> slime littered with tables and chairs and a general air of helplessness.
>
> Bill Maag, Riverside's superintendent in charge of service, said
> they had no idea how costly the flood would be as he surveyed the
> shambles that was the theater-dining room.... Actresses and chorus
> girls in the downstairs dressing room piled out in various stages of
> costume changes. All managed to escape the swiftly rising waters....
> Riverside Hotel switchboard operators...got on chairs and in true

The "Thanksgiving Day Flood of 1950," as it was known, caused massive damage to both the Riverside and Mapes Hotels. Here, just outside the Riverside's Virginia Street entrance, water and flotsam rush by. Nevada Historical Society.

Shown here is Virginia Street during the 1955 flood. Although this one was even worse than the flood of 1950, the Riverside Hotel, at left, suffered little damage due to all the precautions taken by management. In the center of the picture is the twelve-story Mapes Hotel, opened in late 1947, that gave the Riverside Hotel its first real competition. The Virginia Street Bridge sits between the two hotels, but is unrecognizable due to the depth of the water completely covering it. Courtesy Jerry Fenwick.

story-book fashion kept the switchboard open until water put the board out of commission.

The flood caught the guests in the main theater-dining room [unaware].... Among the guests present at the time the water forced its way into the Riverside were the owners of the hotel, Mr. and Mrs. George Wingfield, Sr., Mr. and Mrs. Noble Gretchell, and U.S. Senator and Mrs. Pat McCarran....

The damage to the Riverside Hotel, in the thousands of dollars [later estimated at $250,000], is extensive. The rugs were coated with an ankle deep layer of silt. Five oil burning boilers in the basement will have to be taken apart piece by piece.

Both the Riverside...and the Mapes...were able to conduct their guests to safety.... Both hotels are conducting "business as usual."[6]

If any good did come out of the flood for the Riverside, it was the fact that it gave George Wingfield the opportunity to brick in the original storefronts on Virginia Street and allow expansion of Wertheimer's casino area.

With the flood of 1950, northern Nevadans were sure they had seen the worst Mother Nature had to offer. But in 1955 they would discover just how wrong they were when a bigger storm, dubbed the "Storm of the Century," roared into the Truckee Meadows. For ten days during the Christmas season a series of storms brought rain and snow to the area. Wary downtown business owners, including George Wingfield at the Riverside, didn't wait for the flood this time: they took precautions ahead of the storm. "Christmas shopping gave way to sandbagging along the river," the *Reno Evening Gazette* wrote on December 22. Mert Wertheimer closed the hotel's Theatre Restaurant, and George Wingfield ordered all the hotel's equipment and supplies moved from the basement to the upper floors. Finally, two days before Christmas, the floodwaters arrived, ripping through downtown streets. It was so bad that President Eisenhower declared Reno a federal disaster area.[7]

"The water got higher and higher, and higher," recalled Paul Leonard, the *Reno Evening Gazette*'s assistant managing editor. The newspaper plant was located downtown at the time. "The water...roared right over the tops of the downtown bridges, and split the city in two.... Really!...The water was going down practically through the Riverside Hotel, and on down Court Street," he wrote. Fortunately, Wingfield's and Wertheimer's precautions saved the Riverside from any major damage. Santa's annual visit to the hotel to give gifts to children from the Sunny Acres Children's Home, and the hotel's annual Christmas dinner, had to be cancelled; but a local produce company came through with a large truck, and the children's gifts were delivered directly to the home.[8]

While the 1950s may have been turbulent times for the weather, politics, the economy, and the social fabric of the city, it was relatively uneventful for the Virginia Street Bridge. The bridge—which would celebrate its fiftieth anniversary unnoticed in 1955—endured both floods with no discernible damage.

In 1951 the bridge did receive a little notoriety when it was once again featured in a Hollywood movie. *Reunion in Reno* by Universal-International Pictures starred Mark Stevens, Peggy Dow, and Gigi Perreau in a story of a young girl who visits Reno seeking a divorce from her parents. Crowds gathered to watch a scene being shot that was described by the newspaper as "newly-divorced women going through the widely-ballyhooed but seldom seen Reno 'tradition' of tossing their wedding rings into the Truckee." As often happened with movies shot in Reno, many extras were hired from the local citizenry, so although not a cultural milestone, the movie did provide some local amusement and a few days of pay for some Renoites. It would be a decade later, in 1961, that the ultimate Reno divorce movie would be released. *The Misfits*, written by Arthur Miller, directed by John Huston, and starring Marilyn Monroe and Clark Gable was expected to be a blockbuster film. Although it turned out to be a financial and critical disaster, it still helped promote the city and its waning divorce business. Finally, in 1951 city planning director Raymond Smith won no popularity contest when he recommended that Virginia Street downtown be turned into a pedestrian mall and the Virginia Street Bridge closed down. The suggestion gathered no support, and was never seriously considered.[9]

If the 1950s were a turbulent time for Nevada, the decade was even more turbulent for the Riverside Hotel as the site approached its 100th year of habitation. In August 1951 Lou Wertheimer, brother of Mert who ran the gambling, entertainment, and dining concessions at the Riverside, filed for a license to join his brother as a partner in the Riverside lease. Mrs. Mapes had decided that she wanted her son to run the entire Mapes Hotel operation, a plan that had cut Lou Wertheimer loose. His new license was granted, and the brothers were licensed to run 105 slot machines, four craps tables, two roulette games, and ten twenty-one games at the Riverside.[10]

The Wertheimer brothers were very different types of men, despite their similar backgrounds. Mert, older by five years, had managed to avoid any major scrapes with the law, even though the brothers had operated illegal gambling games in three states. Once in Nevada, he became a prominent figure in the move to set up strict controls over gaming. Lou, on the other hand, had been arrested a number of times and was a much rougher character than his brother.[11]

The Riverside had featured occasional entertainment for its guests as early as the turn of the century. Local singers, piano players, poets, and dance bands had periodically appeared at the hotel. But it would be Mert Wertheimer, beginning in the early 1950s, who would make big-name entertainment a staple at the Riverside Hotel. It all began when Mert hired Ted Lewis for the grand opening of the expanded and remodeled bar, buffet, and casino area in July 1950. He followed that with the city's first "girly" show, a six-week run of "The Parisian Follies," featuring a chorus line of beautiful ladies dancing the can-can, a replica of Parisian night life, and lots of glamour. Initially there was some resistance in the community to this kind of show, but gradually people came to accept it, and eventually embraced it. A young University of Nevada–Reno graduate and Reno wife and mother, Claudia Hoffer, reflected the attitude of many young Renoites when these revues began to come to town. "I loved to go to the Riverside and see the women dancers and their great costumes. They were really fancy, big costumes and dancing. That was very nice."[12]

Ron Smith, a young radio and TV announcer who had recently relocated from the San Francisco Bay area, also remembered "The Parisian Follies" warmly. "[It] was very fresh and new.... It had French performers and they were, indeed, topless. For its time, that was a little titillating."[13]

Mert Wertheimer's idea that big-name entertainment would attract more customers to his gaming tables wasn't a new idea. Benjamin "Bugsy" Siegel had been doing it quite successfully at his Flamingo Hotel in Las Vegas since its opening in 1946; and the Mapes Sky Room had also made quite a splash with its entertainment in the late 1940s, as had the Riverside itself under Nick Abelman. But in August 1951 Wertheimer hired Frank Sinatra for a two-week engagement in the Theatre Restaurant. Sinatra had been absent from the nightclub scene for years, and his career was at a low point. When asked by a Reno entertainment reporter why he had decided to appear at the Riverside, Sinatra said, "I made my start singing for the public in the supper clubs, and now [ten years later] I want to prove to myself I can do it again." But in typical Sinatra fashion, he would attract controversy. Sinatra had been having marital problems with his longtime wife Nancy, and it was rumored that he planned to divorce her and marry Ava Gardner. But any time reporters attempted to confirm the rumor from the man himself, Sinatra would fly into a rage and begin throwing punches. Edward A. "Ed" Olsen, a Reno correspondent for the Associated Press, and Bill Berry, who covered the Reno divorce scene for the *New York Daily News*, decided to go to the airport to greet Sinatra with boxing gloves hung mockingly over their shoulders. When the ill-tempered Sinatra got off the plane and saw the two reporters, instead of flying into a rage he began laughing and invited them to join him in his room at the Riverside for a chat. During that meeting he told the men the story he had been denying for months: that he would be divorcing Nancy and marrying Ava.[14]

Harry Spencer, a young hotel publicity man at the time, and his buddy Frantz Johnson from the *Nevada State Journal* were also excited when they learned Sinatra was coming to town. Johnson suggested that if Spencer could arrange for Sinatra to sit for a photo, they could sell it to United Press Association (which became United Press International in 1958) for $25.00, a healthy chunk of change in the day. Spencer approached Eddie Dowd, Wertheimer's publicity man, who talked to Sinatra. "The Voice" said he'd be happy to pose for a photo between shows. When the duo approached him, Sinatra—who was then sporting a wispy mustache—said he'd like a girl in the picture too. The girl turned out to be Ava Gardner, and the two men got the first photo of the two together. They were able to get a hefty $50.00 fee from United Press Association for the newsworthy picture. On opening night at the Riverside, guests got more than they had bargained for when Sinatra introduced another celebrity, Clark Gable, who was sitting in the front row of the theater. Fans hooted and hollered when Sinatra went into the audience to shake hands with Gable, and the full house enjoyed a great evening of music. However, the two-week engagement that had started with a bang ended in a whimper, when Sinatra's voice gave out during the second night, the result of Reno's dry climate. He missed a couple of shows before returning to finish his gig. Despite Sinatra's flagging voice, and his public treatment of his first wife Nancy, he still had admirers at the Riverside. Matt Mathews was the barber at the hotel, and he gave "Ol' Blue Eyes" a haircut during his stay. Matthews remembers him being a fine fellow who paid him $20 when a haircut was only $2. Sinatra's Reno gig was followed by a similar show in Las Vegas, and he told reporters there that by the time he was finished with both appearances he would have been in Nevada for six weeks, the state's residency requirement to obtain a divorce.[15]

The marquee entertainment Mert Wertheimer kicked off in the 1950s, coupled with the outstanding talents Nick Abelman and George Wingfield had featured in the 1940s, would make the two-decade era memorable. The Riverside had featured such top-rated acts as the Mills Brothers, Liberace, Jimmy Durante, Lena Horne, Pearl Bailey, Carol Channing, and Ella Fitzgerald. There were also Frankie Avalon, Danny Kaye, Sophie Tucker, Johnny Ray, and the Sons of the Pioneers, to name just some of the A-listers who graced the Riverside's stage. Another top-flight name to appear on the hotel's marquee was world-famous trumpeter and bandleader Louis "Satchmo" Armstrong. In a letter on Riverside Hotel stationery to a friend in New Orleans in early 1952, Armstrong wrote, "And since here I am in Reno (not getting a divorce) just doing a show here at the Riverside Hotel with my band." Publicist Harry Spencer also recalled two particular shows they booked while he worked at the Riverside. In one, the main attraction was singer Kay Starr, still enjoying the accolades for her number one *Billboard* hit, "Wheel of Fortune." Her opening act was a young comic duo named Rowan and Martin who had just broken into show business. The second act, Spencer recalled, was a beautiful young singer–dancer named Margaret Olsson, soon to be known an Ann-Margret, whose manager paid for her appearance so she could get the exposure. It wasn't just the tourist market that was attracted to these Riverside shows: locals loved them too, and were always welcome. James Bernardi was fifteen when he moved to Reno with his family in 1957. A few years later, when he was in high school, Bernardi said he and his date would go to the Riverside after a school dance and have a sandwich and coke and catch the Jimmy Durante show, all for $12.00. "You didn't have to be twenty-one to go into those showrooms," Bernardi said. Jerry Fenwick, whose family owned the state's first Sherwin-Williams paint and artists' supply store, said going to the Riverside was for special occasions. He recalled the Riverside's house band, the Bill Clifford Orchestra. "The band was the backup for the [main] act. These people would then appear at schools to teach kids about music…. They were an integral part of the community," Fenwick said.[16]

Entertainment didn't come at a bargain price for the Riverside and the rest of Reno's top hotels and clubs. Marketing and public relations man Mark Curtis, who also wrote a column for *Variety*, wrote that in the early to middle 1950s star attractions normally cost $2,500 to $5,000 a week, with the biggest stars, such as Nat King Cole, getting up to $7,500 a week. Chorus girls—the Riverside's chorus was the "Riverside Starlets"—earned $75 to $125 a week, musicians earned about $135 a week, and house bandleaders about $270 a week. Second-tier entertainers, usually used as opening acts or lounge shows, picked up between $500 and $1,000 a week, depending on their stature.[17]

Occasionally, the Riverside also offered less-expensive entertainment for local residents. Marilyn Melton is a third generation Nevadan; her late husband Rollan was the editor, then publisher, of the *Reno Evening Gazette*. Around 1952, when Marilyn was a student in the art department at the University of Nevada–Reno, she and a male friend were enjoying a walk downtown. For reasons she couldn't recall, the two were walking barefoot, and by the time they reached the Riverside their feet were getting uncomfortably hot. They casually walked into the Riverside's new Lanai Apartments on Island Avenue facing the river, sat down at the large bubbling fountain pool, and dunked their feet. It wasn't long before security arrived, but the young couple avoided trouble by hot-footing it out of the hotel through a kitchen exit.[18]

Perhaps one of the greatest entertainment bargains the Riverside ever offered to the local folks occurred later that year, in September. At that time television was just starting to make an appearance in many American cities and homes, but smaller cities like Reno were not able to receive television signals yet. There were only a handful of TV sets in the entire Reno–Sparks area, and most of those had been brought to town by new residents, and sat unused in their living rooms. With the 1952 baseball World Series coming up, featuring two fan favorites—the New York Yankees and their arch-rivals, the Brooklyn Dodgers—George Wingfield and Mert Wertheimer sensed an opportunity. They partnered with Nevada media entrepreneur Donald Reynolds and arranged for a closed-circuit broadcast of the World Series to be shown on TV sets scattered around the hotel, the lounge, and the corner bar. They even set up huge viewing windows with TV sets around the patio area, with a big sign announcing, "Riverside TV Knothole Gang." During the series—won by the Yankees in seven games—people lined up by the hundreds inside and outside the hotel to watch every pitch, most seeing the brand new medium for the first time. The huge interest spurred Reynolds to open Reno's first TV station, KZTV (now KOLO-TV) channel 8, the following year.[19]

Unfortunately, there was also a darker side to the hotel entertainment scene. Many of the top stars who played the Riverside, the Mapes, and some Lake Tahoe venues weren't allowed to stay in the hotels. Jack Douglass, longtime Reno gaming executive and general manager of the Riverside in the early 1960s, said, "The blacks couldn't stay in our hotel. They had to go to the black boarding houses down on Montello Street [just north of today's I-80, and west of Hwy. 395]. Every time there was a black entertainer in town in those days that's the way it was." Longtime casino marketing executive Roy Powers said that when he worked at the Riverside, part of his responsibility was to find lodgings outside of the hotel for entertainers like the Mills Brothers and the Ink Spots.[20]

The same Jim Crow treatment applied to black customers who came in to gamble. "A very classy black couple started shooting craps one Sunday morning," Douglass recalled. The pit boss walked over to the couple, thanked them for coming in, but told them they couldn't stay since the white customers—of whom there were only about three at that hour—might object. That was the policy at all the large hotel–casinos in Reno.[21]

During the 1950s and early 1960s, Reno's black population was less than 5 percent. Despite that, the city had a long history of racial injustice, even though racism had been fairly rare throughout most of the nineteenth century. But in 1925—the year KKK membership peaked nationally—four crosses were burned in Reno and 2,000 men were initiated into the local Ku Klux Klan chapter, or klavern, as it was called. The Reno Klavern had disbanded during the Great Depression, but many of the attitudes still smoldered decades later, to the point that some black Nevadans referred to Reno as the Mississippi of the West. Black Americans were not even allowed to purchase a house in Reno before 1952, and after that only in a blacks-only neighborhood called Black Springs in the North Valley area. The hotel–casino discriminatory policies were not written in their business manuals, but they were definitely part of the business culture. Delores Feemster, a native-born Renoite of an Italian father and an African American mother, obtained a job at the Riverside working in the restrooms. Although she was half black and half white, in that era she was considered to be "black." Because she had a light complexion, however, she was able to rise through the ranks to better positions, though her experience was the exception rather than the rule. The city's hotel–casinos were especially hung up in the past in what one newspaper reporter called a White Curtain. Not only did they not hire blacks except for low-paying maid and service positions, but they also did not want them as customers.[22]

With very few exceptions, these discriminatory practices in Reno continued all the way up to the passage of the Civil Rights Act of 1964, which finally ended the city's most shameful era.

The Riverside Hotel of the 1950s—particularly the corner bar—was one of the city's favorite watering holes for lawyers, divorcees, businesspersons, gamblers, entertainers, reporters, state and local politicians, and everyday in-the-know citizens. Public-relations man Mark Curtis described the legendary bar: "Red brocade wallpaper, historic Nevada photos in big ornate gilded frames, a horseshoe bar, and a piano player who took requests created the intimate but exciting atmosphere." It was said that Nevada kingmaker Norman Biltz could always be found at his own table in the corner bar, dispensing favors or bargaining for the upper hand in an upcoming legislative session. Biltz ran the operation for powerful Democratic U.S. senator Pat McCarran, doing much of his work out of the corner bar. In 1952 McCarran had handpicked one of his law firm associates, Alan Bible, to run against Senator George "Molly" Malone (Republican, U.S. senator) so that the Democratic party could control both Senate seats. But a virtually unknown candidate, a young man named Tom Mechling, a writer for *Kiplinger Newsletter* in Washington D.C., filed to run against Bible in the Democratic primary. The energetic Mechling and his wife, who had once worked for McCarran, knocked on doors all over the state, and in a tremendous grassroots effort upset Bible by 475 votes. McCarran was apoplectic: in Nevada, you just didn't cross Pat McCarran.[23]

With his momentum, it looked like Mechling would also upset Republican Malone, who carried a lot of political baggage. But then the young man made a colossal blunder. He met with Norman Biltz at the corner bar, and the next day in a radio commercial he accused Biltz of trying to buy him off. But Biltz had been forewarned of the scheme, and he had secretly taped their conversation, which proved that it was Mechling who asked to be bought off, and Biltz had refused him. McCarran then endorsed the Republican (Malone), and Mechling lost the general election. The whole affair had a bad smell to it, and McCarran decided to drop out of sight for a while until the smell had dissipated. He left Washington and nobody knew where he had gone.[24]

Ed Olsen of the Associated Press wanted to interview McCarran about the incident, but he couldn't locate him. Olsen didn't like McCarran at all: "Senator McCarran was always an enigma to me.... I could never get anything but pomposity out of him and gobbledygook most of the time.... We were never the greatest of friends," Olsen said in dramatic understatement. "And one night I was in the Riverside with Melvin Belli...and he nudges me and he says, 'Isn't that your Senator over there?'" Sure enough, across the room sat Pat McCarran with sunglasses on, eating dinner all by himself. So Olsen headed for McCarran's table. McCarran growled, "What do you want?" to the journalist, and Olsen said he wanted a story about where McCarran had been for the last six or eight weeks. "You're nothing but a goddamn Communist that's been following me across the country," McCarran roared. "And with that," Olsen said, "he picked up the table with all its dishes and food and steak and cups and everything and threw it at me! He tipped the whole thing over in the middle of the dining room and got up and stomped out.... It was certainly a shocking experience."[25]

---

In mid-1954 George Wingfield announced plans for another expansion, a three-story addition to the Riverside. The $500,000 project would increase the hotel's capacity by almost 50 percent to 200 rooms and apartments, the announcement noted; the project included another $100,000 to be spent on furnishings and carpeting for the new rooms. San Francisco architect Frank Green, who had also designed the extensive 1949–50 expansion, was again in charge. The target date for completion was January 1955, just in time for the national convention of the Cattlemen's Association, one of Reno's largest annual meetings. The three-story addition would be built on the south side of the hotel, overlooking the pool area; due to the added height, however, each room would also have an unobstructed view of the river; each room would also have its own sun porch. There would also be a one-story addition on the west side of the hotel.[26]

By the mid-1950s the Riverside was still enjoying its reputation as the "in" place to dine, especially for an important occasion. For instance, a couple celebrating a silver anniversary in the Theatre Restaurant could dine like royalty: a champagne cocktail, followed by cold vichyssoise, roast rack of spring lamb for two with Belgian endives, boiled pearl onions and cream, and fondant potatoes, finished off by fresh strawberry shortcake and a split of 1937 Château d'Yquem from France, said to be the world's best dessert wine. The bill for such extravagance, according to a 1955 Theatre Restaurant menu? $25...of course, not including the tip.

---

Marketing itself as a winter sports area had never been Reno's strength, but George Wingfield believed that the newly opened Reno Ski Bowl, on the eastern slope of Slide Mountain, would be a powerful magnet in drawing winter sports fans to Reno, and to the Riverside Hotel. The newspaper article announcing the hotel's expansion noted, "For almost 100 years the site on which the Riverside stands has been catering to the comfort of visitors and travelers. Firmly established as 'Reno's first address' the hostelry was a landmark on the Truckee even before there was a Reno."[27] When the 1960 Winter Olympics were awarded to Squaw Valley at Lake Tahoe two years later, Wingfield's decision to expand proved to be prescient, even though he had sold the historic hostelry by that time.

That sale was announced on December 17, 1955. Wingfield, whose gaming lease with Mert and Lou Wertheimer and their partners, Mathis and West, had been in effect since 1951, had consisted solely of a verbal agreement and a handshake. The men were all old friends and past business partners. This deal, however, called for a more formal arrangement. The buyers, who paid $4,010,000 for the Riverside and all its property, were Mert and Lou Wertheimer, Raymond "Ruby" Mathis, and Elmer G. "Baldy" West. West would sell his share back to the others less than two years later as a result of a so-called difference of opinion between the four partners, and he would become president and part owner of the Horseshoe Casino on North Virginia Street. The remaining partners also replaced Arthur Allen, who had managed the property for sixteen years, with Lee Frankovich, who had worked at Harrah's in both Reno and Lake Tahoe.[28]

With the Riverside Hotel's future brightened by the expansion and the additional focus on winter sports, it's puzzling why George Wingfield chose this time to sell the hotel he had nurtured since 1927. Nearing his eightieth birthday, and having regained all of the personal popularity and respect he possessed before his Depression-era collapse, Wingfield perhaps explained it best in a letter to his friend Bernard Baruch when he wrote, "The mining is all I care to do." All of his other entrepreneurial activities, including the Riverside Hotel, had lost their appeal for the old man once called a Sagebrush Caesar. He did make one thing clear to the Wertheimers, however: he expected them to honor their contract as well as the tradition of keeping the historic hotel as the state's finest hostelry. Patting the shoulder holster he often wore under his coat, he threatened that if the brothers didn't abide by all the terms of the contract, they would see him coming up the street and would know why.[29]

On August 18, 1956, Wingfield's family and friends staged a reception to celebrate his eightieth birthday. The reception was held at the Wingfield home on Court Street, and scores of the honoree's friends stopped by to extend their best wishes. Later in the evening an elaborate dinner was held at the Riverside, where the new owners acted as hosts for fifty of Wingfield's closest friends and associates. Telegrams of congratulations were read from his good friend Bernard Baruch, and another friend, Herbert Hoover, both welcoming Wingfield into the octogenarian club. George Wingfield—one of Nevada's most powerful economic and political figures for more than a half-century—passed away on the day before Christmas in 1959.[30]

George Wingfield had introduced big-name entertainment to the Riverside and to the Reno market, but it was Mert Wertheimer who had made it a regular attraction. He had modernized the operation, and had helped make casino gambling a respected avocation while leasing part of the hotel. Now, as one of the owners of the entire operation, it appeared that the famous Riverside Hotel was on track to continue serving the crème de la crème of the traveling public and the local "in" crowd, as it had been doing for generations. However, that did not turn out to be the case. Mert was seventy-four, and his brother Lou was sixty-nine, and unknown to the Reno public was the fact that both men had been ill for some time. Realizing that they could not continue with the demanding work schedule of running a major hotel–casino, they quietly began searching for a buyer for the property that they had only recently purchased themselves. On January 20, 1958, it was announced that Mert and Lou Wertheimer and Ruby Mathis had sold the hotel to the Crummer Corporation, headed by wealthy Reno financier, land developer, philanthropist, and businessman Roy E. Crummer. The sale price was reported to be between $4 and $5 million. Illogically, given the Wertheimer brothers' health, the three former owners leased back the casino from Crummer on a ten-year lease and continued operating the gambling concession. Operation of the restaurants, bars, and entertainment, however, reverted to Crummer. Roy Crummer was no newcomer to hotel management; he had previously been involved in ownership of the Mark Hopkins Hotel in San Francisco and the elegant Town House Hotel in Los Angeles, which eventually became the Beverly Hilton. From 1959 until the early 1970s when a fire destroyed it, he also owned the popular gourmet restaurant named The Lancer on Mount Rose Highway overlooking Reno. Crummer appeared to be an excellent choice to carry on the Riverside Hotel's ninety-nine-year reputation for excellence.[31]

Crummer immediately announced that the new manager of the establishment would be I. E. "Bill" Nitschke, a former FBI agent who had previously managed The Lancer restaurant. He would be assisted by longtime former manager Arthur Allen, who was brought back into the fold. Nitschke had an interesting background. In the early 1930s a criminal gang was wreaking havoc in a cross-country crime spree. Alfred Brady—who had once bragged that his crime career would make John Dillinger look like a piker—and his two accomplices had murdered a police officer, robbed four jewelry stores of $100,000, hijacked the loot of a number of other gangs, and finally barricaded themselves in a sporting goods store in Bangor, Maine. Nitschke, who was in the FBI's Boston office, was sent to Bangor with a crew of agents with orders to stop the gang's crime wave. An old-fashioned shoot-out ensued, with Tommy guns blasting away from both sides. By the time the smoke cleared, Brady and one of his henchmen lay dead, and the other man had been subdued and arrested. It was determined that Nitschke and his team had fired forty-five bullets, and forty-three of them had found their targets. Nitschke would later provide technical assistance to director Mervyn LeRoy during the filming of Warner Brothers' 1959 hit movie, *The FBI Story*.[32]

In October 1958, after seven years performing at the Riverside's Theatre Restaurant, the Bill Clifford Orchestra resigned to return to San Francisco. Nitschke replaced the band with the Eddie Fitzpatrick Orchestra, also originally from San Francisco, who had spent the previous ten years playing in the Skyroom at the Mapes Hotel. The band had left the Mapes when Charles Mapes Jr. decided to end entertainment in the Sky Room, which in itself was a turning point for the Biggest Little City. During the 1950s—and long before Las Vegas would gain the distinction—Reno had often been called "The Entertainment Capital of the Nation."[33]

The Wertheimer brothers had little time to continue the tradition of excellent service they had brought to the Riverside Hotel's casino. On May 20, 1958, Lou passed away, and two months later, on July 20, Mert died of leukemia, bringing to an end the careers of two of Reno's most enduring gambling figures. Less than a month later, with his two partners and long-time associates gone, Ruby Mathis sold the ten-year Riverside gaming lease to Virgil Smith, a native of Winnemucca, Nevada.[34]

Many knowledgeable gaming men praised the type of gaming operation Mert Wertheimer had run. Everyone knew he had a shady past, and there were even occasional rumors that some of the games at the Riverside were fixed. But nothing ever seemed to stick to the man. Robbins Cahill was the first chairman of the Nevada Gaming Control Board, and he ran that agency for most of the time Mert Wertheimer was active in Nevada gaming at the Riverside. One of Cahill's major tasks was ferreting out the criminal element that was pervasive in the 1950s, but he had nothing but grudging praise for Wertheimer: "We could never find anything [negative] in Mert Wertheimer's record.... There was nothing particularly detrimental to Mert. Mert Wertheimer was a good operator.... He started the type of operation in the Riverside that continued for a number of years.... He had the stars of that era under the same stature that Las Vegas got, and he ran the type of place [that] was *the* swank place in Reno for a number of years" (emphasis in original).[35]

As for Mert Wertheimer the man, most people liked him, despite his somewhat rough exterior. Reno newspaper gaming columnist Stan

Delaplane was a regular at all of the city's casinos, as he made his rounds looking for tidbits of information for his column. He wrote that Mert spent most of his time sitting at a small table on the casino floor keeping his eye on everything that took place around him. "The action was always good. But Mert always pretended it wasn't," Delaplane wrote. He said Mert once told him, "I only sit here on the chance someone will drop his poke and I can get my foot on it." In the 1920s Mert had been kidnapped by Detroit gangsters for refusing to pay protection money, and he was held for $250,000 ransom. To pass the time, he played the card game hearts with one of his kidnappers. After some time, he related to Delaplane, he was holding a lot of markers he had won from the kidnapper. "Big George," Mert told his kidnapper, "if you would pick up your markers, maybe I could pay my bill and be on my way." That was the kind of loose, fun-loving character the man was, and, as Stan Delaplane commented, "It won't be the same around Reno without Mert Wertheimer."[36]

The list of owners of the Riverside Hotel that has occupied the same site on the south side of the Truckee River for more than a century-and-a-half is a long one. Most owners saw the hotel as a means to an end: making money, creating an asset for future appreciation, or perhaps both. But dollars aside, as the historic value of the Riverside Hotel grew over the years, many of these earlier owners also began to see themselves as caretakers of an institution. Harry Gosse, George Wingfield, and even Mert Wertheimer all showed signs of this emotional attachment to the place, over and above whatever financial rewards it might have brought them. They treated the Riverside as if it were more than just a fine hotel, and as a result, for almost the first full century of the existence of the hotel on the Truckee River (1859–1958), "It was the best of times," as Charles Dickens wrote in *A Tale of Two Cities*.

Unfortunately, all that would soon change.

## Notes

1. First quote from Glass, *Nevada's Turbulent '50s*; second quote from Laxalt, *A Lean Year*, 1–2.

2. Glass, *Nevada's Turbulent '50s*, 39–41; Watson, "Tarnished Silver," 56–58.

3. Quote from "Heavy Rains Continue Over Stricken Region," *REG*, 11/21/1950; "Council Shies at Repairing Historic Rock Street Bridge," *NSJ*, 10/18/1949; "Pictures of the Worst Flood: Last Bit of Rock St. Bridge," *NSJ*, 11/26/1950.

4. "Two Days of Work Shows Results," *NSJ*, 11/23/1950.

5. "Heavy Rains Continue Over Stricken Region," *REG*, 11/21/1950; "Two Days of Work Shows Results," *NSJ*, 11/23/1950.

6. Quote from "Riverside and Mapes Hotels, Hard Hit by Flood, at Work Repairing Terrific Damage," *NSJ*, 11/22/1950; "Reno Businesses List Flood Loss," *REG*, 11/30/1950.

7. Quote from "Half-Built Bridge Folds Under Water, Flood Debris," *REG*, 12/22/1955; "Reno Braces for Overflow of River's Muddy Torrent," *REG*, 12/22/1955; "River Lowers at Late Hour," *NSJ*, 12/24/1958.

8. Quote from Leonard, "Tales of Northern Nevada," 127–29; "Day and Night" column, *REG*, 12/28/1955.

9. Quote from "Movie Scenes Shot in Reno," *REG*, 05/01/1951; "Ward Five Elections," *REG*, 04/18/1955.

10. "License Pleas Presented but Not Sahati's," *REG*, 08/14/1951.

11. Cahill, "Recollections of Work in State Politics," 212; Kling, *Rise of the Biggest Little City*, 174.

12. UNOHP and OLLI, "The Cultural Side of Reno: Claudia Hoffer," quote on p. 228.

13. UNOHP and OLLI, "The Cultural Side of Reno: Ron Smith," 582.

14. Quote from Curtis, *It Was Great While It Lasted*, 31–32; "Day and Nite, by Onlooker," *REG*, 08/07/1951; Olsen, "My Career as a Journalist," 58–59.

15. Harry Spencer, interview with the author, 12/26/2013; "Ava Attends Sinatra Show," *REG*, 08/18/1951; "Gable, Sinatra Meet in Reno," *REG*, 08/22/1951.

16. Harry Spencer, interview with the author, 12/26/2013; Crawford, "The End of an Era," *RGJ*, 01/12/1987; first quote from Armstrong, *Louis Armstrong*, 155; second quote from UNOHP and OLLI, "The Cultural Side of Reno: James Bernardi," 3; third quote from UNOHP and OLLI, "The Cultural Side of Reno: Jerry Fenwick," 123.

17. Curtis, *It Was Great While It Lasted*, 5.

18. Reno resident Marilyn Melton, interview with the author, 10/24/2013.

19. Pearce, "Throwback Thursday," KOLO-TV.

20. Quotes from Douglass, "Jack's Story," 225–26; Hagar, "A Look Behind Reno's White Curtain," *RGJ*, 02/27/2008.

21. Douglass, "Jack's Story," 225–26.

22. Miller, "The Biggest Little Struggle," 21–22, 36, 45–47; Rusco, *"Good Time Coming?,"* 196; Townsell-Parker, *A Cry for Help*, iii, 37, 42–43.

23. Quote from Curtis, *It Was Great While It Lasted*, 30–31; Barbano, "Déjà Vu All Over Again," *Sparks, NV, Tribune*, 10/10/2010.

24 Barbano, "Déjà Vu All Over Again," *Sparks, NV, Tribune*, 10/10/2010.

25. Olsen, "My Career as a Journalist," 54–55, 64; all quotes, p. 64.

26. "Three Story Addition for Reno's Riverside Hotel," *NSJ*, 07/18/1954.

27. "Three Story Addition for Reno's Riverside Hotel," *NSJ*, 07/18/1954.

28. "$4,010,000 Is Paid for Riverside Hotel," *NSJ*, 12/17/1955; Kling, *Rise of the Biggest Little City*, 174; "West Withdraws from Riverside," *NSJ*, 01/22/1956; "Lee Frankovich New Riverside Manager; Replaces A. V. Allen," *NSJ*, 01/03/1956.

29. Raymond, *George Wingfield*, 261, 264–65, quote on p. 261.

30. "Geo. Wingfield Honored on Eightieth Birthday," *NSJ*, 08/19/1956; Raymond, *George Wingfield*, 270.

31. "Crummer Corp. Buys Riverside Hotel in Reno," *REG*, 01/20/1958; "Sell Luxury Hotel," *NSJ*, 01/21/1958; Kling, *Biggest Little City*, 95.

32. Kling, *Biggest Little City*, 95; "Riverside Hotel's Manager is Handy Man with Firearms," *NSJ*, 03/16/1958.

33. "Fitzpatrick Orchestra Takes Riverside Stand," *NSJ*, 09/30/1958; Kling, *Biggest Little City*, 141.

34. Kling, *Biggest Little City*, 141; Kling, *Biggest Little City*, "Wertheimer, Lou," and "Wertheimer, Mert," 174.

35. Cahill, "Recollections of Work in State Politics"; quote on p. 211.

36. All quotes from Delaplane, "A Postcard from Stan Delaplane," *REG*, 07/21/1958.

# CHAPTER 12

# IT WAS THE WORST OF TIMES

## THE 1960s

IRONICALLY, 1960—the centennial year for the hotel that became the Riverside—was the beginning of "the worst of times" for the historic site. A succession of new owners, almost stumbling over one another to gain control of the hotel, had no interest whatsoever in the past. The famous hostelry went into a tortuous tailspin that would last for forty years before an unlikely savior stepped in on the cusp of a new millennium and made it relevant again.

Virgil Smith, the Riverside's new casino concessionaire, had a long background leasing and operating gaming concessions in Reno's hotels and clubs, including those at the Palace Club, the Golden Hotel, Belle Livingstone's Cowshed, the Cedars, and a number of others. Smith and Bill Harrah were longtime friends, and Smith had even advanced Harrah the money to open his now-famous Reno hotel–casino. Smith and Roy Crummer were friends, too, and when Crummer bought the Riverside, Smith asked if he could lease space for a single roulette wheel. Quickly, however, he found himself with the entire casino concession when the Wertheimer brothers suddenly passed away.[1]

Roy Crummer's ownership of the historic hotel would last less than two years. Despite the short time period, the Crummer era was the pivotal point in the eventual downfall of the Riverside Hotel. Longtime Reno gaming executive Jack Douglass, who Virgil Smith approached to join him later when he purchased the Riverside from Crummer, said, "I didn't realize it at the time, but under Crummer the property had been losing money, which is why he wanted to sell.... Also we were getting behind in paying our bills, maybe sixty days." Crummer was an experienced high-end hotel owner, and an extraordinarily successful businessman, and the hotel's gaming leases during that period—which paid Crummer a percentage of the revenue—were held by some of the most experienced operators of the day: the Wertheimers and Virgil Smith. Despite those positive factors, according to Douglass, the Riverside was losing money. It's true there was more competition in Reno during the late 1950s and 1960s, but it was mostly geared toward the masses, not toward the high-end audience the Riverside had always attracted. The 1950s and 1960s were decades of explosive growth in the middle class, and the high-end audience was shrinking. Also, one of the Riverside's pillars of profit, the divorce trade, was ebbing away, as other states relaxed their divorce laws and reduced the demand for migratory divorces.[2]

Las Vegas, too, was drawing attention away from Reno, even though Reno was countering some of that loss by promoting itself as a year-round vacation destination. A new four-lane freeway from California and Reno's new municipal airport were both on the cusp of opening, and, to top it off, the 1960 Winter Olympics at nearby Squaw Valley were scheduled, promising to introduce a whole new international audience to the Biggest Little City.[3]

Despite all the positive factors, the fact remains that the Riverside's slide had begun, and things would only get worse for the historic structure as the 1960s unfolded.

The first time the public became aware that Roy Crummer was trying to get out of the Riverside was on December 10, 1959, when he announced he had sold it to Virgil Smith for $5 million on a deal that would close on December 29 of that year. Smith had been scrambling to put a group of investors together, but when the announcement was made he had yet to finalize anything. Over the next few months the names of Smith's partners began dribbling into the newspapers, one or two at a time. In the end, the final owners and their respective stakes in the holding company would be Smith, 50.15 percent; two of the owners of the building that the Cal Neva Hotel–Casino occupied (Beverly Hills dentist Dr. Robert Franks, 25 percent, and Arizona resident Sam Levy, 3.6 percent); longtime Reno gaming executive Jack Douglass, 14.25 percent; and Reno businessman Harold Munley, 7 percent. Majority owner Virgil Smith announced that Lee Frankovich would remain as general manager of the hotel; and said, "We have plans for major expansion and renovation of the hotel which will be announced in the very near future."[4]

Virgil Smith's tenure as majority owner of the Riverside would be even shorter than that of the Wertheimer brothers. On April 19, the Nevada

Gaming Commission granted Smith's sale of his remaining interest in the hotel to Dr. Franks and the three other partners. Smith's health was failing, and, according to his attorney, that was the reason he wished to divulge himself of all interest in the Riverside. However, gaming commissioners approved the sale reluctantly. "The complicated and apparently changing financial structure of the Riverside appeared to bother the commissioners," the newspaper noted. There was also one condition applied to the sale. Gambler David High—a man who had been trying to get his foot in the door in Reno casinos for years—had been hired by Franks to be the assistant entertainment director at the hotel. Commissioners were concerned about High's chummy relationship with the Mob, so much so that they had denied his earlier request for a gaming license at the Cal Neva. Thus, the commissioners' approval of Virgil Smith's sale was based upon High having no part in the Riverside, "directly or indirectly." The commissioners also expressed concern that Smith had earlier sold about 43 percent of his shares to Franks, Levy, and Munley without informing the Nevada Gaming Commission. So once all this dust had settled, Smith was completely out; the Beverly Hills dentist, Franks, was now the majority partner with 44.11 percent; Munley and Douglass each held 13.09 percent; and Levy held 6.55 percent. The remaining 23.16 percent was held in small quantities by various other men and by the holding corporation itself for future sale, all of which caused a great deal of grief for the confused commissioners.[5]

Jack Douglass, the most experienced gaming man among all the owners, quickly got fed up with Franks, who had very little—perhaps none at all—experience running hotels and casinos, and with the whole tangled web of ownership. Douglass said, "Dr. Franks…would come up about every second weekend. We would have a meeting and he would harass everybody about this or that. He was always comping his friends into the hotel, too. He insisted on picking out the entertainment for our showroom…[and] he kept sending up entertainers [from Hollywood]."[6]

But Douglass also had more serious concerns involving David High, the Mob-connected gambler the Gaming Commission had said could have nothing to do with the Riverside: "Well, I would come to work sometimes in the evenings and Dave High would be hanging around outside on the sidewalk. And half the time Emmett, partner Harold Munley's son, would be out there talking to him…. Something was fishy. I got the feeling that maybe through Dave High and our minor partners, Doc Statcher [Joseph "Doc" Statcher] a known Mob associate, was investing. There was money I couldn't account for." Douglass would end up selling his interest a few months later.[7]

Whatever Douglass suspected, however, didn't last too long. In late September it was announced that Franks (now 64 percent owner), Munley (30 percent), and Levy (6 percent) had sold the Riverside for around $5 million, the same price they had paid for it ten months earlier. The new buyers—pending approval by the Nevada Gaming Commission—were two Hollywood men, William "Bill" Miller and Donald O'Connor. Miller was a former investor in the New Frontier Hotel in Las Vegas, and had had ties with the Dunes and Sahara Hotels. His role with those hotels had been as an impresario, putting together entertainment acts and packages. O'Connor was a well-known Hollywood singer–dancer–actor. According to Miller, there would be two separate holding companies involved in the new ownership. He would own 90 percent of the casino holding company and O'Connor would own 10 percent, while they would each own 50 percent of the real estate and hotel holding company. Miller planned to serve as general manager of the entire operation, and he said they would take over the facility in late November.[8]

It had actually been Miller who had previously helped Douglass sell his shares. Miller had come to Reno to scout the property, and he and Douglass got together. Douglass told him, "Look, I want out. I'm uncomfortable here!" He told Miller he wanted $50,000, his original investment, and an additional $15,000 for a profit. "Give me $65,000 and I'm gone," he said. He then added that if the others in the group wouldn't buy him out at that price, "I'm going to Carson [City] to tell them about my suspicions [about David High and Doc Statcher]." Miller met with Franks and the other partners, and they took Douglass seriously. "As far as I know, I was the only one to get his money back, and with a profit besides," Douglass boasted.[9]

By the time all this reached the Gaming Commission for approval in November, another wrinkle had been added. The casino holding company would now be owned 95 percent by Miller, and 5 percent by the ubiquitous Dr. Robert Franks. Donald O'Connor was out of the casino holding company altogether, but he and Miller still held equal 50 percent shares in the real estate and hotel holding company.[10]

Miller got in hot water with the Gaming Commission almost before the ink was dry on the official licensing paperwork. While he was at the New Frontier in Las Vegas, Miller had made the acquaintance of a fellow employee named Gerald Layne who worked in the casino. When Miller took over the Riverside he brought Layne to Reno to be the casino manager, and even promised him he could purchase a 5 percent stake in the casino holding company. But on January 8, 1961, Layne left the Riverside with $15,000 in his pocket to play poker in a private, high-stakes game in Placerville, California.

On the way to the game, Layne completely vanished. A few days later his car
was found at Lake Tahoe, but Layne—like banker Roy J. Frisch twenty-seven
years earlier—has never been seen or heard from again. Layne's name was
submitted in absentia to the Gaming Commission for that 5 percent stake,
but he was turned down because he had been convicted of being in possession of a carload of crooked cards and dice and a loaded pistol a few years
earlier. Present or absent, gaming commissioners said, Layne could not buy
an interest in the Riverside; if he ever did return, they advised Miller, he
couldn't even work there any longer.[11]

As soon as Bill Miller had arrived at the Riverside, he knew it was in
trouble. "This place is a real loser," he told Jack Douglass. "It can't make it;
we've got to make some changes." During his first press conference, he laid
out some of the changes he believed the hotel, and the city of Reno, would
have to make in order to stay relevant: better downtown parking, more marketing and promotion in the Bay Area, attractively priced charter flights to
the West's leading cities, promotion of summer and winter sports attractions, and better hotel and club entertainment offerings.[12]

The last suggestion was one Miller immediately began introducing back
into the Riverside. He eliminated the two-shows-a-night policy Mert Wertheimer had started, and his first booking was for a rising new singer named
Paul Anka. In the Theatre Restaurant, now renamed the Olympics Room,
and the ever-popular corner bar, he booked such top-name entertainers as
Billy Williams, Sarah Vaughn, Gogi Grant, and Dennis Day. However, Miller's
favorite acts were the revue shows. He had first introduced European-style
revue shows to Las Vegas, including "Minsky's Follies," and now he began
lining up similar shows at the Riverside in what he called Jewel Box Revues.
But he stirred up a real hornets' nest when he opened "Le Crazy Horse
Revue," a female impersonator show straight from the Champs Elysées in
Paris. "Adults Only," "No Cameras Allowed," the ads said, and although the
opening night crowd was delighted, many local citizens were not. A group
of local ministers, led by Baptist minister Clyde Mathews, were the most
vocal. "[It] was a lewd show as ever'd been in Reno," Reverend Mathews
hotly charged. Having said that, he naturally had to see it for himself, and in
the company of a couple of local politicians he obtained a front-and-center
table. "It was beyond the bounds of anything that had ever been in Reno,"
he fumed after the show. While many locals like Mathews complained, little
was done to stop the show. Finally, in March 1962—the show had been going
on since the previous June—the Reno City Council passed an ordinance ban-
ning female impersonator shows. Soon thereafter, two officials from the city

attorney's office and three vice squad officers showed up at the Riverside, and Miller relented, closing the show.[13]

While this squabble was going on over the revue, two new minority shareholders had purchased small percentages in the Riverside. They were Frank Cunardi and Roy Denhart. However, anybody in Reno who believed the Riverside Hotel ownership merry-go-round was over was sadly mistaken. On June 14, 1962, it was announced that Miller had sold his majority stake in the hotel in a deal involving "a little in excess of $5 million," according to the newspaper. The new majority owner was Raymond Spector, a New York advertising man, investor, and principal stockholder of cosmetic company Hazel Bishop, Inc. Spector had purchased 88 percent of the stock in the Riverside Hotel; and he would be the seventh owner of the property in less than seven years.[14]

Spector had an interesting history. A successful New York ad agency principal throughout the 1930s and 1940s, he had teamed up with chemist Hazel Bishop in the early 1950s when she invented the first so-called kiss-proof lipstick. As their chief ad man, Spector had taken the Hazel Bishop brand and made it one of early television's biggest advertisers, and a huge early success. In the process he had also earned himself a position as the cosmetic firm's chairman of the board. But Spector the ad man was spending over one-third of the company's gross revenues on advertising, and when sales slowed due to new competitors for "kiss-proof" lipstick, profits plummeted. He forced company namesake Hazel Bishop out, but in 1955 he was forced out himself, although he regained control of the foundering company in 1961. When he purchased the Riverside Hotel the following year he was already financially skating on thin ice.[15]

Coming to Spector's rescue was James R. "Jimmy" Hoffa and his Teamsters Union, which financed $2.75 million of the purchase price from their Central and Southern States Pension Funds. No newcomers to Nevada's hotel scene, the Teamsters Union had also financed the Fremont and Dunes Hotels in Las Vegas. The Nevada Gaming Commission had no problem with the Teamsters' money, but were quick to point out that the money would not be connected with the operation of the Riverside's casino, but only with the purchase of the actual physical assets of the historic property. The newspaper wrote, "It is believed the [Teamster] money was used to consolidate at least three mortgages outstanding against the Riverside at the time of its purchase, thus putting it in the best financial condition in years.... Mortgages paid off were reliably reported to be those of George Wingfield Jr.; the Washoe Hotel Corp., the Wertheimer brothers and their partners; and the

Beverly Hills Development Company, which was Roy Crummer." This information had not heretofore been made public, but the required payments on this large debt went a long way toward explaining why so many past owners had had trouble making a success of the Riverside. Spector had to issue a deed of trust to the Teamsters to obtain the loan, and his monthly payments would be $20,265.[16]

Ralph and Estelle James, Jimmy Hoffa biographers, wrote that the Teamsters' pension funds often extended loans on collateral that other institutional lenders wouldn't touch. One extreme example of this, the pair wrote, was the Teamsters' loan to the Riverside Hotel: "For years [this hotel] had made the rounds of California's mortgage brokers, seeking loans which the brokers consistently refused to recommend to their clients.... The Riverside...suffered from age, from Reno's relative decline as a gambling center, and from the negative attitude of most institutional lenders to Nevada properties.... The skeptical judgment of the local mortgage brokers was quickly vindicated: the Riverside went bankrupt in December 1962, less than six months after the loan was granted."[17]

Despite that bankruptcy, Raymond Spector would start off reasonably well. He remodeled the casino area, the restaurant, and the lobby; being unfamiliar with the hotel's long history, however, he made his first major blunder when he eliminated a major portion of the corner bar—a Reno institution and favored gathering place for longer than most Renoites could recall—to install a keno bar.[18]

At some point in the early 1960s—possibly when Bill Miller had owned the hotel and had suggested this idea—the Riverside Hotel launched a promotion of "fun package" flights from the San Francisco Bay area to Reno, the forerunner of similar excursion packages that became popular years later. It was an instant success, bringing about five hundred people a week from the Bay Area to the Riverside Hotel. However, the Federal Aviation Agency took a dim view of the program when it discovered that the Riverside had subleased five planes from Admiral Air Service and Columbus Airways. The agency charged that the Riverside was acting in the capacity of a certified air carrier, and asked the federal court to issue a restraining order against the hotel and the two air carriers. The court issued such an order, and in December an injunction was issued that stopped the practice altogether.[19]

Despite the remodeling, the large Teamsters' loan, and the newspaper's claim that the hotel was in its best financial shape in years, six months after all that positive news, on December 20, 1962, the historic Riverside Hotel was forced to close its doors when Spector was unable to meet his $35,000 payroll. In all, 350 employees would be affected by the closing. The next day the Riverside Casino Corporation, the holding company, filed a bankruptcy petition in federal court in Carson City. The petition listed ten pages of creditors. It was a black day for the Riverside Hotel; it was only the third time in 103 years that the site would not be entertaining overnight guests, the other two times being when the hotel had burned to the ground.[20]

The historic hotel would remain shuttered for seven months.

On December 31, 1962, just a few days after the hotel had closed, an agreement was filed with the Washoe County Recorder granting an option to H. Hughes Porter to purchase the Riverside Hotel on or before February 20, 1963, through his company Hughes-Porter, Inc., made up of ten local investors. Porter, a wealthy local businessman, was active in the community and had just recently lost a race for a seat on the Washoe County Commission. He was also the owner of the Hughes Porter building at 225 West First Street, a neighbor of the Riverside. On the deadline, Porter exercised the option and purchased the Riverside for a reported price in excess of $3.5 million. Raymond Spector, who testified in the hotel's bankruptcy proceedings that he had personally lost over $1 million during his brief ownership, was disallowed from getting his hands on any of the Porter money until the court released it. Porter told the newspaper, "We expect to be able to open the doors sometime after April 1. But from what we've been able to determine, the hotel will need more than a quarter million dollars for refurbishing and redecorating."[21]

One little-known fact about the Riverside Hotel during the seven months it was closed was that the Smith family, who owned the very successful Harolds Club just down Virginia Street, seriously discussed buying the property around this time. Four Smith family members composed the hotel–casino's board: Raymond I. "Pappy" Smith, his son Raymond A. Smith, his grandson Harold Smith Jr., and his wife Dorothy Smith. She admitted during a 1963 tax trial that the four board members disagreed on many occasions, and one of those disagreements was over whether to purchase the foundering Riverside. The newspaper also wrote that there were five other parties interested in the property, but the only other one identified was New York businessman Joe Wolf.[22]

In May the San Francisco firm Porter had hired to do the refurbishing announced a few of the plans. The corner bar would be moved to a better location, and restored to its former glory. The bar's old entry would remain where it was, but a corridor would lead to the new space, and to the enlarged casino. The showroom would be made smaller with 217 seats, and would be decorated more lavishly to provide a feeling of intimacy. A small gourmet dining room, the Ram's Head, was added, away from the casino and showroom for quiet and privacy. The overall décor, the head designer remarked, would be classic-modern, with colorful new carpets throughout the hotel. The remodeling would also include a new coffee shop, remodeling of the other existing restaurants, and renovation of the hotel rooms and apartments.[23]

Hughes Porter had no intention of being a hotel keeper. He was a real estate investor, and he saw the Riverside Hotel in the same light as he saw his neighboring Hughes Porter building. So no sooner was the remodeling and renovation completed than it was announced that he had leased both the hotel and the casino to a ten-man group of Nevadans and Californians. The Nevada men were Reno attorney Jack Streeter, Calvin Swift, Leonard Wykoff, Donald Hall, Clifford Sanford, and John Sommers; and the California men were Ferdie Sievers, Richard Fraser, James Ensign, and Dr. Neill Johnson. Sanford and Sommers were former executives in the Holiday Hotel–Casino, and brought gaming experience to the group. The group was incorporated as Riverside, Inc.[24]

On July 25 the Riverside Hotel reopened, with a full-page newspaper ad announcing the fact. The ad's headline summed up the hopes and dreams of the new gaming lessee: "Remember how great the Riverside used to be? IT IS AGAIN!" The casino opened with 200 slot machines, two craps tables, one roulette game, eight 21 games, and tons of hope.[25]

For the next nine months the local newspapers carried numerous articles about banquets, luncheons, fraternal meetings, and special celebration dinners at the hotel. Locals had embraced the new Riverside, and were returning to it as a favored spot in the city. The Reno Press Club was formed by area news professionals and public relations people, and obtained a room for the group to use, which would eventually grow to seven rooms. On April 25, 1964, the next big change was announced: Hyatt Corporation, with hotel holdings in six western cities, announced it would operate the hotel portion of the property on a fifteen-year sublease from Riverside, Inc.; Riverside, Inc. would continue operating the gaming side of the business. Don Pritzker, president of Hyatt Corporation, said that assuming operation of the hotel was "a real challenge because of its past history."[26]

By this time entertainment had returned to the Riverside Hotel—not the big name acts that had once graced the stage, but still a talented variety of singers, dancers, comedians, and popular revues. Three days after Hyatt

After being closed for seven months, the Riverside Hotel was about to reopen after extensive remodeling and renovation by new owner Hughes Porter, and a new team of hotel and casino lessees. In this July 19, 1963, photo, the marquee announces, "Grand Opening Count Down…6 Days." Notice the swimming pool in the right side of the photo, behind the windows, the first hotel pool in Reno. Nevada Historical Society.

subleased the hotel, Riverside, Inc., which still controlled the casino and entertainment portion of the business, announced that a new director of gaming, entertainment, and advertising, Lee DeLauer, had been hired. A graduate of the University of Nevada, Reno, DeLauer had begun his business career running an off-campus mess hall for the university. He spent some time with the Stateline Hotel–Casino, then spent eight years with Harrah's Club. Arriving at the Riverside, DeLauer promised an even stronger entertainment policy was on the way, with twilight-to-daylight entertainment offerings. But DeLauer also had bigger ambitions. In a complicated financial maneuver, he purchased 50 percent of the issued stock in Riverside, Inc. The issued stock was only half of the total stock, the other half being held in Riverside, Inc.'s treasury for future sale, so DeLauer's purchase represented only 25 percent of the total authorized stock. He paid $125,000 for his stock, and purchased it in equal amounts from the eight remaining stockholders, each of whom still held a 6.25 percent interest in the company after the sale. None of this maneuvering involved the Hughes Porter Company that owned the property.[27]

Could all these changes indicate a period of much-needed stability was on the horizon for the troubled hotel–casino? Not at all. After only seven weeks of operating the hotel, dining rooms, and bars, Hyatt Corporation sold its sublease back to Riverside, Inc. in a deal engineered by the corporation's largest stockholder and new general manager, Lee DeLauer. "We are a local group and we want to make the Riverside what it used to be—a local hotel. We didn't feel divided premises could work," DeLauer said in announcing the change. Hyatt, however, did sign a consulting contract with the new operating group, but it did nothing to alter the downhill direction in which the famed property was spiraling.[28]

It took the DeLauer group only a few months to discover that their plans weren't working. And despite the fact that group after group after group had discovered the sad reality of trying to turn the Riverside Hotel around, there always seemed to be another group in the wings anxious to try it. In November 1964 three new investors purchased a majority interest in both Riverside, Inc., the operating lessee, and the physical property itself from Hughes Porter, Inc. in a reported $3.7 million deal. After the sale was approved, Bernard Einstoss would own 55 percent of the Riverside Hotel and John P. Richards and Andrew DeSimone, 10 percent each. The remaining 25 percent would be owned by Lee DeLauer and five of the other previous owners of Riverside, Inc., the operating lessee. The Nevada Gaming Control Board approved the sale within a week.[29]

Einstoss was no newcomer to the gaming business. He had been a partner with Lou Wertheimer in the gaming concession at the Mapes Hotel when it had first opened in 1947. He had also run gaming at the Cal Vada Club, later the Bal Tabarin, at Lake Tahoe, and had been one of the partners in the opening of the Horseshoe Club. The other two majority stockholders also had gaming experience. In granting the licenses to the new partners, even Ed Olsen, the chairman of the Nevada Gaming Control Board, the Nevada Gaming Commission's investigative arm, was skeptical, saying, "[The Riverside] has a financial problem. Its chances of surviving the winter without new capital are pretty slim."[30]

By early December the new majority owners had taken charge of the property. They named Walter Ramage, most recently manager of the Mapes Hotel, as manager of the Riverside Hotel. An additional change was also brought to light: the three men had ended up purchasing 100 percent of the hotel and the casino operating company, rather than the 75 percent earlier announced. They had completely bought out DeLauer and his partners. A revised purchase price was not divulged. But, unfortunately, this new arrangement wouldn't last long either. On Christmas Eve 1964 it was announced that two other men would be buying in: James H. Lloyd of Reno and Bernard Richter of Oakland, California, each paid $50,000 for a 12.5 percent stake. Thus, as 1964 came to a close, the owners of the Riverside Hotel were Einstoss at 50 percent; and Richter, Lloyd, Richards, and DeSimone at 12.5 percent each.[31]

It didn't take long for the next change to take place. In November 1965 Bernard Richter purchased John P. Richards' shares for $25,000. Then on Christmas Eve 1965 James H. Lloyd purchased the stock interest of Bernard Einstoss, who was retiring due to poor health, for an undisclosed amount. Lloyd had been involved in mining and hotel keeping in Nevada for thirty years, and had been one of the partners in the purchase of the Golden Hotel from George Wingfield in 1946. The ownership of the operating company now looked like this: Lloyd with 50 percent, Richter with 34 percent, and DeSimone with 16 percent. As the top man, Lloyd made the now-customary claim of all new owners: he had plans, he said, for considerable remodeling and a new and greater entertainment format. "Yeah, sure!" most Renoites mused.[32]

Sadly for the historic property, the new ownership group was the tenth in the past ten years.

Although the Riverside Hotel had lost much of its luster, one guest who stayed in the hotel in early 1966 proved that the name "Riverside" still carried some cachet. Equally important, it proved that the white curtain of the 1950s was gone forever. In January of that year the newspaper's society editor interviewed hotel guest Mrs. Louis Armstrong. She explained that she and her husband generally traveled together, but that she was there as the guest of Governor Grant Sawyer to visit the Nevada State Children's Home, while Louis was performing in New York.[33]

It was also true that majority owner James Lloyd meant what he said when he promised a new and greater entertainment format, as jazz stylist June Christy graced the Riverside's stage soon afterward. However, the entertainment calendar also featured some less lofty shows: "The Pussycat Frolics," the "Les Girls Revue," and even a heavyweight tag-team wrestling match that would have caused Harry Gosse and George Wingfield to turn over in their graves.

In mid-1967 another of those larger-than-life characters that Nevada always seemed to attract showed up in Reno. William Silas "Si" Redd, the son of Mississippi sharecroppers, had spent thirty-five years selling pinball machines, jukeboxes, kiddie rides, and other coin-operated amusement machines in states in the South, Midwest, and New England. When he arrived in Reno, Redd had just purchased the northern Nevada distribution company for Bally Manufacturing Company, and he was about to get his first taste of another type of coin-operated amusement devices, the slot machine, or one-armed bandit as they were popularly called. In 1967 these were totally mechanical machines, operated by gears, wheels, and springs; it was basically the same spinning reel machine in 1967 that it had been in 1899 when San Francisco businessman Charles Fey invented it. But Bally had just invented the first electromechanical slot machine, with larger and faster play and pay-off capability, and thus a higher hold, or margin, for the casinos. It was these machines, named "Money Honey," that Si Redd had come to Reno to sell.[34]

But business had been slow for Redd, as casino owners were reluctant to change out their old slot machines for these new space-age gadgets. Besides, in most casinos slot machines weren't considered very important; they were reluctantly given valuable space on the casino floor simply to give the wives and girlfriends something to do while their "menfolk" played poker, shot craps, or played blackjack. After a couple of frustrating weeks, Redd walked into the Riverside Hotel's casino and met with slot manager Clyde Keeting. When Redd promised Keeting he only had to pay a percentage of the *increase* he made on each new machine, Keeting couldn't resist, and he gave Redd his first big order: a hundred Money Honey slot machines. Redd was jubilant, and the new ploy that had sold Keeting on the Bally slots helped launch his business in a big way. But the Riverside deal…well, it didn't work out quite the way Redd had hoped.[35]

A couple of days later, unrecognized by other gamblers at such an early hour, John Sheehan took his turn when the dice were passed his way at the craps table. At 1:45 AM on Saturday, September 16, 1967, there were few people in the Riverside Hotel's casino, and fewer still at the craps table where Sheehan stood. Only one other casino patron seemed to be paying any attention at all to Sheehan's activities, a man named Don Winne. For a little less than an hour Sheehan played, then like most losers, he turned abruptly and walked toward the door. Winne joined him and the two men left the casino together. Ten minutes later they returned, and Sheehan again went to the craps table and began another session.[36]

Twenty-two minutes later, as Sheehan concentrated on the game, Winne observed another man approach the table, shoot the dice and lose, then walk away. The stick man, who controls the dice on the table, then handed the dice to the casino floor man who was sitting near the middle of the dice table. Winne, now clearly focused on the floor man, noted that the man handled the dice in a different manner than he had done previously before rolling them down the green felt to Sheehan. Sheehan had about $20 spread around the table at the time. He picked up the dice and immediately left the table, heading for the middle of the pit with the dice clutched tightly in his hand. In a flash, the stick man and floor man rushed Sheehan, and physically began trying to pry the dice from his closed fist.

It was at this point that Sheehan and Winne identified themselves as assistant deputy state attorneys general working on assignment for the Nevada Gaming Control Board. They told the two casino employees, in no uncertain terms, to back off. They did. At 6 PM that evening the Riverside Hotel's casino was closed down for cheating.

The confiscated dice were "mis-spots," or rigged dice. They were falsely numbered to give the house an advantage over the players, making it impossible for the shooter to hit certain numbers once he had established his point. If the shooter, on the other hand, uses mis-spots, he can rig the dice so he will win more often. This ploy seldom works for the shooter, however, as professional craps dealers are trained to look for mis-spots, while players are not.

It was determined that several casino employees were involved in the cheating, but the Gaming Control Board's complaint was issued against the casino licensees: James Lloyd, Bernard Richter, and Andrew DeSimone. Gaming Board president Frank Johnson announced that the hotel, restaurants, and entertainment could continue to operate, but table games and slot machines were closed down. He said that Sheehan and Winne had been sent to the Riverside to perform the sting because the board had been receiving complaints for months about cheating going on at the Riverside's casino. He also announced that the chief of the state's gaming enforcement division had been fired for his division's inability to spot the cheating and put an end to it.[37]

Edward Olsen, the ex–Associated Press correspondent who had become the state's chief gaming enforcement officer in the late 1950s, was not surprised by the charges against the Riverside. He later wrote,

That damned Riverside problem we worked on for—oh, what was it, a year. And rumors, rumors, rumors—you had them all over the place. We tried to tell him [an unidentified investor in the hotel]...that there were some problems in the joint, and if he was going to become a major investor he'd better cast around for some different people...because he knew nothing about gambling. He did make some changes but nothing substantive.... We couldn't prove the problems.... We never nailed it down.... I must have picked up $1,000 worth of Riverside dice over the period of [a] year and never found a thing wrong with it.[38]

As for Si Redd and his hundred slot machines that saw only two days of use, he admitted he got lucky. He was able to move them across the street to the Holiday Hotel–Casino so he lost no money in the transaction. Redd would go on to turn the casino business on its ear with his development of video poker, the most successful slot machine of all time, and the eventual founding of International Game Technology, or IGT, today the world's largest slot machine manufacturer and software developer. It all started in Reno.[39]

The day after the Riverside casino closure, despite the Nevada Gaming Control Board's statement that entertainment could go on, hotel management announced that the "Riverside Revue," due to open in a couple of days, would not open as scheduled. The six employees who made up the house band were out of work, along with some forty others employed in the gambling side of the Riverside. From that point on, things moved swiftly. By year's end a trustee had been appointed to keep the Riverside operating. Licenses of the three owners, Lloyd, Richter and DeSimone, and the Riverside corporate gaming license, were all revoked, and the owners announced that they were seeking a buyer for the entire property. On February 2, 1968, the historic hotel was sold at auction—really just a paperwork transfer—as the Teamsters Union Pension Fund took it over as the $1.9 million holder of the first deed of trust.[40]

Two days later, on February 4, for the second time in the decade, the Riverside Hotel closed down completely. Despite the sad occasion, on the afternoon of the closing Reno sentimentalists gathered at the corner bar for one last drink. Most shared an optimistic sentiment: don't worry; it'll open up again pretty soon. As the 3:00 PM closing time neared, general manager Edward Kinney said, "We're not going to throw anyone out of the place if they happen to be having one last drink in the corner bar." A good-sized crowd was there, but the mood was mostly subdued—kind of like a celebration of life party for a deceased friend—which indeed the Riverside Hotel had been for many years, and for many people.[41]

Five months later, on July 17, it was announced that the Teamsters Union Central States Pension Fund had sold the Riverside to Houston business-man Russ Bennett, who would head a syndicate of investors in the purchase. The group would spend $1.5 million on improvements before reopening the hotel, Bennett remarked, although the purchase price of the hotel was not announced. Apparently the deal fell through, as two months later another sale of the property for slightly less than $3 million was announced by the Teamsters Union. This time it was Alabama businessman Winfield Moon, who was described as the principal shareholder, along with partners I. J. Saccomanno and Jake Clegg, two Houston lawyers. The group said they planned to lease out both the hotel and casino. They also announced they would spend $500,000 on the property before leasing it, and that it would be ready for opening before Christmas. However, just two weeks before Christmas the newspaper ran the following article lamenting the still-empty hotel's plight:

> One-hundred-eighty-six rooms stay vacant, four bars gather dust, and a vault stands with a huge steel door ajar—The Riverside Hotel is shuttered and its doors are chained.
>
> For many years the casinos lining Virginia Street were nationally dubbed the neon canyon and the Riverside stood at the end of the canyon with lights and entertainment. But today the padlocked hotel is a paradox in a city which planners say is stifled in growth by the lack of hotel rooms to house conventions and large tourist influxes.... The last production to play the hotel before the loss of the gaming license was backed by one of the smallest budgets revue producer Barry Ashton has [ever] worked with.
>
> ...The Reno Press Club which cleared away seven rooms for its quarters is gone. KONE radio [which had broadcast from the hotel] is gone. A Beauty parlor, a valet shop and a barber shop are gone.... Once the Prospectors' Club...moved to the Mapes [their] room was rented for parties.[42]

In late May the following year, 1969, the hotel reopened, but since none of the owners had applied for a gaming license, the casino remained shuttered. The new owners had made good on their promise to renovate the property. A sale was held to dispose of the aging furniture and kitchen and restau-rant equipment, and the renovation and refurbishing went ahead, although the extent of the changes is not known. A few local events and meetings returned to the hotel, but it was obvious that Renoites were cautious about committing themselves and their organizations to the hotel that had disappointed them so many times in the past.[43]

The owners opened talks with the Pig 'N Whistle restaurant chain to buy the Riverside, and later with Standard Computers, Inc. of Los Angeles, which had recently bought Circus Circus Hotel and Casino in Las Vegas. However, neither of these potential buyers came through. A newspaper article announcing these activities also reported that Winfield Moon was no longer a shareholder, his stake having been purchased by Anthony Scardino, who, like the other two owners was a Houston man.[44]

In November agents of the IRS seized and closed the hotel for nonpayment of employee withholding taxes, saying that $46,283 was owed for the quarter ending September 30. Fifty guests were registered at the time of the closure, but agents allowed them to leave at their own leisure. The IRS said the hotel would be auctioned off if payment was not made by November 18, but by the deadline the amount had grown to $88,283. The debt was paid off, however, when a new buyer stepped in at the last moment and purchased the Riverside property. The attorney for the new owners said a New York corporation, Bonafide Productions, Inc., had purchased all the stock from the preceding owners. Bonafide would eventually be identified as Marvin Rappaport and Burton Rosen, both of New York City, and Ben Cohen of Miami. The attorney for the three men also assured all vendors, many of which carried large balances with the previous owners, that they would be paid in full.[45]

The decade of the 1960s would end for the Riverside just as it had begun: in an untenable financial condition, with owners who cared only about squeezing the historic property out of every possible dollar. Many wondered if the Riverside Hotel would ever attract its white knight, or if was it doomed to end its long tenure as the most iconic landmark in Nevada's Biggest Little City.

For the famed property, the 1960s had indeed been "the worst of times."

## NOTES

1. Kling, *Biggest Little City*, 157–58; "Approve Shift at Riverside," *REG*, 08/19/1958; "Riverside Sold—$5 Million," *REG*, 12/10/1959.

2. Quote from Douglass, "Tap Dancing on Ice," 145.

3. Barber, *Reno's Big Gamble*, 171, 173, 180.

4. Quote from "Virgil Smith New Owner of Hostelry," *NSJ*, 12/10/1959; "Applications Are Filed for Riverside Interests," *REG*, 01/04/1960.

5. "Smith's Sale to Franks Given OK," *NSJ*, 04/20/1960; both quotes from "Commission Approves: Control Change for Riverside," *REG*, 04/20/1960.

6. Quote from Douglass, "Tap Dancing on Ice," 147–48.

7. Quote from Douglass, "Tap Dancing on Ice," 147–48; Kling, *Biggest Little City*, 141.

8. "Sale of Riverside Hotel Announced by Attorneys," *REG*, 09/29/1960; "Second Turnover in Year," *NSJ*, 09/20/1960; "Vegan Takes Over Hotel, Offers Ideas," *NSJ*, 11/23/1960.

9. All quotes from Douglass, "Tap Dancing on Ice," 149.

10. "Hotel Ownership Shift Done," *NSJ*, 11/19/1960; "Game Board Approves Miller for 95% Pct. of Riverside," *NSJ*, 11/22/1960.

11. "Riverside Hotel Casino Manager Object of Search," *REG*, 01/09/1961; "Fail to Find New Leads in Layne Mystery," *REG*, 01/12/1961; "Board Ousts Missing Reno Game Executive," *REG*, 01/14/1961.

12. "Vegan Takes Over Hotel, Offers Ideas," *NSJ*, 11/23/1960; quote from Douglass, "Tap Dancing on Ice," 148; "It's 'Bye, Bye Blues' for the Riverside," *REG*, 03/31/1971.

13. "Billy William Headlining," *REG*, 04/01/1961; adv. for "Riverside Bills Le Crazy Horse," *REG*, 06/03/1961; first and second quotes from H. Clyde Mathews, "Oral Autobiography"; "Disputed Show Closed Down," *REG*, 03/15/1963.

14. Kling, *Biggest Little City*, 141; quote from "Riverside Sale Confirmed by Present Owner," *REG*, 06/14/1962.

15. Hazel Bishop, Inc., "Cosmetics and Skin: Hazel Bishop."

16. Quote from "Teamsters Make Riverside Loan," *NSJ*, 11/27/1962; Kling, *Biggest Little City*, 141.

17. James and James, *Hoffa and the Teamsters*, 250–51.

18. "Riverside's Site Part of History," *REG*, 12/20/1962.

19. "'Fun Package' Flights Halted by U.S. Court," *NSJ*, 11/30/1962; "Judge Issues Order Against 'Fun Excursions,'" *REG*, 12/10/1963.

20. "Riverside Hotel Closed Up; Unable to Meet Payroll," *REG*, 12/20/1962; "Hotel Files Bankruptcy; Host of Creditors Listed," *REG*, 12/22/1962.

21. "Riverside Option Filed Here," *REG*, 12/31/1962; quote from "Riverside Funds Stay in Nevada," *NSJ*, 02/21/1963.

22. "Tax Trial in Third Day," *REG*, 01/16/1963; "Investors Eye Reno's Riverside," *NSJ*, 12/22/1962.

23. "Sleeping Riverside Starts on Comeback Trail," *NSJ*, 05/08/1963; "Riverside Hotel Re-Opens Door to City Today," *NSJ*, 07/25/1963.

24. "Holiday Lodge, Riverside Hotel Licenses Sought," *NSJ*, 07/02/1963.

25. Adv. for Riverside Hotel, *NSJ*, 07/25/1963; Kling, *Biggest Little City*, 141.

26. Quote from "Hyatt Corp. Acquires Riverside Hotel Lease," *NSJ*, 04/25/1964; "Reno Press Club to Be Formed," *NSJ*, 10/19/1963.

27. "Lee DeLauer Takes Post at Riverside," *REG*, 04/28/1964; "Sierra East" column, *REG*, 04/30/64; "Art Long's Nite Notes" column, *REG*, 05/02/1964; "Hotel Game Interest Sought," *NSJ*, 06/02/1964; "Art Long's Nite Notes" column, *REG*, 06/13/1964; "Riverside Bid Tops Gaming Board Agenda," *NSJ*, 06/05/1964.

28. Quote from "Local Interests Assume Riverside," *NSJ*, 06/12/1964.

29. "Riverside Ownership Change Asked," *REG*, 11/14/1964; "State Allows Investment in Reno's Riverside Hotel," *REG*, 11/17/1964.

30. Quote from "State Allows Investment in Reno's Riverside Hotel," *REG*, 11/17/1964; Kling, *Biggest Little City*, 45.

31. "Manager Post Given to Ramage," *NSJ*, 12/06/1964; "Two Request Riverside Investment," *NSJ*, 12/24/1964.

32. "Richter Gets OK for Riverside Deal," *NSJ*, 11/17/1965; "Einstoss Sells Lloyd Interest in Riverside," *REG*, 12/24/1965; Kling, *Biggest Little City*, 142.

33. "Top O' The Morning" column, *NSJ*, 01/02/1966.

34. Harpster, *King of the Slots*, chap. 6.

35. Harpster, *King of the Slots*, 81.

36. The story of the sting is found at "Riverside Gaming Move Revealed by Probers," *NSJ*, 09/18/1967.

37. "Riverside Gaming Move Revealed by Probers," *NSJ*, 09/18/1967; "Riverside Hotel Gambling Closed," *NSJ*, 09/18/1967; "Linked to Riverside Cheating Charges," *NSJ*, 09/21/1967.

38. Olsen, "My Career as a Journalist," 128–29.

39. Harpster, *King of the Slots*, 81.

40. "Riverside Show Called Off," *NSJ*, 09/19/1967; "Riverside Trustee Named," *NSJ*, 09/26/1967; Riverside Loses Gaming Permit," *NSJ*, 12/29/1967; "Sentimentalists Gather for Last Drink at 'Corner Bar,'" *NSJ*, 02/04/1968.

41. "Sentimentalists Gather for Last Drink at 'Corner Bar,'" *NSJ*, 02/04/1968.

42. "Texas Man Leads Group of Buyers," *NSJ*, 07/17/1968; "Riverside Hotel Sale Completed," *NSJ*, 09/07/1968; extract from "Closing Followed Troubled Years," *NSJ*, 12/13/1968.

43. Adv. for "Renovation Sale," *NSJ*, 06/01/1969; "Texan Wants Gambling License for Riverside," *REG*, 05/06/1970.

44. "Non-payment of Taxes Alleged," *NSJ*, 11/04/1969.

45. "Non-payment of Taxes Alleged," *NSJ*, 11/04/1969; "Tax Service Threatens to Auction Riverside," *NSJ*, 11/07/1969; "Riverside Hotel Has New Owners," *NSJ*, 11/19/1969.

# CHAPTER 13

# THE WHITE KNIGHT

ON MAY 6, 1970, escrow was opened on another sale of the Riverside Hotel. William Bonner Phares, a successful Texas land developer, apartment builder, and attorney, applied to the Nevada Gaming Control Board for a license to reopen the hotel, which was still closed despite the necessary payoff made to the IRS. Phares planned to purchase 100 percent of the operation, at an undisclosed price, and would reopen and operate both the hotel and casino. The only condition on the sale was that Phares gain approval for a gaming license. On June 19 he won that approval, and he said he would immediately embark on a $250,000 remodeling project. Concerned commissioners asked Phares if he had the money to take on the Riverside Hotel where so many others had failed for lack of capital. Phares assured them he did. The biggest expense would be payments on the first mortgage held by the Teamsters' Union Pension Fund, which amounted to $2.1 million payable over the next twenty years. Phares had been approved to operate two dice tables, one roulette game, eleven twenty-one games, one keno game, and two hundred slot machines. He said the Riverside Hotel offered "tremendous potential," and said he would reopen the property in July.[1]

Was the Riverside Hotel finally about to turn the corner? Was the white knight on the horizon? One Renoite sent a letter to the editor of the newspaper reflecting the beliefs and attitudes of many in the city:

> Among the many depressing sights in down town Reno there is none more depressing than the empty Riverside Hotel. Once the pride and show place of the "Biggest Little City" for so many decades, it now presents the sad, desolate, deserted appearance of a ghost town. When an errand makes it necessary for me to walk down town from my apartment building I make it a point to avoid passing the Riverside

Hotel as it saddens me to recall the many joyous occasions I spent under its elegant, hospitable roof.

There have been many reports in the paper from time to time that some interested responsible party is negotiating for its purchase and planning to restore the hotel to its former glory, but what has become of these potential buyers? Is it the gambling commission or politics that is keeping the Riverside closed?[2]

William Phares would be the thirteenth owner of the Riverside Hotel in fifteen years, and this did not begin to count all the changes within each ownership group that had occurred. It was time for some good luck to come the Riverside's way, and to many Phares sounded like the perfect answer. But unfortunately, fate intervened. On July 3, 1970, the month the Riverside was set to reopen, William Phares was driving home near Port Arthur, Texas, when his car plunged off the highway into a canal. Phares, who was forty-one, was drowned.[3]

The Phares's deal had not quite been completed at the time of his death, thus the sale was declared null and void, and the Riverside once again went to public auction in October. "There were many spectators, but few buyers. It seems as if no one wanted Reno's Riverside Hotel," the newspaper lamented following the auction. Once again the hotel reverted to the Teamsters' Union Pension Fund for its $1.8 million mortgage when there was not a single bid for the property. Despite the failure, a representative of the Teamsters said he had high hopes of "selling the hotel real quick." An hour after the unsuccessful auction was over, a second one was held to sell the building's contents, and again, lacking any bidders, ownership of the contents reverted to the pension fund as well.[4]

But the wild ride continued. In December, buyer number fourteen surfaced when Investment Services of Oklahoma bought the hotel for $2.15 million. The buyers' attorney announced that they were negotiating with four separate groups—two local Reno groups and two from out of town—to lease the property, but the attorney would not identify the potential lessee groups.[5]

On May 17, 1970, a large headline blazed across the front page of the *Nevada State Journal* newspaper, startling most Renoites with its explosive news: "Howard Hughes Expands North, Buys Harolds." Harolds Club, the storied thirty-five-year-old hotel–casino owned by the Smith family, was credited as having changed the face of Reno's casino scene—not only with its futuristic employment practices, but also by almost single-handedly creating a mass middle-class gaming market in the city. For the Smith family, however, things had not been the same since family patriarch, Raymond I. "Pappy" Smith, had passed away three years earlier. So they decided it was time to sell the property. The sale would create unforeseen waves that would eventually provide that potential white knight that the Riverside Hotel desperately needed.[6]

Fred Beck, of Sheboygan, Wisconsin, had leased the keno, horserace book, pan, and poker games at Harolds since 1940. When Fred passed away in 1954, his second wife, Jessie, who had worked at Harolds since the late 1930s, took over Fred's business, and ran it successfully for the next sixteen years. But when Howard Hughes's Summa Corporation purchased Harolds Club, Jessie Beck's lease, by this time limited only to keno, was terminated. Jessie had a reputation as a sharp operator, and she was known for her friendly and sunny disposition. When the Hughes's ouster occurred, Jessie, who was around sixty-five, had no intention of retiring.[7]

The Hughes's Summa Corporation had paid Beck what was described by one of her coworkers as a token amount of money when they cancelled her keno lease, but Reno casino historian and author Dwayne Kling stated that she had made millions of dollars over the years with her keno lease. So her financial condition was solid enough to buy her own place. "We have looked at at least 32…places in Nevada," the silver-haired grandmother said. By the end of 1970 she had narrowed her list down to three places: Karl Berge's Silver Club in Sparks, Bill & Effie's Café and Truck Stop (eventually Boomtown), and the Riverside Hotel.[8]

On January 5, 1971, Beck made an announcement that she was prepared to purchase the Riverside from the Oklahoma investment group. "It's always given me a bad feeling to see it empty.… I do think it will work…[and] I'll risk every cent I have to make it work," she said. The Beck Corporation, set up to be the holding company for the Riverside, would pay $3.15 million for the property, providing a nifty $1 million profit for the savvy Oklahoma investors, the first group to actually profit from owning the Riverside in many, many years. Beck's realtor said the corporation would complete the rehabilitation of the hotel that had been started by previous owners and on which more than $1 million had already been spent. Beck said, "I don't want anything gaudy looking. I don't need a lot of signs. I'll just let my customers know where we are—that'll be enough." Ownership of the property would be Jessie Beck at 74 percent; her son, John E. Brown, who would serve as general manager, at 7.4 percent; and family members Nancy C. Brown Risley at 2.8 percent; Virginia L. Brown Mathisen at 3.4 percent; and son John E. Brown at 12.4 percent for his minor children. By mid-February the Gaming Control Board had approved the sale.[9]

The hotel's opening was scheduled for April 1. But Beck proved just how attuned to the Reno market she was when she announced that the famed corner bar would open ahead of everything else, on February 11, the day her gaming license was approved. The remainder of the renovations, which amounted to $350,000, continued, and a large bulletin board was posted on the front of the hotel showing the day-to-day progress of the work. "The Gambling Grandma," as Beck would affectionately be called by Renoites, had another ace up her sleeve: two days after the corner bar had opened, the hotel's half-finished showroom was the site of the wedding reception for Beck's grandson John and his wife, the former Georgia Burris, both twenty years old and students at the University of Nevada, Reno. Tables had been reinstalled around the room, the dust and clutter cleared away, and a red carpet installed for the event that drew more than five hundred guests. The next day, the shrewd Beck was rewarded with a full-page story and pictures of the wedding in the morning newspaper, a message to all Reno residents that the Riverside Hotel was back.[10]

On April 1, 1971, the Riverside Hotel reopened. The casino had been shuttered for three-and-a-half years, and the rest of the property for just over three years. General manager John E. Brown announced that 365 people had been hired, mostly from Reno, a tremendous boost for local employment that had been stagnant due to the recession of the early 1970s. Hotel guests were delighted to find the historic structure had been redecorated in a style Jessie Beck described as "the spirit of the West." A gold and red color scheme was used in repainting and recarpeting throughout the hotel, and 183 of the 188 rooms were ready for occupancy. Each room also had new furniture and a color TV set. Additional downtown parking spaces had been obtained. Brown said the Riverside would follow a cabaret-style entertainment policy, led off by the Polynesian revue, Eva Lani and the South Seas Islanders.[11]

A little light humor marked the grand opening celebration. There was a Reno tradition that owners or proprietors of other casinos in town would always attend the opening of a new casino and place a courtesy wager, normally about $100, on the craps table, then continue shooting the dice until the wager had been lost to the house. A very shy Bill Harrah—who seldom gambled—went to Beck's opening, strode up to the craps table, and made his obligatory courtesy bet, the very first wager placed in the new casino. He won. Letting the bet ride, Harrah won again. After the third or fourth win, Harrah had a stack of chips on the table, and the normally taciturn man was obviously embarrassed. A crowd began to gather, and Harrah continued to let the money ride. At some point—nobody could recall years later how much Harrah had won—he finally crapped out, to the crowd's distress, but much to Bill Harrah's great relief.[12]

Beck had hired an experienced staff of key executives to operate the business, led by her and her son John E. Brown. In the 1940s Brown had been a bellhop at the Riverside, and it was there he had met his future wife Helen, who was a waitress in the coffee shop. Arthur Allen, who had served as manager of the hotel from 1940 to 1956, returned to the Riverside as hotel manager. He remarked at the opening ceremony, "It seems like I've lived to see a miracle. All the businessmen in town are here—they're all admiring our work." Many of the other key executives followed Beck from Harolds, including Harry J. Bergemann, director of industry affairs; Jim Hunter, director of public relations; and Don O'Donnell, casino manager. The remodeled casino had been licensed for eight table games, one keno game, and a hundred slot machines.[13]

The morning newspaper lauded the Riverside's comeback in an editorial, praising Jessie Beck:

> It is much more than just the opening of another business in downtown Reno…. Many Reno residents…were frankly fearful that this 'dean' of major hotels in the state would never again sleep another guest, feed another patron, host another cocktail party or deal the cards to another player.
>
> There is an intangible factor that applies only to this particular hotel being open for business. It may not be understood to any except long-time residents. But they have looked on the Riverside as an indestructible symbol of the past that, somehow, assured Reno's future. Through the years until the hotel was closed the first time, just before Christmas in 1962, the Riverside maintained its reputation.
>
> As the famous hotel resumes its place in the community, it will have the good wishes of the people in Reno and of all Northern Nevada.
>
> Everybody is happy that the Riverside "has come back."[14]

The next few years were just like the good old days at the Riverside, now officially rechristened as Jessie Beck's Riverside. The Reno Press Club returned to its quarters at the hotel, and local organizations again began scheduling their banquets, press conferences, pageants, and luncheons at the city's favorite meeting place. The corner bar was again buzzing with activity. Entertainment was back, too, with popular solo acts and revues. The hotel business bounced back as well; in late 1974, despite the recession, the Riverside announced it had 100 percent occupancy in October and was booked up for every weekend until June of the following year.[15]

All the credit for the resurrection of the state's oldest hotel was being given to the Gambling Grandma, Jessie Beck. Shortly after reopening the hotel, Beck was honored by the chamber of commerce as Civic Leader of the Year. Later, the newspaper lauded her generosity to military personnel, saying, "Jessie Beck gives away everything from rolls of nickels…to free cocktail parties for servicemen." The fact was, Beck had a soft spot in her heart for servicemen. She had lost a son in the Vietnam conflict, and there was nothing she wouldn't do to help and honor members of the military, including hiring vets whenever possible. The University's ROTC Cadet Battalion held their annual formal military ball at the Riverside, and Beck was named the Queen of the Ball. The U.S. Department of Defense awarded her its highest civilian honor, the Award of Merit, in 1968, and Governor Paul Laxalt named her a Distinguished Nevadan in 1969.[16]

Despite the Riverside's early successes, however, by the mid-1970s things were not going as well as Beck had hoped. She was getting older—she was in her early seventies by this time—and she seemed to have lost her touch. One of the casino's pit bosses said the gregarious Beck would sit down at a blackjack table, replacing the dealer, and would spend eight or ten straight hours dealing blackjack—often making mistakes—and chatting with the players. This would cost the replaced dealer all of his or her tips, and led to growing frustration among the employees. She also had a policy of paying entertainers to come in as early as 4:00 PM for a gig, and there would only be one or two people in the audience. For two years in a row in the mid-1970s, she cut every employee's pay in half for a two-month period over the Christmas holiday, when business was slow. The first year she did that, she did repay the lost wages later, but the second time, she did not repay employees for their lost wages.[17]

James Bernardi was fifteen years old when he and his family moved to Reno in 1957, and he had many fond memories of the Riverside of his youth. He left Reno, but returned in early 1972 to be the chair of the University of Nevada, Reno, Theater Department. Much had changed by the mid-1970s, he admitted during his oral history interview: "When we came back, the [JA] Nugget [in Sparks] was in operation…. There was a showroom there that was actually doing more…. The Riverside and the Mapes were fading into nothing. They were old buildings and they just didn't have quite the same draw that they once had. The Nugget and Harrah's became much more the places by then." Bernardi's opinion reflected that of many people in the community.[18]

For Jessie Beck and the Riverside Hotel, the handwriting was on the wall. Beck likely sensed it, and she had been unsuccessfully seeking a buyer for the property for over six months. Her well-meaning but unsuccessful attempt to save the historic property may have been partially her own doing, but there were also factors at play that were well beyond her ability to control. First and foremost, the nearly 120-year-old site and the 50-year-old building that occupied it were relics of a bygone era. They were simply no longer relevant. The Riverside was not able to compete in a 1970s decade, often referred to as the "Me" decade, where the needs and wants of the individual trumped the needs and wants of the community. Locals as well as visitors were veering away from tradition, and moving toward pleasures that were more self-indulgent.

Then there was the increased competition. The eleven-story Eldorado Hotel–Casino had opened downtown in 1973; Harrah's, already a prodigious competitor, was expanding; and construction was under way on the Circus Circus Hotel and Casino, also located downtown. Perhaps the largest factor from a competitive point of view, however, was still on the horizon: a fearsome new competitor named the MGM Grand. Kirk Kerkorian, owner of MGM pictures, had opened the MGM Grand Hotel–Casino in Las Vegas (now Bally's) in 1973 with 2,084 rooms at a then-staggering cost of $106 million. It was the largest hotel in the world at the time. In 1975 when Kerkorian announced he planned to build a thousand-room hotel–casino in Reno, it may have been the last straw for the struggling Riverside. The MGM Grand Reno, now the Grand Sierra Resort, opened on May 3, 1978—only eight weeks after Beck's sale of the Riverside—with 141 table games and 2,000 slot machines.[19]

Harrah's Hotel–Casino had been expanding for years, buying adjacent properties and growing its huge hotel–casino complex. In March 1978 Harrah's bought the Riverside from Jessie Beck, and in a three-way real estate deal traded the Riverside to Richard "Pick" Hobson for his sixty-two-year-old Overland Hotel–Casino on the corner of Commercial Row and Center Street. No price was given for the Riverside's sale. The Overland site eventually became a multistoried garage for Harrah's growing empire.[20]

Hobson, sixty-seven at the time, had been active in Reno's gambling scene since 1929, two years before it was even legalized. In the 1940s and 1950s he had owned the Frontier Club before he sold that business to

Harrah's in 1956, and when he obtained the Riverside he also owned and operated the Gold Club in Sparks and the Topaz Lodge on Topaz Lake near the
California–Nevada border. At the time of the Riverside purchase, Hobson's
general manager said, "The operation will go right on. We will run it in the
same good manner Mrs. Beck has."[21]

Given all this new competition, and the Riverside's drift away from rel-
evancy, one has to wonder why an experienced casino operator like Pick
Hobson would have wanted the Riverside at all. He simply traded one failing
old property for another. But regardless of Hobson's motivation, Jessie Beck
was delighted. Asked if the sale meant this would be her last time hanging
around the gaming tables at the Riverside, she responded with a big grin,
"Oh no, honey! I'll be around here for a long time." Then asked why she had
sold, she replied, "They came up with enough money." These casual remarks
simply reflected the plucky style of Reno's "Gambling, Grandma." Jessie Beck
passed away on July 17, 1987, at the age of eighty-three, in the same year her
beloved Riverside Hotel would close for the final time.[22]

If Pick Hobson had inherited many of the economic and competitive
woes Jessie Beck left behind, there were even more troubles facing him
and his new Riverside Hotel. Just two months after his purchase, Resorts
Casino–Hotel opened on the Boardwalk in Atlantic City, New Jersey, the first
legal casino in the United States outside of Nevada. It was soon joined by
others; although Atlantic City did not have the disastrous effect on Nevada
casinos that many had anticipated, it still did extract a toll by wooing eastern
gambling junkets and conventions away from Nevada's hotels and casinos.
The entire nation also suffered from an economic downturn from 1978 to
1982 that affected all Nevada casinos, including Hobson's.[23]

Despite all the negative factors, Hobson was a hard-nosed, experienced
casino man. Under the large neon sign atop the hotel that flashed "'Pick'
Hobson's Riverside," he carried on. For the first four years under his ownership, the business remained in the black, according to his later bankruptcy
filing. A 1980 magazine article promised, "Today, under the guidance of R. H.
"Pick" Hobson, the hotel is like a grand old lady, a bit worn and wrinkled but
comfortable and filled with memories. It's that sentimental attachment that
moves hotel guests to specify a certain room whenever they're in town. Their
reasons range from remembering a honeymoon decades ago to a pair of yellow chairs that appeal to a frequent guest." Room prices ranged from $22 to
$75, and for top dollar one could request the suite that was once the home of
former owner Jessie Beck, and before her, the temporary digs of many rich

and famous divorcees. In the once-proud corner bar, DJ Jack Joseph spun records of music of the 1940s for dancing and listening.[24]

Beginning around 1982, the lingering recession and the competition began catching up with the Riverside. In December of that year, the hotel–casino that had once been the Riverside's primary competitor, the art deco-styled Mapes Hotel, closed down when it was unable to meet its operating costs. But Hobson, always the optimist, kept going.[25]

In 1986, despite the falling fortunes of his hotel, Pick Hobson was able to take pride in the fact that in August the historic property he owned was officially listed on the National Register of Historic Places. It earned the honor six years after its near neighbor, the Virginia Street Bridge, had been so honored. Paradoxically, only three months later, staggering under $4.66 million in debt and a decreasing market share, Hobson filed a Chapter 11 bankruptcy petition. A month later he closed the casino, saying, "We explored every possible avenue before making this decision, and felt that we simply had no other choice." Perhaps the final straw for Hobson was announced in a headline in the same issue of the newspaper as his casino closing: "Harrah's Plans $10 Million Refurbishing of Reno Hotel." Harrah's had been purchased by Holiday Inn in 1978. Despite the closure of his casino, Hobson said he did plan to keep the hotel, restaurants, and bars open.[26]

The executive director of the Gaming Industry Association of Nevada indicated that the Riverside casino's closing was symptomatic of the gaming economy, and listed a number of other Reno casinos that had closed their doors over the past two years. The Riverside had 250 employees at the time of the closing, but an undisclosed number of these people remained on the job in the hotel and food service departments. However, more than three hundred Riverside creditors, owed more than $1.4 million, would be left empty-handed due to the bankruptcy. A local realtor told the newspaper that Hobson had been quietly shopping the Riverside around for $5.5 million for about a year, and that there were presently three parties interested in the property.[27]

On November 1, 1987, with expenses far outweighing revenues, Hobson was forced to close the hotel and restaurants too, putting the final thirty employees out of work. Just over three weeks later a U.S. bankruptcy judge approved Hobson's bankruptcy plan, and the Riverside Hotel was turned over to its chief creditors, Valley Bank of Nevada and its sister company VB Liquidation Corporation, which now had the task of selling the 188-room landmark property to recover their mortgage debt.[28]

When word was spread by the national media about the closing of the Riverside Hotel, many of the big-name stars who had played the hotel in the 1940s and 1950s expressed their regrets. "It was a hot joint to play," said Sammy Davis Jr., "the first place I worked in the state of Nevada." Sammy had played the Riverside just after World War II as part of the Will Mastin Trio in the Wertheimers' elegant 250-seat Theatre Restaurant. He followed that gig with one at the Mapes. "With the Mapes lying there, and the Riverside closing, I feel sad," he said. "It's a personal attachment, a performer feeling the loss of part of his business." "God, that used to be my favorite," said singer Kay Starr. "It was wonderful—except for the river overflowing one time when I was working there. People just kept gambling in water up to their knees."[29]

Some years later, when there was talk of demolishing the Riverside, Hobson proudly told a reporter that despite the creditors who got burned, "When the Riverside closed, I paid every employee every single nickel they were owed in wages.... Even vacation pay. Some places that closed didn't do that." He also scotched a rumor that was prevalent at the time of his closing that his financial problems were due to a number of keno tickets that had hit big. Not so, he said, adding, "When I bought the Riverside was the year five new hotel–casinos opened up.... The newer, bigger places just inhaled us. But that's business. That's the way it is."[30]

Given the Grand Dame hotel's track record over the past two decades, many people believed it had gasped its last breath. Reno historian Alicia Barber wrote, "Both the Mapes and the Riverside...now stood boarded-up on highly desirable property, serving no economic purpose, and certainly bringing in no tourist revenue." But there seemed to be some sort of magic attached to the Riverside Hotel. Perhaps it was its long history, or perhaps the enviable reputation of its earlier days. But whenever things looked the darkest, it seemed that someone was always willing to take a gamble on the old relic.[31]

In 1988 an unidentified investor group announced a plan to purchase the hotel, and when that failed, Washoe County considered buying it for $3.1 million to convert it into county offices. In November another deal was in the works. A Canadian businessman, Peter Ng, signed a contract with Valley Bank to take over the property. His plan was to lease out retail space in the building and lease out the casino operation, but by March 30, 1989, the deadline set to finalize the purchase, Ng had not completed the deal. Only three months later, however, Ng was back in the picture, heading up a Hong Kong investment firm, Riverside Hotel Enterprises, composed primarily of

Canadian citizens. This time the group came through, buying the Riverside for $1.9 million from Valley Bank.[32]

Renoites were stunned—and also somewhat skeptical—when in December Ng announced his group's plans for the hotel–casino. He said the new owners would begin a $10 million renovation of the Riverside Hotel by the spring of 1990. For a property that had been trading in the $3 to $5 million range for decades, it was difficult to swallow such an enormous number. "I want to see it return. It's the last landmark we've got left downtown," said Dick Wiseman, the real estate agent representing the owners. The Riverside will become "like the Fairmont Hotel in San Francisco; it'll be plush," Wiseman said. Ng's plans this time around were to take out the entire first floor's northern wall to create a new entrance, which would be adjacent to the city's planned $6 million Truckee River beautification project. This space would feature several first-floor indoor shops and boutiques right along the riverfront. The city's effort, launched earlier in the year under the name Western Nevada Clean Committees, was tied into a nationwide project entitled Keep America Beautiful. The city's river beautification project was due to be completed in the fall, and would feature a multitier plaza on the riverbank, greatly enhancing, and being enhanced by, Ng's plan for the hotel.[33]

Beautifying and enhancing the Truckee River where it meanders through downtown Reno had been talked about for at least three-quarters of a century. Most of the ideas went no farther than feasibility studies, but perhaps the first real effort was a WPA project during the Great Depression. A beautiful little island with walking paths and flower gardens was built in the middle of the river between Virginia and Center Streets. Of course it could only be reached during low water, and even then it required a risky climb down a steep hillside followed by a challenging rock-hopping trip across half the river. It didn't take long before Mother Nature tired of the whole thing and completely washed the peaceful little park away.

In 1965 the next serious effort called for pedestrian walkways, bridges, landscaping, and other elements of private and public beautification, and that was followed four years later by a similar program with another catchy name. Both efforts failed. But a few things had succeeded by the beginning of the 1990s: beautifying Wingfield Park and making it more accessible,

*Overleaf:* The Truckee River Island Park, built during the Great Depression by the WPA, or Works Progress Administration, was a beautiful, tranquil little spot, filled with flowers and plants. Here, with the Virginia Street Bridge in the background, one can see the walking trail that loops around the small park. Special Collections Department, University of Nevada, Reno Libraries.

the West Street Plaza development with footbridges to Wingfield Park, and the beginnings of the Raymond I. Smith Truckee Riverwalk, named after the downtown Harolds Club patriarch, which would be completed by late summer of 1991.[34]

The decades of the 1970s and 1980s, like the 1960s before them, were tumultuous years for the aging Riverside Hotel. They had begun with high promise when a wealthy Texas businessman named William Phares had purchased the hotel, only to die before he could take possession, and they were ending on another high note, with the promise of an exciting new chapter that could spell rebirth for the historic structure. Only time would tell if this new promise would be met.

During the decades of the 1960s, 1970s, and 1980s, while events surrounding the Riverside Hotel were mostly chaotic, the life of the Virginia Street Bridge was relatively tranquil. In 1960, the year the concrete bridge celebrated its fifty-fifth birthday, the City of Reno honored civil engineer and Reno pioneer Thomas (T. K.) Stewart by naming a street after him. Stewart Street runs east to west from Kietzke Lane to Virginia Street, only about one-quarter mile south of the site where he was instrumental in building the fifth Virginia Street Bridge. Of the bridge, he prophetically said during its planning phase, "I mean to prepare plans and specifications for a cement bridge that will last for generations." And so he had.[35]

In 1970 the bridge received one of its few facelifts. The city had embarked on a public project named RENOvation, and beautifying and restoring parts of the Virginia Street Bridge were included. During the floods of 1966, when much of the bridge was under water, the original wiring for the sixty-five-year-old light fixtures had shorted out, and for four years the twenty-four globes sitting atop the six iron light fixtures had remained dark. Some of the piping and the ornamental leaves on the beautiful wrought-iron fixtures had also rusted and needed repair. By August 7, the work was due to be finished and the lights would be turned back on after a long absence.[36]

Despite the work, the problem continued. Every time the new automatic photocell turned the lights on at sundown, some unknown glitch immediately turned them off again. City engineers were perplexed until it was discovered that an old mechanical timer in the basement of the Riverside Hotel that had operated the old lights was somehow overriding the new photocell. Once the mystery was solved, the lights began glowing all night long, to the delight of Reno residents.[37]

In 1972, echoes of the Virginia Street Bridge's past reverberated. Myron Lake's last home, today the Lake Mansion at 250 Arlington Street in Reno, is operated by the not-for-profit group Very Special Arts of Nevada, or VSA. In 1971, to save the building from demolition as downtown office space expanded, it was moved from its original California Street at Virginia Street location to a site near the Convention Center on South Virginia Street. After the move, the building was being readied for its reopening, but one project remained to be done. Lyle Ball, vice president of Washoe Landmarks Preservation, Inc., the company in charge of the mansion's restoration, said that two bridges—exact replicas of the Lake's Crossing Bridge—would be built over a canal that ran beside the mansion. This would have been a good idea, but it appears that it was never carried through. In 2004, when the Convention Center needed the space, the house was moved again, this time to its present location.[38]

However, the bridge, and the hotel as well, would receive their due recognition two years later during the nation's bicentennial celebration. A local women's nonprofit organization, Reno Service League, staged a three-day 1874 Bi-Centennial Fair & Exposition in late May to celebrate the city as it had been a hundred year earlier. Storefront replicas of downtown Reno in 1874 were constructed. Both Myron Lake's Lake House hotel and Lake's Crossing Bridge—the forerunners of the Riverside Hotel and Virginia Street Bridge—were big hits with all the fair's attendees. People were dancing in the aisles and feeling the spirit of 1874 while they watched—or participated in—a frog jumping contest, an arm-wrestling challenge, and the Hart's Liberty Review. The event was so well attended that the Service League members staged it for the next five years as well, according to some sources.[39]

Finally, in 1980 the Virginia Street Bridge—then seventy-five years old and in its fifth iteration—received its highest honor: It was listed on the U.S. Department of the Interior's National Register of Historic Places, joining dozens of other famous and fabled spans across the nation. The bridge was honored because of its architectural, engineering, and transportation significance. The honor for once and for all times cemented the structure's place as being significant to the historic development of Reno, Nevada.

## Notes

1. "Texan Seeks Gambling License for Riverside," *NSJ*, 05/06/1970; quote from "Texan Licensed for Riverside," *NSJ*, 06/19/1970.

2. "Whither Riverside?," Letters to the Editor, *NSJ*, 06/06/1970.

3. "Riverside Applicant's Death Ruled Accident," *NSJ*, 07/07/1970.

4. "Reno's Riverside Hotel Sold for $1.8 Million," *REG*, 10/07/1970, including quotes.

5. "Oklahoma Firm Buys Riverside," *NSJ*, 12/11/1970.

6. "Howard Hughes Expands North, Buys Harolds," *NSJ*, 05/17/1970.

7. Kling, *Biggest Little City*, 8–9.

8. Salas, "A Family Affair," 188; Kling, "Luck Is the Residue of Design," 166–67; quote from "Riverside Hotel Sale Anticipated," *NSJ*, 01/05/1971.

9. First quote from "Riverside Hotel Sale Anticipated," *NSJ*, 01/05/1971; "Papers Signed for Reno Hotel," *REG*, 01/06/1971; "Riverside Gaming Tops Key Hurdle," *NSJ*, 02/11/1971; "Riverside Hotel Wins Approval of Game Board," *REG*, 02/11/1971; second quote from "Jessie Beck Talks About Opening the Riverside," *REG*, 01/09/1971.

10. "Riverside Corner Bar Opens Today," *NSJ*, 02/10/1971; "Reno's Grand Old Hotel Comes to Life for a Party," *NSJ*, 02/21/1971.

11. "Riverside Hotel Nearly Prepared to Open April 1," *NSJ*, 03/27/1971; quote from "We're Building a Hotel Around It," *REG*, 02/27/1971.

12. Dixon, "Playing the Cards That Are Dealt," 90; Dwayne Kling, interview with the author, 09/30/2013.

13. Quote from "Arthur Allen Named Manager of Riverside Hotel," *NSJ*, 01/29/1971; "Bergmann Goes to Riverside from Harolds," *REG*, 02/06/1971; "It's 'Bye, Bye Blues' for the Riverside," *REG*, 03/31/1971; "Riverside Gaming Tops Key Hurdle," *NSJ*, 02/11/1971.

14. "Editorials," *NSJ*, 04/01/1971.

15. "What Recession? Reno-Tahoe Fall Tourism Boom," *REG*, 11/06/1974.

16. "Jessie Beck, Carol Channing Win Chamber of Commerce Annual Awards," *REG*, 06/07/1971; quote from "Hospitality of Casinos Gesture of Goodwill," *NSJ*, 07/08/1973; "Military Ball Saturday in Reno," *NSJ*, 11/14/1974; Kling, *Biggest Little City*, 9.

17. Chuck Clifford, ex-Riverside pit boss, interview with the author, 09/29/2013.

18. UNOHP and OLLI, "The Cultural Side of Reno: James Bernardi," 12.

19. Kling, *Biggest Little City*, 46, 22, 107-8.

20. "Riverside Hotel Sold," *NSJ*, 03/10/1978.

21. Quote from "Riverside Hotel Sold," *NSJ*, 03/10/1978; Kling, *Biggest Little City*, 79–80.

22. All quotes from "Casino Fun Goes on for Mrs. Beck," *NSJ*, 03/10/1978; Kling, *Biggest Little City*, 9; Beck's obituary, *REG*, 07/18/1987

23. Schwartz, "The Great Vegas Turnaround."

24. "Judge Oks Riverside Bankruptcy Plan," *RGJ*, 11/25/1987; quote from Hage, "One Night Stands," 43.

25. Online Nevada Encyclopedia, "Mapes Hotel and Casino, Reno."

26. Quote from "Riverside Casino Closes," *RGJ*, 11/01/1987; "Judge Oks Riverside Bankruptcy Plan," *RGJ*, 11/25/1987.

27. "Judge Oks Riverside Bankruptcy Plan," *RGJ*, 11/25/1987; "Riverside Plan Costs Creditors," *RGJ*, 11/05/1986.

28. "Judge Oks Riverside Bankruptcy Plan," *RGJ*, 11/25/1987.

29. Crawford, "The End of an Era," *RGJ*, 01/12/1987, including quotes.

30. "The Heart of Reno's History," *RGJ*, 01/07/1996, including quotes.

31. Barber, *Reno's Big Gamble*, 224.

32. "Riverside Buyer Missed Earlier Purchase Attempt," *RGJ*, 06/20/1989; "Riverside Sold; New Owners Plan to Remodel, Reopen," *RGJ*, 06/17/1989; "Owner Says He'll Fix up Riverside," *RGJ*, 02/15/1995.

33. Quotes from "$10 Million Riverside Project," *RGJ*, 12/19/1989; Truckee River Info Gateway, TruckeeRiverInfo.org.

34. "New Ideas for Truckee River," special supplement, "Restoration in Downtown Reno," *RGJ*, 07/28/1990; "Riverside Hotel Getting New Lease on Life," *RGJ*, 05/29/1991.

35. Quote from "Stewart Honors Engineer, Builder," *NSJ*, 04/17/1960.

36. "RENOvation Outlines Three-Pronged Attack," *REG*, 03/04/1970; "City Crews Make Props for Bridge," *NSJ*, 02/07/1970; "Work Begins on Bridge Restoration," *NSJ*, 07/30/1970.

37. Cobb, "Sweeping Away the Cobwebs" column, *NSJ*, 08/19/1970.

38. Walton-Buchanan, *Historic Houses and Buildings of Reno, Nevada*, 3; "Summer Lake Mansion Opening Seen," *NSJ*, 11/03/1972.

39. "Fun at the Fair," editorial, *REG*, 05/30/1974; "1874 Bi-Centennial Fair & Exposition," adv., *REG*, 05/31/1974; "Reno Fair Leaves Them Dancing," *REG*, 06/01/1974.

# CHAPTER 14

# A DECADE OF RECKONING

FOR THE RIVERSIDE HOTEL and Virginia Street Bridge, the 1990s would be a decade of reckoning. One of the historic landmarks would be saved by the private sector through the steely determination of a small group of preservationists and art advocates. The other's fate would merely be postponed by the inertia of the public sector.

As the new decade started, the Reno City Council and the City Planning Commission rejoiced in Peter Ng's plans for the Riverside. "I think it's spectacular," said Timothy Collins, Planning Commission chairman. "It's a real asset…for downtown. Hopefully it will stimulate further restoration of the Mapes." More and more, the two shuttered hotels were being discussed in the same breath, as if the fate of one was tightly bound to the fate of the other. However, this would not turn out to be the case.[1]

Ng had added more details of his Canadian group's plans for the hotel since his earlier announcement. The Riverside would be restored to its original Victorian décor, in addition to the mini-mall of exclusive boutiques on the first floor and in the lower level, he said. A courtyard would also be created on the ground level of the hotel that would tie into the design city planners envisioned for the multitier plaza in front of the hotel. On the second floor a steakhouse restaurant would be built, along with a rooftop terrace overlooking the river. These changes would complement the $6 million Truckee River beautification project and the Riverwalk in the immediate downtown area that were due to be launched in the spring. "We're becoming a little more like San Antonio.… We have finally discovered the river," Dick Wiseman, the Riverside owners' spokesman, said of that city's famed Riverwalk, which had become a vital part of San Antonio's urban fabric and a major tourist attraction.[2]

Historically, the Riverside Hotel had been the only Reno institution to take advantage of its location on the Truckee River. As Reno historian Alicia Barber noted in her history of the city, "Only the various incarnations of the Riverside Hotel truly had taken advantage of the riverfront with a combination of veranda and picture windows." Now, however, it was widely hoped that Reno's river beautification project and the restoration of the Riverside Hotel would finally be the genesis of an expanded city core for the 122-year-old city.[3]

By the early 1990s the Riverwalk (today more broadly referred to as the Riverwalk District) had progressed, but was still a work in progress. A book devoted to the project described it: "The Riverwalk offers a scenic walkway that spanned the banks of the Truckee River and would stretch from the current location of the National Automotive Museum to McKinley Park School, built in 1909. Art and sculptures were introduced along the sidewalks, and seven fountains were installed along the walkway. There were also outcrops of gazebos, seating areas, and historical markers."[4]

Not all Renoites were enamored with the Riverwalk in its earliest days, however, believing it to be a poor comparison to what San Antonio and Portland, Oregon, had done. Pick Hobson, the onetime owner of the Riverside, had this comment: "It's stupid.... I just don't like it, that's all."[5]

Despite the ongoing enhancements in the Riverside Hotel's surroundings, however, the arrival of spring in 1991 brought only more promises from Peter Ng. He had found a firm that wanted to lease and operate the Riverside, he announced, and a tentative agreement had been reached. Pending final approval, however, the long-awaited renovation would have to be postponed until late July. When Ng's late July date arrived, instead of renovations there was only another proposal. Wouldn't it be nice, he said, if a municipal court took up residence in the Riverside Hotel? He offered the city the chance to lease 50,000 square feet for a courtroom complex on an upper floor on the South Sierra Street side of the hotel. In turn, his group would build a restaurant, shops, boutiques, and fountain-decorated courtyard on the first floor, and would renovate the hotel rooms as a business hotel. As Peter Eng—he had either changed his last name to Eng by 1993, or the newspapers had decided to change their spelling of the name—continued to generate ideas, but little else; city officials and downtown planners began to lose patience. The downtown area had long since lost its luster for local residents, and the long-shuttered Riverside and Mapes properties were seen as crucial elements in a hoped-for downtown renaissance. City historian Barber pointed out that the construction of large downtown casinos had driven out small businesses, and the last of the major downtown retailers, J. C. Penney, had left for the suburbs in 1991. The area was littered with closed businesses, and, as Barber noted, "Reno's downtown teetered precariously on the brink of seediness." The newspaper echoed the sentiment of many, writing that it was time to set a deadline for the owners of the Mapes and Riverside to revitalize their properties or face losing them to the City Redevelopment Agency through seizure. "Perhaps the best of efforts will not succeed; maybe these old buildings will have to be torn down and something else built in their place," the newspaper concluded.[6]

Despite everyone's best intentions, the issue with the two hotels dragged on. A year-and-a-half later, Reno's fire chief called the Riverside Hotel "a public nuisance," and demanded that it be brought up to code or torn down. He pointed out that the hotel was occupied again, this time by thousands of pigeons and an endless parade of vagrants. Eng promised he'd comply, saying once again that he had a potential buyer in the wings, and this time throwing out the idea that the hotel could be converted into a new city hall.[7]

Heavy rains during the winter months of 1995 only brought more attention to the deplorable condition of the Riverside. The fire department had to pump eight inches of water off the roof to keep it from collapsing, and the city council was advised by the Washoe County health inspector that the guards it paid to patrol the building could no longer safely enter because of exposure to asbestos, pigeon droppings, and human waste. Fire inspectors also found seven new building code violations. The city council responded by planning to begin advertising for a firm to demolish the building if Eng didn't come through with the money to make all the necessary repairs.[8]

By March 1995 it had become apparent that the Riverside Hotel might have to be demolished. The City of Reno Historical Resources Commission began establishing guidelines for mitigating the adverse effects of demolition, a legal requirement since the building had been recognized on the National Register of Historic Places as a historically significant structure. Historical documentation on the site's history had to be prepared, along with plans, drawings, photos, and other information as required by an official Level II Documentation (today called Standard II Documentation) in order to preserve an accurate record of historic properties that can be used in research and other preservation activities. The task of writing and gathering all this information fell to city employee Stephen L. Hardesty. He completed the resulting package, entitled "The Site of Reno's Beginning: The Historical Mitigation of the Riverside Hotel/Casino," in 1997.[9]

In January 1996, while Hardesty was working on his project, a potential savior appeared for the historic structure. Bob Stupak, the maverick,
publicity-seeking founder and part owner of the Stratosphere Hotel–Casino
in Las Vegas, which was due to open in mere months, expressed an interest
in buying the Riverside if he could buy and reopen it for $12 to $20 million.
The odds of that happening, professional gambler Stupak speculated, "are
about 50/50." One of the keystones in the deal—in addition to the condition
of the structure—would be whether or not sufficient parking could be found
for the property, always a problem in the past as well.[10]

For the next six months, despite the April bankruptcy filing of the Stratosphere Corporation in which he held a 16 percent position, Stupak pressed
on in his quest to purchase the Riverside. Some people believed Stupak was
not really interested in the hotel, that he was only seeking publicity. However, before his bid ended he would spend a significant amount of money on
architectural specs and formal presentations, indicating that his interest was
serious. One of his proposals, should the historic property become his, was
to build a thrill ride that would travel, in seven seconds, two hundred feet
up a three-hundred-foot structure rising on the Virginia Street side of the
hotel. It would be similar to the Big Shot ride at the Las Vegas Stratosphere,
but, according to Stupak, "faster, quicker and better" than its counterpart.
He also claimed that the Riverside would have the highest gambling limits
in Reno under his ownership.[11]

By July 1996 Stupak's option to purchase was about to run out, and he was
faced with renewing the option or pulling out of the deal. Stupak decided
to pull out, fearing that Eng would find some last-minute technicality and
back out, leaving him with nothing. Eng, meanwhile, said he was considering tearing the hotel down and building a retail-office complex on the site.[12]

While the Riverside was losing perhaps its last chance for resurrection,
the fight to save the Mapes across the river took another turn. In September the City of Reno purchased the Mapes from owners Robert Maloff and
George Karadanis for $5 million, ending years of speculation and contro-
versy. This would not be the endgame for the hotel, however, but merely
another step in determining its final fate.[13]

The year 1997 came in like a lion when, on January 1, Reno suffered another
devastating flood, one that would later be adjudged by the Army Corps of
Engineers as a 100-year flood (other sources adjudged it as a 117-year flood).
A series of wet Pacific storms quickly filled Lake Tahoe—the source of the

Truckee River. When the lake reached what an outdated statute claimed was its maximum height, the gates of the Tahoe Dam were opened, and a torrent of water rushed downstream, where it inundated parts of Reno, including the entire downtown area, causing $650 million in damages. "Downtown Reno looked like a military encampment, with a foot-high barrier of sandbags extending the length of First Street," reported the *Reno Gazette-Journal*. Damage to the Riverside Hotel was extensive, further hampering the efforts of preservationists to save the historic structure.[14]

As in floods past, the ninety-two-year-old Virginia Street Bridge was again a major impediment to the raging waters, as the twin arches of the bridge were quickly clogged with the debris that rushed past, forcing the water up over the bridge and into the downtown area. City workers labored overnight to remove the parking meters on the bridge so they wouldn't be destroyed, or act as flotsam-catchers.[15]

The bridge had first been identified as being structurally deficient by the Nevada Department of Transportation (NDOT) in 1992; two years later NDOT completed an assessment of the bridge. The report noted three possibilities for the aging structure, and the cost and estimated lifespan of the bridge under each option. First, do nothing, at no cost, and with an estimated lifespan of five years. Second, modify and rehabilitate the present structure and preserve its historical significance, at a cost of $1.6 million and a lifespan of twenty-five years. And third, replace the bridge at a cost of $2.7 million if it were widened, or $2.4 million if not, with an estimated lifespan of fifty years. NDOT recommended the second option, "modify and rehabilitate."[16]

Soon after, NDOT and the City of Reno, the bridge's owners, entered into an agreement to study repair options. Because of the bridge's historic importance, these studies were necessarily conducted under the auspices of the National Environmental Policy Act. An environmental assessment completed in 1996 approved the rehabilitation of the bridge through the federal Highway Bridge Replacement and Rehabilitation Program. NDOT would begin the rehab design in 1997 after the flood, but the plan screeched to a halt when it was determined that the assessment had not dealt with the bridge's hydraulic capacity, meaning the measure of the volume of water that could pass under it. Like many such studies that require input and cooperation between federal, state, and municipal agencies, the project would be terminated in 1999 pending recommendations that would evaluate the downtown reach of the Truckee River. The decade would end with no final decision on the fate of the deteriorating Virginia Street Bridge.[17]

In early February 1997, with the Mapes Hotel now in its possession, the Reno City Council took a historic step when it voted five to two to condemn the Riverside Hotel and acquire it by rights of eminent domain, the first time this new law would have been used by the city. But the council also instructed the city manager to continue negotiating with owner Peter Eng over a price for the hotel in order to avoid having to go through a lengthy court battle to legitimize the city's seizure. Council members also set a deadline for the Eng negotiations, setting the date for demolition of the Riverside to begin in six weeks. By April 9 no progress had been made in the negotiations, so the Reno City Council seized the property and put the hotel in the hands of the Reno Redevelopment Agency. Lacking any further resolution from Peter Eng, on November 14 the Riverside's demolition began when the wrecking ball took down George Wingfield's massive 1951 Riverside addition. For preservationists, it was now "put up or shut up" time.[18]

Local preservationists had not been sitting on their hands; they had been fervently working on saving both the Mapes and the Riverside. They found a San Diego–based real estate development firm, Oliver McMillan, that was interested in the Mapes, but the huge $6 million to $9 million price tag of rehabbing the high-rise building eventually discouraged the company from taking on the project. The smaller Riverside's rehabilitation, however, had been tabbed at much less, at only $1.5 million; but Oliver McMillan wasn't particularly interested in rehabbing that project either, although the company did have an interest in developing some other downtown Reno land it owned.[19]

Dave Aiazzi, a Reno City Council member, threw another iron in the fire when he proposed to Oliver McMillan that they renovate the upper-floor rooms of the Riverside into apartments for divorcees, and use the first floor for a House of Blues nightclub. Despite all the outlandish plans that were now floating around, Mayor Jeff Griffin put a cap on it, saying he'd favor restoring the Riverside, despite his numerous votes to condemn it, but added, "If it's not found to be economic, boom! It's out of here in mid-October." Griffin was referring to the fact that the city already had one firm standing by to remove the asbestos in the Riverside at a cost of $290,300, and another firm ready to demolish it for $737,000.[20]

It was about this time that two other organizations stepped into the picture with a plan that would eventually prove to be the Riverside Hotel's salvation.

Sierra Arts Foundation was founded in 1971 as northern Nevada's first nonprofit arts support group. They provided educational opportunities for artists, as well as training, financial support, and promotion and marketing assistance. They also provided venues in the community for artists to perform or display their work. However, at the time Patricia Smith accepted the position as executive director of the organization in 1992, Sierra Arts had fallen on hard times and was only one step away from having to close its own doors. But through the hard work of Smith and a small staff, and a few vitally needed financial grants, by 1997 the organization was back on its feet. Smith said she had first learned what the term "live/work space" meant some time earlier. Just like it sounds, it is where artists have their living space and their working space together in one unit. One day when Smith and her Sierra Arts program director, Jill Berryman, were downtown working on an "Artists in the Street" show and sale event, Smith pointed at the Riverside and jokingly said, "I think that's where we ought to have live/work space. Gee, that'd be really neat."[21]

Sometime later the two ladies attended an Americans for the Arts convention in Minneapolis, where they went on a tour of a live/work space building put up by a local nonprofit company named, appropriately, Artspace. They met with Artspace president Kelley Lindquist and pitched him on converting the Mapes Hotel to a live/work space building. Lindquist agreed to visit Reno with his team, but after touring the Mapes the group indicated it was not conducive to good reuse because the retrofit to make it earthquake proof would be too expensive. Not wanting to miss the Artspace opportunity altogether, Smith quickly recommended they look at the Riverside across the river, despite its deplorable condition. To everyone's surprise, Lindquist and his team were quickly won over at the prospect of converting that historic property into live/work apartments.[22]

Artspace had been launched in 1979 when the Minneapolis Arts Commission founded the nonprofit organization to advocate for local artists' space needs. After a decade, however, it became clear that a more proactive approach was called for, and the company evolved from advocate to developer. Its first live/work space project was in nearby St. Paul, in the city's decaying warehouse district. As *Fast Company*, a magazine of entrepreneurial activities, wrote in an extensive article about Artspace's first project, "The Northern Warehouse district may be one of the clearest case studies of the role of artists in rejuvenating decaying neighborhoods—and sticking around afterward."[23]

When Patricia Smith of Reno's Sierra Arts and Kelley Lindquist of Minneapolis's Artspace began talking in the late 1990s, Artspace had just begun to branch out from its home state into the national artists' live/work-space scene. The decision of the two organizations to work together to save the Riverside Hotel for a higher purpose must have seemed like kismet to both Smith and Lindquist. Today, the nonprofit real estate developer owns or co-owns thirty-three arts facilities across the country, providing nearly two thousand affordable live/work units in twenty states for artists and their families, and one million square feet of nonresidential space for creative enterprises. Their Reno partner, Sierra Arts Foundation, still provides local management for the Riverside Artist Lofts, and maintains offices and a gallery on the ground floor of the hotel.[24]

Hoping to do their bit to ensure the artists' lofts would become reality, a group of local artists and art students, under the direction of Sierra Arts, prepared sixty-two paintings with themes that celebrated the arts. The paintings were placed in the first, second, and third floor windows of the vacant Riverside just in time for the opening of the U.S. Conference of Mayors in Reno in June 1998. "I think it's great," said Reno mayor Jeff Griffin, who had been leading a campaign to clean up downtown's derelict buildings before the visiting mayors arrived.[25]

A great deal of work remained to be done, however, to raise funds to purchase the hotel from the city and to convert the decrepit old building into livable spaces. After a feasibility study, Artspace's plan was to convert the five upper floors into thirty-five artist live/work spaces. The firm would go into a partnership with a San Diego firm, Oliver McMillan, that would renovate the hotel and add shops and restaurants, although that firm eventually bowed out of the enterprise. Shortly thereafter, the Reno City Council, acting as the Reno Redevelopment Agency, accepted Artspace's proposal, and agreed to sell the Riverside to the Sierra Arts Foundation for $350,000. Sierra Arts and Artspace formed a $7.9 million partnership, subsidized by the U.S. Department of Housing and Urban Development, for the renovation. Money for the renovation came from historic and low-income tax credits, a federal disaster recovery grant, a Nevada cultural grant, and a federal home grant. Subsequently, the two partners recovered the rest of the purchase price of the hotel by selling the valuable water rights that went with it.[26]

The renovation wasn't without its problems. The first big issues were the removal of all the asbestos and lead paint, and then mold that was discovered in the basement as a result of all the flooding over the years. Completing these tasks set the initial schedule back by almost six weeks. While this was ongoing, architects were frantically searching through library collections for the original 1927 building plans, as the renovation called for the finished project to look much as Frederic DeLongchamps had designed it in the mid-to-late 1920s. But from that point on, the work progressed smoothly. The building was completely gutted inside so little remained beside the concrete floors. From there, the interior was completely rebuilt into the thirty-five individual apartment units. New plumbing, electrical, and HVAC (heating, ventilation, and air conditioning) units were added to each work/live space. Most units had ten-foot high ceilings, and heating and cooling ductwork was left exposed to achieve the industrial look that was just coming into vogue.[27]

The Mapes Hotel, unfortunately, did not meet with similar success. With the hotel under city ownership, the clock continued ticking down on the endgame for the forty-eight-year-old hotel. The National Trust for Historic Preservation placed the Mapes on its 1998 list of most endangered historic places in America in an effort to help save it, and an unprecedented surge of local public support arose toward the same goal. But nobody stepped forward with the estimated $5 million to $9 million it would take to rehabilitate the property. Despite continued efforts to save it, on Super Bowl Sunday, January 30, 2000, the building many in Reno considered the city's albatross was imploded. It would eventually be turned into a public plaza with a winter ice skating rink, trees, fountains, bleachers, and other amenities. When the new Virginia Street Bridge was completed in 2016, the space was renamed Ice Rink Plaza. It featured expansive seating area on the riverbank, and was the location for all the public art treatments installed as part of the bridge project.[28]

Neal Cobb, a local historian, author, and preservationist, probably had the most succinct comment on the twin fates of the Riverside and the Mapes when he said, "[The Riverside Hotel] is the one we were worried about. We thought it was a shoo-in to save the Mapes, but we had it backwards."[29]

### NOTES

1. "Reno Planners Endorse $10 Million Riverside Hotel Renovation Proposal," *RGJ*, 02/08/1990, including quote.

2. "Reno Planners Endorse $10 Million Riverside Hotel Renovation Proposal," *RGJ*, 02/08/1990, including quote.

3. Barber, *Reno's Big Gamble*, 217, including quote.

4. Quote from Rhiana and Meredith, *Images of America, Reno's Riverwalk District*, 8.

5. First quote from Rhiana and Meredith, *Images of America, Reno's Riverwalk District*, 8; second quote from Powers, "The Heart of Reno's History, *RGJ*, 01/07/1996.

6. "Plan Converts Hotel to Judicial Use," *RGJ*, 07/31/1991; first quote from Barber, *Reno's Big Gamble*, 215; second quote from "Deadline for Mapes and Riverside? Yes," editorial, *RGJ*, 09/08/1993.

7. "Chief: Bring Riverside up to Code or Tear It Down," *RGJ*, 01/21/1995, including quote.

8. "Riverside Hotel Endangered by Heavy Rains," *RGJ*, 12/13/1995.

9. Hardesty, "The Site of Reno's Beginning," 3–4.

10. "Stupak Still Hoping to Buy Riverside," *RGJ*, 05/01/1996, including quote.

11. "Stupak Committed to Big Ride for Reno," *RGJ*, 06/04/1996, including quote.

12. Voyles, "Stupak Folds on Riverside Deal," *RGJ*, 07/10/1996.

13. Barber, *Reno's Big Gamble*, 224.

14. McLaughlin, "Tahoe Dam 1997 Flood"; quote from "River Swamps Downtown," *RGJ*, 01/02/1997.

15. "River Swamps Downtown, *RGJ*, 01/02/1997.

16. NDOT, "Summary of Assessment of Virginia Street Bridge, Structure No. B-178."

17. NDOT, "Summary of Assessment of Virginia Street Bridge, Structure No. B-178"; City of Reno, "Reno Bridges–Flood Projects, Background."

18. "Riverside Closer to Wrecking Ball," *RGJ*, 02/04/1997; Hardesty, "The Site of Reno's Beginning," 20; "Riverside Demolition Starts," photo and caption, *RGJ*, 11/14/1997.

19. "Mapes Supporters Deserve More Time," *RGJ*, 11/14/1997; Roy Close, vice president, Special Projects: Artspace, 10/11/2013, e-mail to the author.

20. Voyles, "Riverside Getting Last Look to See if it's Salvageable," *RGJ*, 07/17/1997, including quote.

21. UNOHP and OLLI, "The Cultural Side of Reno: Patricia Smith," 521–22, 528; quote on p. 529.

22. UNOHP and OLLI, "The Cultural Side of Reno: Patricia Smith," 529–30.

23. Artspace website, www.artspace.org; quote from Badger, "The Key to a Thriving Creative Class?"

24. Badger, "The Key to a Thriving Creative Class?"

25. Quote from Anglen, "Artwork Restores Vitality to Historic Riverside Hotel," *RGJ*, 06/09/1998.

26. Voyles, "Artspace Proposes to Make Top Floors of Riverside Hotel into Lofts for Artists," *RGJ*, 01/10/1998; "Council Gives Final OK to Riverside," *RGJ*, 02/05/1998; Barber, *Reno's Big Gamble*, 231; Cox, "Old Landmark, New Lofts," *RGJ*, 12/03/2000; Roy Close, vice president, Special Projects: Artspace, e-mail to the author, 10/11/2013; Powers, "Riverside Hotel Renovations on Track," *RGJ*, 05/10/2000.

27. Powers, "Riverside Hotel Renovations on Track," *RGJ*, 05/10/2000; Magliari, "Home Is Where the Art Is."

28. Barber, *Reno's Big Gamble*, 224–30; "Mapes Supporters Deserve More Time," *RGJ*, 11/14/1997.

29. UNOHP and OLLI, "The Cultural Side of Reno: Neal Cobb," 54.

# CHAPTER 15

# RESURRECTION

PERHAPS IT WAS FITTING that the oldest occupied site in Reno, Nevada, and the site that first offered protection from the harsh elements and a bed for the night for weary travelers, was resurrected at the dawn of a new decade, a new century, and a new millennium.

Back in 1994 the city of Reno had begun facing the problems of its decaying downtown core. In response they had developed a new entity named the C.I.T.Y. 2000 (Cultural In The Year 2000) Arts Commission. This commission was charged with arts and culture development in the downtown core area. By the new millennium, however, little progress had been made, so the city updated the plan and decided to refocus on a seven-year vision to revitalize the downtown core, especially that portion along the river within what was then described as the Arts and Culture District. The official opening of the Riverside Artist Lofts would spearhead that plan, although the plan would later be hampered by the severe recession of 2008 to 2010.[1]

The Artist Lofts formally opened on October 20, 2000. The thirty-five one-, two-, and three-bedroom live/work spaces occupying the top five floors of the Riverside ranged in size from 780 square feet to 1,600 square feet, and initially rented for $297 to $634 a month. To qualify for an apartment, an artist had to earn a minimum of $12,030 a year but not more than $29,925. Achieving the minimum earnings proved that a person was indeed a practicing artist, trying to make a living; requiring an artist not to surpass the high end of the range ensured that only "struggling" artists qualified for the subsidized housing. Representatives from all five branches of the arts qualified as tenants: visual artists, musicians, actors, dancers, and writers. The arts practiced by the Riverside Artist Lofts' first tenants were wide ranging. Among the early artists to secure their apartments were a fashion designer, an oil painter, a makeup stylist, a cello player, and a quilt designer. The lofts were blank spaces, with white walls and unpainted concrete floors; artists were expected to do their own designing and decorating. Early comments made by the tenant artists reflected their unbounded enthusiasm for their new spaces: "You can drip paint on the floor," said one painter excitedly. "It's great; you have to pinch yourself every morning," said a cellist looking out his corner window toward the Truckee River. The fashion designer pointed out the polka dots she had painted on her bathroom walls that provided daily inspiration. Jeff Frame, the architect who designed the lofts, said, "It's a feel-good project. We gave these artists blank boxes. They want these big open spaces."[2]

"The light in my loft is fabulous.... Living here facilitates my art," a folk-singer and songwriter added fifteen months later as the artists prepared for their first open house to share their art and music and their live/work spaces with the general public, an event that has become an annual happening in Reno.[3]

Typical of today's resident artists is Erik Holland. A plein-air painter, art instructor, and cartoonist, Holland was one of the original tenants at the Riverside Artist Lofts, taking up residence in 2000; he is still happily en-sconced in the historic building. Prior to moving to Reno, Holland had spent most of the 1990s living and painting in Alaska, after being raised in Chicago and trained in New York. He is also the unofficial mayor of Nada Dada Motel, a quirky born-in-Reno art event that is now in its twelfth year. Holland de-scribed the sense of community that exists at the Artist Lofts: "It's kind of like being a part of a family...but you still have your own space. Some of the resident artists prefer to have things more regimented, but others prefer less structure.... You can be as involved or non-involved with the internal life of the building as you want."[4]

Holland likes to get outside for at least a few hours every day—regardless of the weather—and capture some of the flavor of Reno with his palette and brush. He's a prolific painter, and he said he often produces a salable work of art in just a few hours' time. "I like Reno a lot.... In the thirteen years I've been here it seems to have grown up; and it's a more and more exciting place to be an artist. I've done very well here; Reno's been kind to me as an artist."[5]

Today at the Riverside Artist Lofts there are a few families, but Holland said singles occupy most of the thirty-five apartments. In at least one sense, the Artist Lofts community is no different than any other community. Two artists, Sarah Fisk, a sculptress and photographer, and Bart McCoy, an oil painter and airbrush artist, started out as singles but ended up as a couple in one apartment. As the story goes, some of the residents were scheduled to

Plein-air painter Erik Holland, shown here in his home studio in this bird's-eye photo, enjoys the live/work space that facilities like the Riverside Artist Lofts provide for professional artists. Photo by Vincent Cascio; courtesy of Erik Holland.

paint murals on the walls in the lobby, and Fisk and McCoy decided to team up. Their resulting mural, a large, single eye looking directly at you, is striking; and despite the artists' differing styles, they produced a cohesive and pleasing piece. So successful was the mural partnership that within weeks the two were married, reminiscent of hundreds of other such unions that the Riverside Hotel produced during the heyday of its divorce—and often, remarriage—business.[6]

In the original deal with Oliver McMillan, the firm was to commercialize the ground-floor space, but that plan fell through as the project moved forward. Sierra Arts Foundation took over one-third of the first-floor space for offices; the Foundation was granted a free thirty-year lease for its space. A gallery and a music studio for the tenant artists would occupy more of the space, and plans called for a few commercial tenants to share the remaining space in the future.[7]

In June 2007 longtime friends Chuck Shapiro and Doug Holter opened the Wild River Grill in one of the Riverside's ground-floor spaces. With a large outside patio sitting right on the riverbank, the restaurant immediately became one of the city's hotspots. A diverse menu, an extensive bar, and live entertainment have kept Renoites and tourists coming back time after time. In 2010 the restaurant expanded, taking over an adjacent space that had been occupied by a coffeehouse. Called the River Room, the new spot is spacious and open, features a full bar and a private dining room, and is designed to be group friendly. The entire establishment has proven to be an excellent addition to the hotel long known for its food, libations, and entertainment.[8]

Perhaps most importantly to Reno old-timers is that the River Room is located where the old corner bar once stood, and before that, George Wingfield's Riverside Bank. The historic hotel had been resurrected, and it was again a vibrant, living space after sitting vacant for fourteen years. The visionaries who had made it happen saw immediate recognition for their work. In 2000 the Riverside Artist Lofts was given a Tourism Development Award at the U.S. Governor's Conference held in Reno; and the following year the building received the James C. Howland Award for Urban Enrichment from the National League of Cities.[9]

For the city of Reno and its citizens, who had been trying for decades to jumpstart the renovation of downtown, perhaps the most concise comment on what the Riverside Artist Lofts meant for the city was made by the executive director of the statewide Nevada Arts Council: "It opened the eyes of our elected officials and members of the public to what downtown could be, and it linked contemporary activity with the historic uniqueness of Reno.... I believe it was pivotal to the transformation of the river corridor and demonstrated that clearly, people would live downtown."[10]

As further proof of that, by mid-decade a number of old and new downtown buildings had been converted to condominiums; and although sales were seriously hampered by the deep recession in the second half of the decade, once that ended people again began buying the condos and making downtown Reno their homes.

Having won the fight for the Riverside and lost the fight for the Mapes, many in the city and state preservation communities were now beginning to turn their attention to the historic Virginia Street Bridge. By virtue of NDOT's 1994 recommendation to modify and rehabilitate the old concrete bridge rather than demolish it and start over, the preservation folks seemed to have gained the upper hand as the new century began. One of the key concerns in earlier studies had been the hydraulic capacity of the old bridge, or the volume of water it was able to channel downstream. The old bridge's twin-arch design with a center pier had always proven to be a bottleneck to unobstructed water flow, and even more so during flood events. In the summer of 2003 a team of experts was assembled to study solutions to the concrete bridge's hydraulic capacity problem in an effort to see if the bridge could be saved. "We are willing to spend funds…to preserve the state's most historic bridge," said Bill Crawford, Nevada's chief bridge engineer.[11]

Engineers designed a plan that would add additional river bypass channels to each side of the existing bridge—forty feet wide on the south end and twenty-five feet wide on the north end—lengthening the bridge by sixty-five feet. This plan became known as the Ferrari Shields design. These bypass channels would allow more water to flow by the bridge, thus increasing its hydraulic capacity. A garage-sized model of the bridge and the river had been designed and would be used to run water through the bridge at differing flows to measure what the overall effect of the new design would be. The test was scheduled to last eighteen months. The bridge was eligible for federal highway funds to restore or replace it. However, NDOT was unwilling to seek the funding until the Army Corps of Engineers, the agency that had ordered the study, had assurances that the bridge design met its requirements for flood control. Eventually, however, the Corps determined that the Ferrari Shields design would not work, and, even if it were feasible, the cost of implementing it would be much higher than the cost of a new bridge. On top of that it would destroy too much riverfront property, including some of the city's most historic sites.[12]

Preservationists, however, were undaunted; they still wanted to save the historic old bridge. But they had two powerful entities that believed the old bridge must go: flood control officials and environmentalists. Flood control experts' primary concern was that there was no way the concrete bridge could be altered to reduce the damage it caused to the river itself and to the riverbanks during flood events. Their opinion was that only a new bridge, absent any destructive piers that clog the river's flow, would suffice if the community hoped to mitigate future flood damage.

Environmentalists agreed that only by starting over with a new bridge could the Truckee River ecosystem be rehabilitated, which was their main concern. Their mission statement explained their position:

> Over the last 150 years, more than 30 dams and water supply diversion structures were constructed along the Truckee River. In the 1950's and 60's, the bed of the Truckee River was blasted, dredged and straightened in an effort to reduce flooding upstream in the Truckee Meadows. Together, these activities wreaked havoc on the river's ecosystem, significantly reducing the native vegetation which had lined the riverbanks, lowering water levels, eliminating critical habitat, and

impeding fish spawning in the river. Today, approximately 90% of the riparian forest that existed along the river at the beginning of the 20th century has been lost, along with 70% of the hundreds of species of nesting birds that were once common along the river.[13]

In July 2005 the weighty and confrontational issues on what to do with the Virginia Street Bridge were put aside for a day when everyone joined together for a birthday party for the historic century-old structure. Following a number of speeches on the bridge's history, a ceremonial "ring toss" was performed. Attendees were all given toy gold rings tied to the end of ribbons to "throw" into the Truckee River in one coordinated group fling. Following the ceremony there was a reception in the Sierra Arts Gallery inside the historic Riverside Artist Lofts, complete with a birthday cake decorated with historic images of the bridge.

As if mocking the ceremony, another devastating flood on the last day of 2005 aided flood-control advocates' and environmentalists' bridge objectives when it left a large hole in the concrete bridge's foundation, seriously compromising the preservationists' hopes of rehabilitating the old structure.[14]

On March 28, 2007, the Reno City Council unanimously sided with flood-control experts and voted that the old bridge would be torn down and replaced. Two weeks later the Flood Project Coordinating Committee agreed, making the decision official. In the final analysis, what this decision meant was that despite earlier agreements to the contrary, historic preservation, although a worthy goal, would of necessity take a backseat to issues of flood control. At this point the federal, state, and local entities that would be responsible for building the new bridge were all in line. The City of Reno, as the official owner of the bridge, would manage the project, in close coordination with the Truckee River Flood Management Authority, which would obtain most of the money for the project, and the U.S. Army Corps of Engineers. Numerous historic groups; other federal, state, and local agencies; and downtown stakeholders would also be involved in the process in advisory capacities.[15]

By the end of the following year the City of Reno had published a "TRAction Visioning Project" report, the first step in defining the city's needs and opportunities, and the constraints that existed for implementing any improvements. A primary objective of the study was to determine both the city's and the public's vision for the "look-and-feel" of the replacement bridges in the downtown area. Certain assumptions were identified. First, the structures would be clear-span bridges, meaning there would be no supporting columns under the bridge; second, the bridges would provide protection against a hundred-year flood event; and third, all bridges would have two feet of freeboard, the clearance between the bottom of the bridge deck and the highest point of the water surface elevation. Lack of sufficient freeboard under the concrete bridge had been another of its major flaws. The report also stated the importance of community input, and set dates for a number of public workshops, and for presentations to concerned civic organizations.[16]

As the first decade of the new century passed into history, it was obvious that whatever design the city adopted for the new Virginia Street Bridge would create controversy. The iconic structure had been such an important part of the life of the city and its residents that it would have been impossible to please everybody.

## NOTES

1. City of Reno, "2012 Cultural Master Plan: Introduction"; UNOHP and OLLI, "The Cultural Side of Reno: Mary Lee Fulkerson," 159–63.

2. All quotes from Cox, "Old Landmark, New Lofts," *RGJ*, 12/03/2000; Powers, "Riverside Hotel Renovations on Track," *RGJ*, 05/10/2000.

3. Hayes, "Lofty Living," *RGJ*, 03/09/2001, including quote.

4. "Art Show Today"; all quotes from plein-air painter Erik Holland, personal interview with the author.

5. Plein-air painter Erik Holland, personal interview with the author, including quote.

6. Plein-air painter Erik Holland, personal interview with the author, including quote.

7. Cox, "Old Landmark, New Lofts," *RGJ*, 12/03/2000; Powers, "Riverside Hotel Renovations on Track," *RGJ*, 05/10/2000.

8. WiredPRNews.com, "The Historical Riverside in Reno, More Than One Hundred Years of Hospitality," 01/28/2013.

9. Barber, *Biggest Little City*, 231.

10. Gadwa and Muessig, "How Art Spaces Matter, II."

11. Voyles, "Saving Virginia Street Crossing," *RGJ*, 10/27/2003, including quote.

12. Voyles, "Saving Virginia Street Crossing," *RGJ*, 10/27/2003; Online Nevada Encyclopedia, "Virginia Street Bridge."

13. Truckee River Flood Project, "Ecosystem Restoration."

14. Online Nevada Encyclopedia, "Virginia Street Bridge."

15. Voyles, "Virginia St. Bridge to be Demolished," *RGJ*, 03/29/2007; City of Reno, "Virginia Street Bridge Project: FAQs."

16. City of Reno, "TRAction Visioning Project."

# CHAPTER 16

# ONE OF THE WORST BRIDGES
# IN THE COUNTRY

AT THE OPENING of the second decade of the new century, replacing the aging Virginia Street Bridge before another flood raged through the Truckee Meadows was at the top of most priority lists. The chairman of a coalition of local governments representing the Truckee River Flood Project referred to the devastating flood of 1997 when he said, "My biggest fear is we're going to flood [again] and people are going to look at us and say we really haven't done much of anything [about the bridge]." Progress had been made, according to the Army Corps of Engineers, but local officials were frustrated with the pace of that progress. In January 2010 the Corps announced that modeling mistakes would delay until 2012 congressional approval of the $1.6 billion being sought. Meanwhile, the Reno City Council had selected a designer for the Virginia Street Bridge. The bridge's $20 million to $25 million price tag, however, was still largely part of the elusive $1.6 billion.[1]

In November 2010 the city council and the Flood Project Coordinating Committee approved spending up to $1.8 million to begin the bridge design process and to gather all necessary permits. The design work was complicated by the fact that the new bridge had to adhere to the Secretary of the Interior's standards for the treatment of historic properties. The design process included public outreach efforts to help determine the exact look and feel the open-span bridge should take. Although the plans included other downtown bridges as well, an engineer with the Reno Public Works Department indicated that the Virginia Street Bridge design would set the standard for the designs of the Sierra, Lake, Center, Booth, and Arlington Street bridges, all of which would need to be replaced in the future. Reno council member Dan Gustin described the bridge replacements as the "linchpin" for Reno's portion of the broader $1.6 billion flood project, which was still awaiting congressional approval.[2]

By late 2011, following months of outreach meetings, and careful study of all the alternatives offered by Jacobs Engineering—the Pasadena, California firm chosen to do the bridge design work—the Reno City Council made its choice for the new Virginia Street Bridge from the five final options offered. The options ranged in style and function, and in price from $20 million to $50 million. The winner was the pony truss design that featured eleven-foot-high curved arches, no supportive piers, and the necessary roadwork between Mill and First Streets. That basic design was similar in nature to the 1877 iron bridge, but it would require that Virginia Street and its sidewalks be raised by three feet leading up to the higher level necessary to satisfy the two-foot freeboard minimum. This upset the Historic Reno Preservation Society because the associated roadwork could affect some historical sites along the riverfront. To ameliorate the problem, it was decided to use split sidewalks rather than one span of sidewalk to achieve the three-foot height difference. The choice also included key aesthetic details of the project. Although the public outreach meetings had also favored the pony truss design, not everyone was in agreement. Even among city council members who voted for the pony truss design, some admitted it wasn't their first choice. Dan Gustin preferred the "hydraulic" design, while Mayor Bob Cashell liked the "rigid frame" design. Ultimately, however, most everyone found the pony truss design to be the most practical overall.[3]

*Civil Engineering* magazine added some important details about the selected design:

> In replacing an earth-filled bridge that is listed in the National Register of Historic Places, designers had to consider aesthetics as well as function. At roughly 160 ft long, the Virginia Street Bridge, in Reno, Nevada, is not a large structure, but its location makes it an important one.... So when city officials decided to replace the 107-year-old bridge, a great deal of consideration was given to the new crossing's functionality and design....
>
> Taking all of the requirements [including flood control] into consideration, the team developed bridge types that were acceptable from both an engineering and a historical standpoint: three static bridges...and two movable bridges.... [City] officials...determined that the movable bridges were less desirable because of their cost and maintenance issues over time....

In contrast to the existing bridge, the new bridge will not have a skewed alignment. It will be approximately 166 ft long and will vary in width from 84 to 98 feet, the widest part being at the center, where 11 to 18 ft wide pedestrian walkways will bow out on either side. The bridge will carry two 12 ft wide traffic lanes, and there will be room along the shoulder for parking or a streetcar line should the city decide to add those features.[4]

Jacobs Engineering handled the selection of the bridge's aesthetic features in a unique, digital-age fashion. With a lot of different aesthetic options available, it would have been very difficult for a person to imagine how one particular aesthetic feature—ornamental iron handrails, for example—might look when combined with another feature, like colored pedestrian walkways. So the firm designed a Build Your Bridge computer application that allowed officials and stakeholders to request any combination of aesthetic features and then fly through a 3-D rendering of that combination to see how all the elements worked together. Different features could then be substituted and another 3-D fly-through compared. In this fashion the final look and feel of the bridge was composed and presented to the Reno City Council for its approval.[5]

Although the $1.6 billion flood control project was still awaiting its funding, $4.8 million had been authorized to begin work on the architectural and engineering plans of the bridge, and another $1.4 million had already been spent on the design work. Engineer Bryan Gant of Jacobs Engineering said the project would start in spring 2014 and could take up to eighteen months to complete. However, that start time would eventually be pushed back to 2015.[6]

By 2013 the Virginia Street Bridge project finally had some sustained forward movement. A January 16, 2013, "Reno City Council Project Update" report outlined the work accomplished and the work still to be done. Architectural renderings of the bridge showed a sleek, modern design highlighted by low concrete arches on each side of the roadway, and broad pedestrian walkways on each side of the bridge. According to the report, the advanced design specifications were 60 percent completed, and construction funding had finally been identified. It would come from the Nevada Department of Transportation, Truckee River Flood Management Authority, and—if necessary—the Washoe County Regional Transportation Commission. Still to come was the selection of the public art for the project, which would again have community input, subject to the Reno City Council's final approval. Reno has a requirement that 2 percent of public works project costs must be dedicated to public art. Simultaneously there was a public "Call for Artists" that would include work on the bridge railing, the pedestrian walkways, and various retaining walls around the project.[7]

In July 2013 a Reno metalworking firm, Tutto Ferro, was awarded a $270,000 contract to design and execute the public art for the new bridge. *Tutto ferro* is Italian for "all iron," although the majority of the firm's work is done in steel. The firm primarily produces one-off steel works of art that have a heavy emphasis on architectural and design elements. Most of the company's work is done for commercial and residential customers, although they have produced some public art pieces as well. The company's work has been featured in *Architectural Digest*, *Dwell*, and *Nevada* magazines. Paolo Cividino, a master steelsmith, is the owner of Tutto Ferro. Born in Italy, Cividino has lived in Nevada for thirty years, and takes tremendous pride in the "Battle Born" state's rugged and diverse landscape, which inspires much of his art. "We live in a magical place," he says, "[and we want] to create a sense of local and regional pride."[8]

From mid-2013 to mid-2015, specific plans for the bridge's public art went through a number of metamorphoses, as Tutto Ferro and the Reno Arts Council attempted to find just the right blend to compliment the striking new bridge. It was finally decided that all the public art would be located on the wall of what would become known as the Ice Rink Plaza River Access area, a riverfront walkway below ground level on the northeast corner of North Virginia Street and the bridge, once the site of the Mapes Hotel.

Final plans for the bridge's public art are extensive. There would be one art piece in concrete and five in steel installed along the wall of the River Access elevation. The concrete panel will be a seven-by-ten-foot relief map of Nevada. It will showcase the mountainous nature of the state with the ranges enlarged for effect, and the cities and towns along the main transportation routes will be represented by steel letters embedded in the concrete. "The cities should provide a context by which the various ranges and landmarks can be located, creating a more engaging experience," a spokesperson for Tutto Ferro said. The five individual steel panels will be lined up along the wall next to the map showing striking sculptural representations of Nevada landmarks Wheeler Peak, the City of Reno, Pyramid Lake, the Sedan Crater at the Nevada Test Site, and the Truckee

River. Locals and visitors alike should be "wowed" by the dramatic impact of the six sculptural panels that Cividino and his artistic staff will have crafted.[9]

As for the aging concrete Virginia Street Bridge, one top-level flood control official described it as "one of the worst bridges in the country." NDOT agreed with that assessment, giving the fabled 111-year-old span a 17-out-of-100 rating. There was no comfort in those numbers for the drivers and passengers in the 11,000 cars, on average, that passed over the bridge every day. But in October 2013 the good news Reno had been waiting for finally arrived. The money to replace the Virginia Street Bridge was always to come in part from the Truckee River Flood Management Authority, an organization that gets its funding from a one-eighth of a cent sales tax imposed in Washoe County in 1998. But the initial figure floated around for their flood control project had been $1.6 billion, and officials eventually agreed that that was economically and politically unrealistic. So the number was scaled down to a more realistic figure, and in December 2013 stakeholders agreed to $446 million for the flood project. Of that amount, regional flood officials had finally approved a $7.25 million expenditure for the bridge. That amount was added to $10 million in federal funding acquired through NDOT, and $2 million committed by the Regional Transportation Commission as a reserve fund. In addition to the $19.7 million total available money for construction, $4.2 million had already been spent on designing the span and procuring all the architectural and engineering plans.[10]

The replacement of the old concrete bridge was finally ready to go, although a specific date could not be set. City officials explained that the first stage of the construction—tearing down the old bridge—could not begin until spring flows from the winter's snow had subsided. As it turned out, the drought in Nevada and California continued for a fourth straight year through the winter of 2014–15, so although very bad news for the two states, it would allow for work to begin in late spring 2015.[11]

With a timetable finally in place, the bridge that had been declared structurally deficient more than two decades earlier by NDOT, and had been at least partially responsible for more than $500 million in damages in the hundred-year flood of 1997, would at last be replaced. When completed in mid-2016, the sixth Virginia Street Bridge would become part of a downtown core that was also beginning to show great economic promise.

The historic 1934 Art Deco Post Office building, originally designed by Frederic DeLongchamps, had been sold by the U.S. Postal Service, and was in the midst of a renovation and repurposing as an upscale retail center. This building, like the bridge and the Riverside Artist Lofts, is on the National Register of Historic Places, and was renovated to preserve its historic integrity. It reopened in early 2016 with a number of tenants occupying the basement area. Also planned for renovation for reuse were the 1948 Truckee Lane Building, sitting right on the river at First Street, and the former J. C. Penney building.[12]

In July 2014 the *New York Times* ran a feature on Reno, pointing out many of the city's problems, but also mentioning some of the positive things happening in the downtown corridor. "Completed in 1995, the bowling stadium [the 78-lane National Bowling Stadium] is scheduled to undergo a $15 million renovation, including the addition of 10 lanes…[and] the United States Bowling Congress agreed to hold championship tournaments here through 2030." The *Times* also mentioned Apple Corporation's $10 billion, ten-year commitment to northern Nevada that includes a downtown office building that may also house other technology firms. Adding to the good news, in late 2015 the local newspaper reported that downtown's biggest eyesore, the huge Kings Inn motel, closed for thirty years, would be converted into luxury flats.[13]

As for the Truckee River itself, it, too, was doing fine. In late 2013 the Nature Conservancy, the organization that oversees the restoration of the river for the Truckee River Flood Authority, announced that restoration work on the lower Truckee was almost completed. The river would be "restored to a state much closer to nature's intention," the newspaper noted, which involved restoring the river's meandering course and replanting indigenous cottonwood and willow trees along the riverbanks.[14]

There may still be a long way to go, but Reno, Nevada, was truly a city on the move by 2016. But whatever else may occur in years to come, the city's oldest and most iconic landmarks—the Virginia Street Bridge and the Riverside Hotel—will continue as they have for more than 156 years to be at the center of everything in Reno.

## NOTES

1. Quote from DeLong, "Flood Planners Say We're Due for Deluge," *RGJ*, 05/08/2010.
2. DeLong, "Flood Planners Say We're Due for Deluge," *RGJ*, 05/08/2010; Gant and

Gottemoeller, "CITY BRIDGES: Biggest of the Little"; quote from "Bridge's Long Story Coming to an End," *RGJ*, 11/06/2010.

3. "Replacement for Historic Bridge," news broadcast, KTVN channel 2, 07/30/2011, 9:19 AM; Duggan, "Reno Picks Design of New Downtown Bridge," *RGJ*, 11/17/2011.

4. Jones, "New Bridge to Replace Historic Reno Crossing."

5. Gant, "CITY BRIDGES: Biggest of the Little."

6. Gant, "CITY BRIDGES: Biggest of the Little"; Bryan Gant interview with the author, January 2013.

7. City of Reno, "Virginia Street Bridge Project: Reno City Council Project Update," 01/16/2013.

8. Quote from "Tutto Ferro Looks to Reno, Region for Inspiration for Virginia Street Bridge," *RGJ*, 07/16/2013; Tutto Ferro website, www.tuttoferro.com; Duggan, "Metal Shop Gets Contract for Bridge Art," *RGJ*, 07/03/2013.

9. E-mails to author from Jonathan Compton, Tutto Ferro, 10/19/2015, including quote.

10. Quote from DeLong, "Bridge Replacement Gets Needed Funds," *RGJ*, 10/12/2013; "Evening News," KOLO Channel 8, 6:30 PM, 10/25/2013; "Flood Project Wins Approval," *RGJ*, 12/14/2013.

11. "Flood Project Wins Approval," *RGJ*, 12/14/2013.

12. Hidalgo, "Betting Big on Downtown," *RGJ*, 10/20/2013; Hidalgo, "Former Reno Post Office Coming Back to Life," *RGJ*, 03/23/2015.

13. Quote from Onishi, "With Gambling in Decline, A Faded Reno Tries to Reinvent Itself," *New York Times*, 07/14/2012; Higdon, "'Great Bones,'" *RGJ*, 12/04/2015.

14. DeLong, "Truckee Restoration Project Nears End," *RGJ*, 11/08/2013, including quote.

# CHAPTER 17

# "LET'S GET THIS BRIDGE BUILT"

WITH THOSE WORDS, on May 20, 2015, Mayor Hillary Schieve—the young businesswoman who had been elected mayor in 2014—closed the official groundbreaking ceremony to replace the iconic but crumbling Virginia Street Bridge, while a large group of officials, businesspeople, and private citizens nodded their approvals.[1]

Just the previous month the Reno City Council had approved a contract for $18.3 million with Reno firm Q&D Construction Inc. to take down the most recent, 110-year-old bridge and replace it with the sixth iteration of the Virginia Street Bridge on the same site as the original iteration built in 1860. May 2016 was the target date for completion of the project. Large, complex construction jobs were not new to Q&D. The fifty-year-old firm owned and managed by the Dianda family counted many of the region's most important corporate and government entities as customers, including St. Mary's Regional Medical Center; the University of Nevada, Reno; Reno-Tahoe Airport Authority; Nevada Energy; and the cities of Reno and Sparks, to mention only a few. Norm Dianda had launched Q&D in 1964 with a kitchen remodeling job hastily sketched on paper napkins over a pasta dinner.[2]

The two on-site managers for the project would be Brian Graham, project manager for Q&D Construction, and Kerri Koski, street program manager for the City of Reno. Charla Honey, a twenty-six-year city employee and engineering manager of the Reno Public Works Department, would oversee the entire project.

Q&D Construction, Jacobs Engineering, the bridge designer, and the City of Reno agreed on an innovative approach for the build that would be faster and minimize the impact on the surrounding community. It was a seven-step plan:

1. Build temporary barricades around the construction and staging areas.

2. Remove the old bridge and divert the river to provide working space.

3. Build temporary supports in the river to hold the bridge structure.

4. Build the new structure in a casting area nearby.

5. Move the completed structure atop the temporary supports.

6. Replace the temporary supports with permanent ones dug into the riverbed, and add the bridge decking.

7. Remove the river diversion and build the new bridge accesses.[3]

Once the work began and the dismantling of the old bridge got under way, Renoites were faced with downtown road closures, not an unusual occurrence since many of the active city's downtown civic events require the same thing. For step 2, the river's diversion was eased by the Truckee River's drought-diminished flow, but the demolition work would uncover a few expensive secrets.[4]

In 1905, the same year the old concrete bridge had been built, the city was also graced with another magnificent new structure. Due to growing membership, the old Masonic Hall of Lodge #13 on Commercial Row at Sierra Street—today the oldest remaining commercial building in the city—was no longer adequate, so members decided to build a new Temple on the site of a livery stable at the northwest corner of the new bridge. The Temple was a beautiful three-story, two-tone Romanesque building that quickly became a landmark in Reno. But following a 1965 fire the entire building had to be razed and replaced with a new structure. However, the old Lodge had left a few surprises behind.[5]

While demolishing the concrete bridge, Q&D workers found contaminated soil in the riverbed, the result of wastewater from the 1905 Masonic Building being piped directly into the river. After digging down a little way in another area, they also discovered large granite blocks that had formed the foundations of the old iron bridge built in 1877. Altogether these surprises cost an estimated $410,000 to remedy.[6]

In mid-June a story appeared in the newspaper about the desirability of offering chunks of the old bridge for sale to the public as historic relics, as the much-revered 110-year-old structure held a great deal of sentimentality for many local citizens. The city council studied the idea, even though adopting it had a number of risks that threatened some of the federal permits that were already in place. In the end, Q&D Construction's Norm Dianda took it upon himself to order a limited number of small pieces of the 112-year-old bridge's rebar encased in resin to be offered for sale, with all proceeds going to the city's National Automobile Museum.[7]

The pony truss bridge pictured here was one of three options offered to Reno city officials to become the new Virginia Street Bridge. Although it wasn't an overwhelming favorite, Reno City Council members agreed it would be the best overall choice. On the far side of the bridge sits the Riverside Artist Lofts, ancestor of the first structure ever built in what would become downtown Reno. Courtesy of the City of Reno.

Step 3, building temporary abutments to support the new bridge, was completed without incident by November 2015, but it was steps 4 and 5 that seemed almost too audacious to be true: building the new bridge itself off-site and then "sliding" it atop the temporary columns that had been sunk into the riverbed.

The industry term for such a plan is Accelerated Bridge Construction, or ABC, and it is most frequently used to minimize traffic impact when building busy interstate bridges. The ABC method was chosen because of the time and financial benefits it offered the City of Reno and its citizens. The two arch-and-beam sets, each weighing about four hundred tons, were built on South Virginia Street right in front of the Riverside Artist Lofts. Q&D Construction Company built them of wood and rebar, and poured concrete in them to complete the forms. Then each of the 185-foot-long × 40-foot-high arch-and-beam sets was slid into place on the temporary supports, using four 100-ton hydraulic rams. To ease the friction as the huge sets made their

In this photo from December 2015, Q&D Construction Company makes the final concrete pours that attach the two arch-and-beam sets to the foundation of the sixth iteration of the famed Virginia Street Bridge. The bridge, the Riverside Artist Lofts, and the adjoining Washoe County Courthouse will forever be remembered as the triumvirate that reigned over Reno's divorce trade for more than a half-century. Courtesy of the City of Reno.

arduous 175-foot journey across the Truckee River, liquid dish soap was poured under them. The entire operation took four days, and many curious Renoites came out to watch in person, or watched it on local television.[8]

While all this was going on, concrete work and curing on the sidewalks, crosswalks, curbs and gutters, and retaining walls also moved forward without a hitch, as did the installation of all the necessary utilities, all work that would be completed on schedule by March 1, 2016. By mid-January the concrete bridge deck had also been poured. Steps 6 and 7 were also completed on schedule and without problems. Finally, Tutto Ferro, the Sparks, Nevada, metalworking firm charged with manufacturing and installing the public art portion of the project, completed its work, and on beautiful, sunny April 12, 2016 the sixth iteration of the Virginia Street Bridge was officially opened at a ribbon-cutting ceremony attended by hundreds of people. The project was both ahead of schedule and significantly under budget. It was a grand day for the entire northern Nevada community.[9]

When the famed bridge across the Truckee River at Virginia Street was officially dedicated in 2016, it marked another important milestone in "The Biggest Little City." It would also be one of the highlights in the rapidly changing face of the city that it represented, a city that Mayor Schieve had bragged about in her most recent State of the City speech late in 2015: "Reno has reinvented itself to become a mecca for entrepreneurs, young professionals, progressive businesses and an arts and culture community that I believe can stand up to any major metropolitan city any day."[10]

Reno and its northern Nevada neighbors have indeed reinvented themselves, becoming one of the nation's hottest new high-tech business locations. Tesla Motors and its partner Panasonic led the way, building the world's largest gigafactory to manufacture lithium ion batteries for homes and cars. But Tesla is not alone: cutting-edge data center developer Switch is building Switch SuperNAP nearby, an industrial campus that will encompass nearly nine million square feet of space, making it the largest data center on earth. Also, technology heavyweight Apple is building Project Huckleberry, its second major data center in northern Nevada, bringing its total space to about one million square feet; and eBay has approved a $412 million investment to facilitate its growing e-commerce and auction business. Many smaller, but no less impressive business investments are also on tap for the region.[11]

Meanwhile, in downtown Reno where the city's first two building sites still huddle next to each other as they have since 1860, there are both blessings and challenges. One of the biggest blessings is a deal, twenty-seven years in the making, that has finally come to fruition, a deal that solidifies the importance of the new Virginia Street Bridge. The deal involves another important Reno citizen, the sparkling little Truckee River. In a complex deal involving a number of important players, the deal allows the Truckee Meadows Water Authority to store and manage drought reserves in the winter, something the agency has not previously been allowed to do. This should double, and eventually triple, the Reno area's upstream drought reserves, putting an end to unsightly situations where the river becomes merely a trickle.[12]

As for many of the other challenges the city faces with the downtown core, the city's daily newspaper summed up the situation in an article by the president and CEO of Economic Development Authority of Western Nevada: "Downtown revitalization is a focus of our mayor and council, a place where significant private investments are planned and the beginnings of a partnership with the university [University of Nevada, Reno] that embraces the potential for a college town environment."[13]

As with anything that might occur in the future, there is always the possibility of unexpected surprises, both positive and negative. But there is little doubt that the 148-year-old city, and the 156-year-old sites of the present-day Riverside Artist Lofts and futuristic Virginia Street Bridge, will continue to reinvent themselves as time goes by.

What else would you expect from the "Biggest Little City in the World"?

## NOTES

1. "Ceremony Marks Start of Virginia Street Bridge," *RGJ*, 05/2/2015.

2. "Virginia Street Bridge FAQs"; "Q&D History," Q&D Construction, Inc.

3. Q&D Construction Inc., "Virginia Street Bridge Replacement's Innovative Construction Method"; private communication between author and Brian Graham, project manager, Q&D Construction, 12/01/2015.

4. Q&D Construction Inc., "Virginia Street Bridge Replacement's Innovative Construction Method"; City of Reno, "Virginia Street Bridge Project: What's Happening."

5. Reno Historical Team, "Masonic Temple"; Reno Masonic Lodge #13, "History of Reno 13."

6. Damon, "Surprising Virginia St. Bridge Finds Boost Cost," *RGJ*, 07/24/2015.

7. "Council Mulls Virginia Bridge Disposal," *RGJ*, 06/12/2015; interview with City of Reno engineering manager Charla Honey, 12/07/2015.

8. E-mail to author from Brian Graham, Q&D Construction Co. project manager, 11/20/2015; Coleman, "The New Virginia Street Bridge Moves Across the River."

9. City of Reno, "Virginia Street Bridge Project: What's Happening."

10. Damon, "Reno Revival," *RGJ*, 09/02/2015, including quote.

11. Tesla Motors, "Tesla Gigafactory"; Hildalgo, "Thinking Huge," *RGJ*, 09/22/2015; "Apple Files 'Project Huckleberry' Permit," *RGJ*, 01/05/2016; Higdon, "eBay Plans $230M Center," *RGJ*, 12/16/2015.

12. "After 27 Years, A Win for All," *RGJ*, 01/10/2016.

13. Kazmierski, "3 Challenges That Could Hurt Growth: One View," *RGJ*, 01/17/2016, including quote.

# BIBLIOGRAPHY

**ABBREVIATIONS**
n.d.: no date available
n.p.: no page available
n.t.: no title available
BLM: Bureau of Land Management
NDOT: Nevada Department of Transportation
*NSJ: Nevada State Journal, Daily Nevada State Journal, Weekly Nevada State Journal*
OLLI: Osher Lifelong Learning Institute
*RC: Reno Crescent*
*REG: Reno Evening Gazette*
*RGJ: Reno Gazette-Journal*
*RWGS: Reno Weekly Gazette and Stockman*
*TE: Territorial Enterprise*
UNOHP: University of Nevada Oral History Program

"Administrative Records of the Secretary of State, 1864–1995." Nevada State Library and
    Archives. Carson City, NV.
Angel, Myron, ed. *History of Nevada with Illustrations and Biographical Sketches of its Prominent*
    *Men and Pioneers*, Oakland, CA: Thompson and West, 1881.
Anonymous. *Illustrated History of Plumas, Lassen & Sierra Counties*. San Francisco: Farris and
    Smith Publishers, 1882.
Armstrong, Louis. *Louis Armstrong, in His Own Words*. New York: Oxford University Press, 1999.
"Articles of Incorporation of the Riverside Hotel Company." Recorded May 2, 1905, with the
    secretary of state, State of Nevada. Nevada State Library and Archives, Carson City, NV.
"Articles of Incorporation of the Nevada Transit Company." Approved March 16, 1903. Nevada
    State Library and Archives, Carson City, NV.
Atkinson, Harry Hunt. "Tonopah and Reno Memories." UNOHP, Reno, 1970.
Badger, Emily. "The Key to a Thriving Creative Class?" *Fast Company*, 08/09/2012. PARS
    International, New York.
Barber, Alicia. *Reno's Big Gamble: Image and Reputation in the Biggest Little City*. Lawrence:
    University Press of Kansas, 2008.
Bartlett, George A. "George A. Bartlett Papers." NC 1253, Special Collections. University of
    Nevada, Reno Library.
———. *Is Marriage Necessary: Memoirs of a Reno Judge*. New York: Penguin, 1947.
Basso, Dave. *The Works of C. B. McClellan: Nineteenth-Century Nevada Portrait and Landscape*
    *Artist*. Sparks, NV: Falcon Hill Press, 1987.
Biltz, Norman H. "Memoirs of 'The Duke of Nevada': Developments of Lake Tahoe, California
    and Nevada; Reminiscences of Nevada Political and Financial Life." UNOHP, Reno, 1969.
Blair, Minnie P. "Days Remembered of Folsom and Placerville, California: Banking and
    Farming in Goldfield, Tonopah, and Fallon, Nevada." UNOHP, Reno, 1968.
Blake, Nelson Manfred. *The Road to Reno: A History of Divorce in the United States*. Westport CT:
    Greenwood Press, 1977. Original published 1962.
Bond, George W. *Six Months in Reno*. New York: Stanley Gibbons, c. 1921.

Bryant, Edwin. *What I Saw in California: Being the Journal of a Tour by the Emigrant Route and South Pass of the Rocky Mountains, Across the Continent of North America, the Great Desert Basin, and through California in the Years 1846–1847*. New York: D. Appleton, 1849.

Bureau of Land Management (BLM). "Military Bounty Land Warrant." Bureau of Land Management, U.S. Department of the Interior, Vol. 1032: 116. http://www.glorecords.blm.gov/details/patent/default.aspx?accession=NV0010__.191&docClass=STA&sid=wfprfvzb.brs#patentDetailsTabIndex=1

Cafferata, Patty. *Lake Mansion: Home to Reno's Founding Families*. Reno: Eastern Slope, 2006.

Cahill, Robbins E. "Recollections of Work in State Politics, Government, Taxation, Gaming Control, Clark County Administration, and the Nevada Resort Association." UNOHP, Reno, 1977.

Cahlan, John F. "Trolley Town." In *Nevada: Official Bicentennial Book*, edited by Stanley Paher, 107–9. Las Vegas: Nevada Publications, 1976.

California Great Registers, 1866–1910. "Charles William Fuller: Image 00007." FamilySearch.org. https://familysearch.org/pal:/MM9.1.1/VTDY-F9C

———. "Charles William Fuller: Image 00008." FamilySearch.org. https://familysearch.org/pal:/MM9.1.1/M6PS-LM1

Carlson, Helen S. *Nevada Place Names, A Geographical Dictionary*. Reno: University of Nevada Press, 1974.

City of Reno. "2012 Cultural Master Plan: Introduction." http://www.reno.gov/government/departments/public-works/reno-bridges-flood-project/virginia-street-bridge/background

———. "Reno Bridges–Flood Projects, Background." http://www.reno.gov/index.aspx?page=1573

———. "TRAction Visioning Project." Draft of final report. Prepared by CH2MHILL Co., December 2008.

———. "Virginia Street Bridge Project: website." http://vsbreno.com/

———. "Virginia Street Bridge Project: What's Happening." http://vsbreno.com/whats happening

———. "Virginia Street Bridge Project: Reno City Council Project Update." 01/16/2013.

———. "Virginia Street Bridge Project: FAQs." http://vsbreno.com/faqs

Coleman, Carol. "The New Virginia Street Bridge Moves Across the River." *FootPrints* 19 (1, Winter), 2016. Historic Reno Preservation Society.

Coman, Katherine, *Economic Beginnings of the Far West*, vol. 2. New York: Augustus Kelley, 1968. Original published 1912.

Curran, Harold. *Fearful Crossing: The Central Overland Trail Through Nevada*. Reno: Great Basin Press, 1982.

Curtis, Leslie. *Reno Reveries: Impression of Local Life*. Reno, NV: Self-published, 1924.

Curtis, Mark. *It Was Great While It Lasted: A PR Man's Reflections on Nevada's Entertainment Heyday*. Reno: Black Rock Press, University of Nevada, 2001.

Davis, Sam P., ed. *The History of Nevada*. Vol 2. Reno: Elms Publishing, 1913.

DeLongchamps, Frederic J. "Frederic J. DeLongchamps Architecture Records, 1899–1962." Mathewson IGT Knowledge Center, Special Collections Department, University of Nevada, Reno.

Dixon, Mead. "Playing the Cards That Are Dealt: Mead Dixon, the Law, and Casino Gambling." UNOHP, Reno, 1992.

Doten, Alfred. *The Journals of Alfred Doten, 1849–1903*. 3 vols. Edited by Walter Van Tilburg Clark. Reno: University of Nevada Press, 1973.

Douglass, Jack. "Tap Dancing on Ice: The Life and Times of a Nevada Gaming Pioneer." UNOHP, Reno, 1998.

——. "Jack's Story: The Life and Times of Jack Douglass, Nevada Gaming Pioneer." UNOHP, Reno, 1996.

Dreibelbis, John A. "A Jaunt to Honey Lake Valley and Noble's Pass." *Hutching's California Magazine*, June. San Francisco, CA, 1857. http://www.yosemite.ca.us/library/hutchings _california_magazine/

Earl, Phillip I. "The Disappearance of Roy Frisch." *Nevada* [magazine], July–August 1998. Nevada Commission on Tourism, Carson City, NV.

Elliott, Isaac H. *Record of the Services of Illinois in the Black Hawk War*. 32nd Illinois General Assembly. Isaac H. Elliott, Adjutant General, Springfield, IL: 1902, 215. http://archive.org /stream/recordofservices00inilli#page/214/mode/2up28

Elliott, Russell R. *History of Nevada*. Lincoln: University of Nebraska Press, 1973.

Fairfield, Asa Merrill. *Fairfield's Pioneer History of Lassen County California to 1870*. San Francisco: H. S. Crocker, 1916.

Fatout, Paul. *Meadow Lake, Gold Town*. Bloomington: Indiana University Press, 1969.

Fey, Marshall. *Emigrant Trails: The Long Road to California*. Reno: Western Trails Research Association, 2008.

Fisher, Joy. 2007, April 21. "Mexican War." USGenWeb Project, Statewide County IL Archives Military Records. http://files.usgwarchives.net/il/statewide/military/mexican/other /mexicanw105nmt.txt

Foster, Julie. "A Distinguished Drive." *Nevada* [magazine]. July–August 2009.

Franzwa, Gregory M., and Jesse G. Petersen. *The Lincoln Highway: Nevada*. Tucson, AZ: Patrice Press, 2004.

Fulton, R. L. *Reminiscences of Nevada*. First Biennial Report of the Nevada Historical Society, 1907–1908. Carson City, NV: State Printing Office, 1909.

Gadwa, Anne, and Anna Muessig. "How Art Spaces Matter, II." Metris Arts Consulting, Reno. https://www.giarts.org/sites/default/files/How-Art-Spaces-Matter-II.pdf

Gant, Bryan, and Frederick Gottemoeller. "CITY BRIDGES: Biggest of the Little." *Roads & Bridges*, 08/09/2013. http://www.roadsbridges.com/city-bridges-biggest-little

Garvis, Jann. *Roar of the Monitors: The Quest for Gold in the Northern Sierra*. Santa Ana, CA: Graphic, 2004.

Glass, Mary Ellen. *Nevada's Turbulent '50s: Decade of Political and Economic Change*. Reno: University of Nevada Press, 1981.

Goodwin, Victor. *Flood Chronology: Lower Half, Carson River Sub-basin, 1861–1976*. Portland, OR: Soil Conservation Service, 1977.

——. "Nevada's Toll, Freight & Stage Roads." In *Nevada: Official Bicentennial Book*, edited by Stanley Paher. Las Vegas: Nevada Publications, 1976.

——. "Wm. C. (Hill) Beachey, Stagecoach King," *Nevada Historical Society Quarterly* 10, no. 1, Spring (1976).

"Grants and Permits for Toll Roads and Bridges." Records of Carson County, Utah & Nevada Territories, 1855–1861. Don Wiggins Manuscript Collection, Nevada Historical Society, Reno, NV.

Gulling, Amy Thompson. "An Interview with Amy Gulling." Interview by Mary Ellen Glass. Oral History Project, Center for Western North American Studies, University of Nevada, 1966.

Hage, Bob. "One Night Stands." *Nevada* [magazine], Mar/Apr 1980. Nevada Commission on Tourism, Carson City, NV.

Hardesty, Stephen L. "The Site of Reno's Beginning: The Historical Mitigation of the Riverside Hotel/Casino." Reno Historical Resources Commission, Reno, 1997.

Harmon, Mella Rothwell. "Divorce and Economic Opportunity in Reno, Nevada During the Great Depression." Master's thesis, University of Nevada, Reno, 1998.

——. "The Extraordinary Career of Frederic J. DeLongchamps." *Nevada Historical Society Quarterly* 49 (3, Fall), 2006.

Hazel Bishop, Inc. "Cosmetics and Skin." http://www.cosmeticsandskin.com/companies /hazel-bishop.php

Henrick, Kim, "Anna Warren and the Riverside Hotel," Historic Reno Preservation Society "Footprints," 18, no. 4, Fall 2015.

——. "Elevenses (or Let's Revisit Reno's Past)." Historic Reno Preservation Society "Footnotes" newsletter, February 11, 2016. www.historicreno.org/index.php/hrps-blog/81-elevense

Hummel, N. A., ed. *General History and Resources of Washoe County, Nevada*. Published under auspices of the Nevada Educational Association, 1888.

IMDb. "Tom Mix." http://www.imdb.com/name/nm0594291/, n.d.

James, Ralph C., and Estelle James. *Hoffa and the Teamsters: A Study of Union Power*. Princeton, NJ: Van Nostrand, 1965.

Jones, Jenny. "New Bridge to Replace Historic Reno Crossing." *Civil Engineering* [magazine], 04/29/2013. American Society of Civil Engineers, Reston, VA.

Kingsbury, F. B. "Pioneer Days in Sparks and Vicinity." Nevada Historical Society Papers, vol. 5, 1925–1926. Reno, NV: Nevada Historical Society.

Kling, Dwayne. *The Rise of the Biggest Little City: An Encyclopedic History of Reno Gaming, 1931–1981*. Reno: University of Nevada Press, 2000.

——. "Luck Is the Residue of Design." UNOHP, Reno, 2000.

Lake, Myron C. "Petition for Divorce." Myron Lake Papers, 1868–1883, MS RNC #128 (Official documents, plaintiff and defendant pleadings, witness statements, etc. from Myron Lake's 1879–80 divorce from Jane Conkey Bryant Lake). Reno: Nevada Historical Society.

Lassen County, California. *Book A of Deeds*. County Recorder's Office. Susanville, CA.

——. *Book C of Deeds*. County Recorder's Office. Susanville, CA.

—— "William Fuller vs. His Creditors, Schedule A." Bankruptcy petition. District Court. Filed July 1, 1868, granted August 19, 1868. FamilySearch.org.

Laxalt, Robert. *A Lean Year, and Other Stories*. Reno: University of Nevada Press, 1994.

"Laws of the Territory of Nevada, Passed at the Second Session of the Legislative Assembly," Virginia City: J. T. Goodman Co., Territorial Printers, 1863.

Leonard, Paul A. "Tales of Northern Nevada—and Other Lies: As Recalled by Native Son, Journalist and Civic Leader." UNOHP, Reno, NV, 1980.

Lord, Eliot. *Comstock Mining and Miners*. United States Geological Survey. Washington DC: Government Printing Office, 1883.

Mack, Effie Mona. *Nevada: A History of the State from the Earliest Times Through the Civil War*. Glendale, CA: Arthur H. Clark Co., 1936.

Magliari, Dana, "Home Is Where the Art Is." *Nevada* [magazine], May/June 2008.

Mathews, H. Clyde, Jr. "Oral Autobiography of a Modern-Day Baptist Minister." UNOHP, Reno, 1969.

McDonald, Russell. "History of Washoe County," 1982. "Forward, Washoe County Code, Supplement No. 13: A Revision and Codification of the General Ordinances of Washoe County, Nevada." Washoe County, NV: Board of County Commissioners, April 2012. http:// www.washoecounty.us/clerks/files/pdfs/county_code/history.pdf

——. "The Life of a Newsboy in Nevada." UNOHP, Reno, 1971.

McLaughlin, Mark. "Tahoe Nugget #9: Tahoe Dam 1997 Flood." http://thestormking.com /tahoe_nuggets/Nugget_9/nugget_9.html

Merry, Robert W. *A Country of Vast Designs: James K. Polk, the Mexican War, and the Conquest of the American Continent*. New York: Simon & Schuster, 2009.

Miller, Joaquin. "Classic Cowboy Poetry: Joaquin Miller." www.cowboypoetry.com/miller.htm

Miller, Geralda D. "The Biggest Little Struggle: Black Activism in Reno, 1954–1965." Master's thesis, University of Nevada, Reno, 2009.

Miramon, Beth. "Reno's Heritage Bridge Is in Jeopardy." Paper written under auspices of Historic Reno Preservation Society, June 2005. Nevada Historical Society, Reno, "Virginia Street Bridge" folder.

———. "Reno's Heritage Bridge: Truckee River Floodwall." Nevada Historical Society, Reno, "Virginia Street Bridge" folder.

Moody, Eric N. "The Early Years of Casino Gambling in Nevada, 1931–1945." PhD Dissertation, University of Nevada, Reno, 1997.

Myrick, David F. *Railroads of Nevada and Eastern California*, vol. 1. Reno: University of Nevada Press, 1992. Original published 1962.

National Park Service. "Washoe County Courthouse." http://www.nps.gov/nr/travel/nevada /was.htm

"National Register of Historic Places Inventory—Nomination Form: Virginia Street Bridge." Filed 05/08/1979, Granted, December 10, 1980. Nevada State Historic Preservation Office, Carson City, NV.

"National Register of Historic Places Inventory—Nomination Form: Riverside Hotel." Filed June 13, 1983, Granted, 08/06/1986. Nevada State Historic Preservation Office, Carson City, NV.

Nevada Department of Transportation (NDOT). "Summary of Assessment of Virginia Street Bridge, Structure No. B-178." Structural Design Division, Carson City, Nevada, December 7, 1994.

*Nevada Highways and Parks* [magazine] (forerunner of *Nevada* [magazine]). March 1937. Carson City, NV: Nevada Department of Highways, State Printing Office, 1937.

Nevada Historical Society. *Second Biennial Report of the Nevada Historical Society, 1909–1910*. Carson City: Nevada State Printing Office, 1911.

*Nevada Newsletter: Reno Nevada, Its Resources*. Promotional magazine. Reno: Nevada Newsletter Publishing Co., 06/25/1927.

Nicoletta, Julie. *Buildings of Nevada*. New York: Oxford University Press, 2000.

Null, Jan, and Joelle Hulbert. "California Washed Away: The Great Flood of 1862." *Weatherwise* [magazine], Jan/Feb 2007.

Olsen, Edward A. "My Career as a Journalist in Oregon, Idaho, and Nevada; In Nevada Gaming Control; and at the University of Nevada." UNOHP, Reno, 1972.

Online Nevada Encyclopedia, "Frederic DeLongchamps." http://www.onlinenevada.org/ articles/frederick-delongchamps

———. "Lew Hymers." www.onlinenevada.org/articles/lew-hymers

———. "Mapes Hotel and Casino, Reno." http://www.onlinenevada.org/articles/mapes-hotel -and-casino-reno

———. "Virginia Street Bridge." http://www.onlinenevada.org/articles/virginia-street-bridge

Paher, Stanley W., ed. *Nevada: Official Bicentennial Book*, Las Vegas: Nevada Publications, 1976.

Pearce, Ed. "Throwback Thursday: In 1952 Reno Gets Its First Glimpse of TV." KOLO-TV. September 20, 2013. http://www.kolotv.com/home/headlines/Throwback-Thursday-In-1952 -Reno-Gets-Its-First-Glimpse-Of-TV-223560511.html

Peckham, George E. "Reminiscences of an Active Life." Nevada Historical Society Papers, 1917–1920. Nevada Historical Society, Reno.

Petricciani, Silvio. "The Evolution of Gaming in Nevada, The Twenties to the Eighties." UNOHP, Reno, 1982.

Potter, David Morris, ed. *Trail to California: The Overland Journal of Vincent Geiger and Wakeman Bryarly*, New Haven, CT: Yale University Press, 1945.

Prouty, Annie Estelle. "The Development of Reno in Relation to its Topography." Master's thesis, University of Nevada, 1917.

———. "The History of Reno's Territorial Development." Undergraduate thesis, University of Nevada, 1908.

Puddington, Grace E. "A Biography of Marguerite H. Gosse Who Introduced the Bill into the Legislature that Became the First Nevada State Nurse Practice Act, of 1923." Manuscript, University of Nevada Special Collections, 1960.

Q&D Construction Inc. "Virginia Street Bridge Replacement's Innovative Construction Method." https://vimeo.com/128425347

Ramsey, Alice. *Veil, Duster, and Tire Iron*. Covina, CA: Castle Press, 1961.

Raymond, C. Elizabeth. *George Wingfield: Owner and Operator of Nevada*. Reno: University of Nevada Press, 1992.

"Reno Has a Downtown Resort Hotel." *Hotel Monthly*, February 1952. John Willy Publications, Chicago.

Reno Historical Team. "Masonic Temple." http://renohistorical.org/items/show/62?tour=5&index=11

Reno Masonic Lodge #13. "History of Reno 13." http://reno13.org/history.htm

Rhiana, Courtney, and Christopher Ryan Meredith. *Images of America, Reno's Riverwalk District*. Charleston, SC: Arcadia, 2013.

Riley, Glenda. *Divorce, An American Tradition*. New York: Oxford University Press, 1991.

Riverside Hotel. "May 11, 1935 Riverside Hotel menu," #76/2/7. Nevada Historical Society, Reno.

Riverside Hotel. "Thanksgiving Dinner Menu," 1912, #76/2/7. Nevada Historical Society, Reno.

Rocha, Guy Louis. http://nvsearch.nv.gov/search?affiliate=stateofnevada&query=Getting%20%E2%80%98Reno-Vated%E2%80%99, click on "Myth #68: Getting 'Reno-Vated': The Ring of Truth." Nevada State Library and Archives, Carson City, NV.

———. "The Mysterious Demise of Key Pittman." *Nevada* [magazine], September/October 1996. Nevada Commission on Tourism, Carson City.

———. "The Mystery of Reno's Beginnings." *Washoe Rambler* 6, no. 2, Summer 1982. Reno, NV: Washoe County Historical Society.

———. "Reno's First Robber Baron." *Nevada* [magazine], Mar/Apr 1980. Carson City, NV: Nevada Commission on Tourism.

Ross, Silas E. "Recollections of Life at Glendale." UNOHP, Reno, 1970, 157–58.

Rowley, William D. *Reno: Hub of the Washoe Country, An Illustrated History*. Woodland Hills, CA: Windsor Publications, 1984.

Ruhl, Arthur. "Reno and the Rush for Divorce." *Collier's* [magazine], July 1, 1911.

Rusco, Elmer. *"Good Time Coming?" Black Nevadans in the Nineteenth Century*. Westport, CT: Greenwood Press, 1975.

Salas, Bill. "A Family Affair: Harolds Club and the Smiths Remembered." UNOHP, Reno, 2003.

Sampson, Gordon A. "Memoirs of a Canadian Army Officer and Business Analyst." UNOHP, Reno, 1996.

Sanford, John. "Printer's Ink in My Blood." UNOHP, Reno, 1972.

Sawyer, Raymond I. *Reno, Where the Gamblers Go!* Reno: Sawston, 1976.

Schwartz, David. "The Great Vegas Turnaround." News Center, University of Nevada Las Vegas. http://news.unlv.edu/article/great-vegas-turnaround

Snyder, John, and Steve Mikesell. "The Consulting Engineer and Early Concrete Bridges in California." *Concrete International*, May 1994.

Statutes of Nevada. Nevada State Archives, Carson City, NV.

Summerfield, Mary Winslow. "On the Way to Reno." In *Nevada: Official Bicentennial Book*, edited by Stanley Paher. Las Vegas: Nevada Publications, 1976.

Territory of Utah, County of Carson. "County Book of Carson County Court, 1855–1861." Microfilm Roll No. 93–08, Nevada State Archives, Carson City, NV.

———. "Bond, C. W. Fuller, for Toll Bridge on the Truckee River." Dated 05/03/1861, approved 05/03/1861. #01010601, TERR-0103 (Box JJ). Nevada State Archives Carson City, NV.

———. "County Court Records A." Dated 1860–1861. TERR-0016. Nevada State Archives, Carson City, NV.

———. "Deeds, Vol. A, 1860–1861." Microfilm Roll No. 93–06, Carson County Recorder. Nevada State Archives, Carson City, NV.

———. "Petition of C. W. Fuller for Bridge Franchise." Filed 02/20/1861, granted 03/05/1861, filed 03/17/1861. #01010505, TERR-0100 (Box GG), File 31. Nevada State Archives, Carson City, NV.

Tesla Motors. "Tesla Gigafactory." https://www.teslamotors.com/gigafactory

Thompson, David, ed. *The Tennessee Letters: From Carson Valley, 1857–1860*. Reno: Grace Dangberg Foundation, 1983.

"Town of Reno…1868." Map Collection. Nevada Historical Society, Reno, NV.

Townley, John M. *Tough Little Town on the Truckee: Reno, 1868–1900*. Reno: Great Basin Studies Center, 1983.

Truckee River Flood Project. "Ecosystem Restoration," truckeeflood.us/233/restoration_projects.html

Twain, Mark [Samuel Clemens]. *Roughing It*. New York: Harper & Row, 1913.

"Typically American, Peculiarly Nevadan." *Pacific Coast Record*, January 1951. Los Angeles, CA.

UNOHP and Osher Lifelong Learning Institute (OLLI). "The Cultural Side of Reno." Interviews listed by interviewee. Reno, 2012. https://contentdm.library.unr.edu/cdm/ref/collection/unohp/id/5481

United States Census, 1880. "John E. Fuller." FamilySearch.org. https://familysearch.org/pal:/MM9.1.1/M6PS-LM1

Vacchina, Elmer. "The Italian-America Experience in Northwestern Nevada, from Territorial Days to the Present." UNOHP, Reno, 2006.

Walton-Buchanan, Holly. *Historic Houses and Buildings of Reno, Nevada*. Reno: Black Rock Press, 2007.

———. "Reno-vated." *Nevada* [magazine], Nov/Dec 2009. Carson City, NV: Nevada Commission on Tourism.

Warren C. A. & Co. "Miscellaneous Index of Filings: Vol. 1, 1875–1912." Washoe County Recorder's Office, Reno. Filed 05/01/1905.

Washoe County, Nevada. "History of Washoe County." http://www.washoecounty.us/clerks/files/pdfs/county_code/history.pdf.

Washoe County Recorder's Office. "Riverview Survey Tract Map T-105." Washoe County Recorder's Office, Reno, 08/15/1896.

Washoe County. *Book 2 of Deeds, Part 1*. Washoe County Recorder's Office, Reno.

———. *Book 2 of Deeds, Part 2*. Washoe County Recorder's Office, Reno.

Watson, Anita. "Tarnished Silver: Popular Image and Business Reality of Divorce in Nevada, 1900–1939." Master's thesis, University of Nevada, Reno, 1989.

Wiggins, Don. "Don Wiggins Manuscript Collection." Nevada Historical Society, Reno, NV.

Williams, Henry T. *The Pacific Tourist: Williams' Illustrated Guide to Pacific RR and California Pleasure Resorts Across the Continent*. New York: Henry T. Williams, 1876.

Willis, F. M. "Truckee Meadows Memoirs." *State of Nevada, Second Biennial Report of the Nevada Historical Society, 1909–1911*. Carson City, NV: State Printing Office, 1911.

Wilson, Thomas Cave. "Reminiscences of a Nevada Advertising Man, 1930–1980, or Half a Century of Very Hot Air, or I Wouldn't Believe It if I Hadn't Been There." UNOHP, Reno, 1975.

Wingfield, George. "George Wingfield Papers." Nevada Historical Society, Reno, NV.

Winn, Mary Day. *The Macadam Trail: Ten Thousand Miles by Motor Coach*. New York: Alfred A. Knopf, 1931.

WiredPRNews.com. "The Historical Riverside in Reno, More Than One Hundred Years of Hospitality." 01/28/2013. http://www.wnd.com/markets/news/read/23334223/the_historical_riverside_in_reno

"Women's Biographies: Anna B. Mudd Warren." Nevada Women's History Project. http://www.unr.edu/nwhp/bios/women/warren.htm

Wren, Thomas, ed. *A History of Nevada, Its Resources and People*, New York: Lewis Publishing, 1904.

Zhang, Xiao. "Nevada Hit Low Point in 1900." "Nevada Outpost." Reynolds School of Journalism, University of Nevada, Reno, 1999. http://www.jour.unr.edu/outpost/community/com.zhang.history1.html

# ABOUT THE AUTHOR

A native of Burlington, Vermont, Jack Harpster was raised in Memphis, Tennessee, and graduated from the University of Wisconsin, Madison, in 1959 with a bachelor of science degree in journalism. He spent forty-three years working in the newspaper industry in Southern California and Southern Nevada. At retirement in 2002, Jack was the executive director of advertising for the *Las Vegas Review-Journal* and the *Las Vegas Sun*, and director of new media for the Stephens Media Group's newspaper division. He and his wife Cathy moved to Reno, Nevada in 2006.

Upon retirement, Jack began writing as a hobby. This is his ninth book, all in the personal or institutional biography genre. Five of his nine books have been published by academic or scholarly publishers, and the others by trade publishers. He has also published dozens of essays and articles on history and biography in national and local journals and magazines.

# INDEX

Page numbers in *italics* refer to illustrations.

Abelman, Nathan, 122, 131–32, 148

Accelerated Bridge Construction (ABC) method, 234–35

Admiral Air Service, 178

Admissions Day, 62

African Americans: discrimination in Reno, 163–64

Aiazzi, Dave, 213

Alameda Street Bridge, 139

alcohol prohibition, 110

Alford, William, 18

Alhambra Saloon and Lodging House, 37

Allen, Arthur, 144, 150, 167, 168, 195

Alvord Lake Bridge, 75

Anka, Paul, 176

Ann-Margret, 162

antidivorce militants, 110–11

Apple Corporation, 230, 236

"Argenta," 38–39

ArkStorm of 1861–62, 26–28, 26–29

Armstrong, Louis, 162

Armstrong, Mrs. Louis. *See* Wilson, Lucille

Artown, 152

Arts and Culture District, 218

Artspace, 214–16

Atkinson, Harry, 145

Atlantic City, 198

Ball, Lyle, 205

Bally Manufacturing Company, 184

Bal Tabarin, 182

banking business, 124–25

Bank of California, 44

Barber, Alicia, 200, 209, 210

barroom: of Lake House, 15, 34

bartenders union, 149

Bartlett, George A., 111–12

Baruch, Bernard, 152, 167

baseball World Series (1952), 163

Beck, Fred, 193

Beck, H. H., 89

Beck, Jessie, 66, 193–97, 198

Beck Corporation, 193

Bell, Lola, 130

Belle Isle, 120

Belli, Melvin, 165

Bennett, Russ, 187

Bergemann, Harry J., 195

Bernardi, James, 162, 196–97

Berry, Bill, 161

Berryman, Jill, 214

Beverly Hills Development Corporation, 178

Bible, Alan, 165

Bi-Centennial Fair and Exposition, 205

Bill Clifford Orchestra, 162, 169

Bishop, Hazel, 177

black entertainers, 163–64

Blitz, Norman, 134–35, 145, 165

Boardman, Horace, 57–58

Bonafide Productions, Inc., 188

Boothe, Clare, 125

boxing matches, 112

Boynton Slough, 48

Brady, Alfred, 168–69

Bragg, Allan C., 38

Bravo, Louis. *See* Oritz, Louis

Bridge Commission, 74, 75, 76, 77, 80–81

bridge of flowers proposal, 140

Bristol, Rebecca, 85

Brown, John E., 193–94, 195

Bryant, Jane Conkey, 31. *See also* Lake, Jane

Bunker, Berkeley, 144

Burris, Georgia, 194

Cahill, Robbins, 144–45, 169

California Gold Rush, 9–10

Californians, 134

California Trail, 9

Cal Vada Club, 182

Cantrell, Ruth, 147

Carnival Week, 90

Carson, Kit, 9

Carson Pass, 9

Carson River, 27

Carville, Ed, 139, 144

Cashell, Bob, 226

casino gambling: in Atlantic City, 198; cheating at the Riverside casino, 184–86; decline Reno in the 1970s, 199; Jim Crow and, 164; legalization in Nevada, 128–29; loss of small businesses in Reno in the 1990s, 209–10; Mapes Hotel and, 148; marquee entertainment and, 160; in Reno in the 1930s, 129, 130–31; in Reno in the 1940s, 144–45; Riverside Hotel and, 129, 131–32, 145, 148–49, 184–86, 194–95; Mert Wertheimer and, 169–70

cattle bridge of 1887, 57

Central Pacific Railroad, 34–38, 45

Chamberlain, W. R., 56–57, 65

Chase, Charley, 15

Chase, John Paul, 133

cheating: at the Riverside casino, 184–86

chorus girls, 160, 162
Christy, June, 183
Chuck Wagon restaurant, 150
Circus Circus Hotel and
    Casino, 197
Circus Day (1915), 107
C.I.T.Y. 2000 Arts Commis-
    sion, 218
City of Reno Historical Re-
    sources Commission, 210
Cividino, Paolo, 228–29
Clegg, Jake, 187
Clemens, Samuel, 26–27
Cleo (dog), 108
closed-circuit broadcasts, 163
Club Cal Neva, 148, 149
"Coast-to-Coast Rock High-
    way," 108–9
Cobb, Neal, 216
Cochran Ditch, 89
Cohen, Ben, 188
Cole, Nat King, 162
Collins, Timothy, 208
Columbus Airways, 178
Comstock Lode, 10
Corey, Laura and William, 86
corner bar: at the Riverside
    Hotel, 132, 164–66, 178,
    179–80
Cortes (steamship), 7
Cotton Brothers, 77, 78
craps: cheating at the River-
    side casino, 184–86
Crawford, Bill, 222
Crocker, Charles, 35–36, 37,
    39
Crocker, E. B., 38–39
Crocker, William, 131
Crocker First National Bank,
    129, 131, 135
Crummer, Roy E., 167, 172–73,
    178
Crummer Corporation, 167
Crystal Bay Development
    Company, 135
Crystal Peak, 35
culinary workers' union,
    149
Cunardi, Frank, 177
Curtis, M. J., 73, 76, 88, 89
Curtis, Mark, 162, 164–65

Daughters of the American
    Revolution, 138
Davis, Sammy, Jr., 200
Davis, Sam P., 19
Dawson, Norman, 115, 116
Delaplane, Stan, 169–70
DeLauer, Lee, 181–82, 183
Delonchant, Felix, 76, 81
Delonchant & Curtis, 76
DeLongchamps, Frederic, 72,
    76, 103, 121, 139
Denhart, Roy, 177
depression of 1880–1900, 71
DeSimone, Andrew, 182–83,
    185, 186
"Development of Reno in Re-
    lation to its Topography,
    The" (Prouty), 28
Dianda, Norm, 232, 233
Dianda family, 232
divorce business: antidivorce
    militants, 110–11; The Mis-
    fits and, 159; number of di-
    vorces in 1931, 136; number
    of divorces in the 1940s,
    142; Reno and, 69, 85–86,
    110–12, 128, 135–38, 142,
    154, 159; Riverside Hotel
    and, 85, 86, 121, 122, 125,
    142; wedding ring myth
    and, 136–38
divorce laws, 85, 110–11, 128
"divorce ranches," 134, 136
Donner Pass, 9, 34
Douglass, Jack, 163, 172, 173,
    174, 175
Dowd, Eddie, 161
Dreibelbis, John, 5–6
Drytown, 10
dude ranches, 134, 136

Eddie Fitzpatrick Orches-
    tra, 169
Einstoss, Bernard, 182–83
Eisenhower, Dwight D., 158
El Cortez Hotel, 134
Elder, George, 49
Eldorado Hotel–Casino, 197
electric trolleys, 79, 80
electromechanical slot ma-
    chines, 184, 186

Eng, Peter. See Ng, Peter
Ensign, James, 180
entertainment: at the River-
    side Hotel, 160–64, 176–77,
    180, 183
environmentalists: opposi-
    tion to rehabilitating the
    Virginia Street Bridge,
    222–23
Eva Lanie and the South Sea
    Islanders, 194
excursion packages, 178
express companies, 44–45

Fairfield, Asa, 6, 7
Farmers Hotel, 19
FBI Story, The (film), 169
Federal Aviation Agency, 178
Federal Building, 72
Federal Bureau of Investiga-
    tion (FBI), 168–69
Federal Land Patent #177, 36
Feemster, Delores, 164
female impersonators, 176–77
Fenwick, Jerry, 162
Ferrari Shields bridge de-
    sign, 222
ferries, 16
Fey, Charles, 184
Fifth Illinois Volunteers,
    55, 56
fire: Lake House destroyed
    by in 1868, 42; Reno and
    the fire of 1879, 53–54;
    Riverside Hotel destroyed
    by in 1922, 102, 115–17
First National Bank, 125
Fisher, Carl, 108
Fisk, Sarah, 219–20
Flamingo Hotel, 160
Flood Project Coordinating
    Committee, 223
floods: of 1876, 33; of 1907, 96;
    of 1950 and 1955, 154–59,
    155–58; of 1997, 211–12;
    of 2005, 223; ArkStorm
    of 1861–62, 26–28; flood
    threat and parapet con-
    troversy with the concrete
    bridge, 106–7
Foley, M. D., 65

Foley, R. L., 64–65

Folsom Prison escapees, 81–82

Fort Defiance, 6

Fourth of July Celebration (1949), 149

Frame, Jeff, 219

Frankovich, Lee, 167, 173

Franks, Robert, 173, 174, 175

Fraser, Richard, 180

Freeman, Sam, 116

Frisch, Roy J., 133

Frontier Club, 197–98

Fuller, Charles William (C. W.): arrival in the west and at Truckee Meadows, 7–8; bankruptcy petition, 12, 19, 25; barroom in the hotel of, 15; building of hotel and bridge, 7, 12–20, 23; ferry operated by, 16; later life of, 25; skew in the Virginia Street Bridge and, 49; trades Fuller's Crossing to Myron Lake, 19, 20, 24–25, 40n6; trading post of, 15; wagon road built by, 16–17

Fuller, Frances, 6–7, 19, 23, 24

Fuller, James, 6–7, 19

Fuller, James P., 8

Fuller, John E., 6–7

Fuller, W. L., 8

Fuller's Bridge, 7, 12–13, 15–20, 23, 49, 76. *See also* Lake's Crossing Bridge

Fuller's Crossing, 12–20; traded to Myron Lake, 19, 20, 24–25, 40n6. *See also* Lake's Crossing

Fuller's Crossing Hotel, 7, 12–15, 19–20, 23, 25. *See also* Lake House; Riverside Hotel

*Fuller vs. His Creditors*, 12

Fulton, Robert L., 28

Gable, Clark, 161

gambling: outlawed in the 1910, 110. *See also* casino gambling

Gant, Bryan, 227

Gardner, Ava, 160, 161

Gates, Charles, 11, 19

*General History and Resources of Washoe County, Nevada* (Hummel), 13, 15

Genoa, 85

Gilette, Tommy, 134

Gill & Madden Company, 48

Glendale, 34

Gold Club, 198

Golden Hotel, 114, 131, 135

Goodwin, Nat C., 65

Gosse, Harry, Jr., 108

Gosse, Harry J.: 1905 concrete bridge and, 75, 77; becomes owner of the Riverside Hotel, 91–92; divorce trade and, 111; hotel fire of 1922 and, 115–17; management of the Riverside Hotel, 66–68, 86–94, 108, 109–10, 118, 120; rebuilding of the Riverside Hotel, 87–94; retirement and death of, 120

Gosse, Josephine, 66, 91, 116, 118

Gosse, Marguerite, 66, 118

Graham, Bill, 132, 133, 134

Graham, Brian, 232

Graham, James M., 37

Grand Central Hotel, 60

Grand Sierra Resort, 197

Great Depression: divorce business in Reno during, 135–38; impact on George Wingfield and the Riverside Hotel, 126, 129–35; impact on Reno, 136; Virginia Street Bridge during, 138–40

Green, Frank W., 150, 151, 166

Greenwood, Caleb, 9

Griffin, Jeff, 213, 215

Grimm, Madame, 110

Gustin, Dan, 225–26

Hall, Donald, 180

Hardesty, Stephen L., 210

Harmon, Mella, 121

Harolds Club, 135, 179, 192–93

Harrah, Bill, 194–95

Harrah's Hotel–Casino, 148, 197, 199

Hart, George, 132

Hazel Bishop, Inc., 177

Heidt, Horace, 134

Henness Pass toll road, 9

Henrick, Kim, 36, 68

High, David, 174

high-tech business, 236

Highway Bridge Replacement and Rehabilitation Program, 212

Highway Day Parade, 109

Hillside Cemetery, 138

Historic Reno Preservation Society, 226

Hobart creek, 107

Hobson, Richard, 197–99, 200, 209

Hoffa, James R., 177–78

Hoffer, Claudia, 160

Holiday Hotel–Casino, 186

Holiday Inn, 199

Holland, Erik, 219, 220

Holter, Doug, 220–21

Honey, Charla, 232

Honey Lake, 5

Honey Lake Valley: descriptions of, 5–6, 10–11; Fuller family, 6–7, 20, 23; Myron Lake and, 23, 24; pioneer settlers, 6–8

Hoover, Herbert, 167

Horseshoe Casino, 167

Horseshoe Club, 182

Hotel Golden, 145

Huffaker's Station, 10

Hughes, Howard, 192, 193

Hughes-Porter, Inc., 179, 182

Hughes Porter Building, 179

Hummel, N. A., 13, 15

Hunter, Jim, 195

Hunter's Crossing, 10

Huston, John, 159

Hyatt Corporation, 180–81, 182

Hymers, Lew, 83

Hymers, Thomas K., 16, 46–47, 48–49, 73–74, 82–83, 99

Ice Rink Plaza, 216
Ice Rink Plaza River Access area, 228
Indiana Automobile Manufacturers Association, 109
"Indian Monte Carlo," 63
Internal Revenue Service (IRS), 188
International Game Technology (IGT), 186
Investment Services of Oklahoma, 192
Island Avenue, 94, 120

J. C. Penny building, 230
Jacobs Engineering, 226, 227
James, Ralph and Estelle, 178
James C. Howland Award for Urban Enrichment, 221
Jamison (or Jameson), H. H., 10
Janesville, 17–18
Jeffries, James, 112
Jessie Beck's Riverside, 195–204
Jewel Box Revues, 176
Jim Crow, 163–64
Johnson, Frank, 185
Johnson, Fritz, 161
Johnson, Jack, 112
Johnson, Neill, 180
Johnstonville, 7
Julian, Estey, 124

Karadanis, George, 211
Keep America Beautiful project, 201
Keeting, Clyde, 184
keno bar, 178
Kerkorian, Kirk, 197
King & Wheelock firm, 47–48
Kinney, Edward, 186
Kirman, Richard, 139
Kling, Dwayne, 148, 193
Koski, Kerri, 232
Ku Klux Klan (KKK), 164
KZTV, 163

labor disputes, 149
Lake, Charles, Jr., 54, 55
Lake, Jane: on the burning of Lake House in 1868, 42; divorce from Myron, 54; divorce petition and description of the Old Lake House, 13, 14; marriage to Myron Lake, 31; at Meadow Lake, 32; son Charles, 54
Lake, M. C., 77
Lake, Myron: ArkStorm of 1861–62 and the rebuilding of Lake House, 28–29; biographical overview, 23–24; dealings with the Central Pacific Railroad and the founding of Reno, 34–38, 39; death and estate of, 54–55; divorce from Jane, 54; divorce petition and description of Lake House, 13, 14; fire of 1879 and, 53; franchise for a toll bridge and toll road, 30; C. W. Fuller trades Fuller's Crossing to, 19, 20, 24–25, 40n6; Lake House at Meadow Lake, 32–33; Lake Mansion and, 30, 54, 55, 205; life and second marriage in the 1860s, 30–32; Mexican War and the reputation of, 55–56; new iron bridge and, 52; operation of Lake House, 25–26, 34, 42–43, 52; painting commissioned by, 30; public takeover of the Lake's Crossing Bridge, 46–47; son Charles, 54; strengthening of Lake's Crossing Bridge, 43–44; tariffs and customers of the Lake's Crossing Bridge, 44–45; Virginia & Truckee Railroad bridge and, 45–46; Washoe County Courthouse and, 45
Lake House (Lake's Hotel): in 1877, 50; ArkStorm of 1861–62 and the rebuilding of, 26–29; barroom of, 15, 34; descriptions of, 25–26, 30, 31–32, 43; dismantling of, 92–93; fire of 1879, 53–54; Myron Lake leases to others, 34, 42, 52; lightning miracle, 43; paintings of, 29–30, 98; rebuilt after the fire of 1868, 42; rebuilt to two-and-a-half stories, 34; renamed Riverside Hotel, 56 (see also Riverside Hotel); replica in the 1974 Bi-Centennial Fair and Exposition, 205; William Thompson's ownership of, 54–55, 56–57; Edwin Vesey and, 52, 53; Horace Vesey and, 52
Lake House at Meadow Lake, 32–33, 41n29
Lake Mansion, 30, 54, 55, 205
Lake's Addition, 36, 45
Lake's Crossing: ArkStorm of 1861–62, 27–28; in the early 1860s, 30–32; Myron Lake, Central Pacific Railroad, and the founding of Reno, 34–39; paintings of, 28–30, 98
Lake's Crossing Bridge: ArkStorm of 1861–62 and the rebuilding of, 28, 29; franchise as a toll bridge, 30; paintings of, 29, 98; Daniel Pine as toll collector, 33; public takeover of, 46–47; rebuilt in 1867, 33–34; rebuilt in 1877 as a public iron bridge, 47–48; replica in the 1974 Bi-Centennial Fair and Exposition, 205; strengthening of in 1869, 43–44; tariffs and customers, 44–45; Virginia & Truckee Railroad bridge and, 45–46. See also Virginia Street Bridge
Lake Tahoe, 211–12
Lambot, Joseph, 75
Las Vegas, 154, 173
Las Vegas Strip, 154
Laxalt, Paul, 196
Laxalt, Robert, 154

Layne, Gerald, 175–76
"Le Crazy Horse Revue,"
176–77
Leonard, John B., 75, 77, 78
Leonard, Paul, 137, 158
LeRoy, Mervyn, 169
Levy, Sam, 173, 174, 175
Lewis, Ted, 150, 160
Lincoln Highway, 108–9
Lincoln Highway Commit-
tee, 109
Lindquist, Kelley, 214, 215
Lloyd, James H., 183, 185, 186
London, Jack, 112
Lowery gang, 24
lynchings, 60–62, 63

*Macadam Trail, The* (Winn),
129
Mack, C. E., 66, 68, 91, 92
Mack, Effie Mona, 28
Mackay, Clarence, 95–96
Mackay, Jim, 95
mail fraud, 133
Maloff, Robert, 211
Malone, George, 165
Mapes, Charles, Jr., 169
Mapes, George, 148
Mapes family, 145, 148
Mapes Hotel: closing of, 199;
Sammy Davis Jr. on, 200;
Eddie Fitzpatrick Orches-
tra and, 169; Bernard Ein-
stoss and, 182; final years
and demolition of, 210,
211, 214, 216; founding and
popularity of, 104, 145, 148;
National Trust for Historic
Preservation and, 216;
Sky Room, 148, 160, 169;
Thanksgiving Day flood
of 1950 and, 155; Lou Wert-
heimer and, 145, 159
marriage business, 69
Masonic Lodge building, 72,
106–7, 233
masseuses, 110
Mathews, Clyde, 176
Mathews, Matt, 161
Mathis, Raymond ("Ruby"),
149, 167, 168, 169

Mathisen, Virginia L. Brown,
193
Maxwell Model K Gentle-
man's Roadster, 95
Mayberry Bridge, 96
Mayberry Crossing, 10
McCarran, Pat, 165–66
McClellan, Cyrenius B., 28–
30, 98
McCoy, Bart, 219–20
McDonald, Joseph, 94–95
McKay, James, 132, 133, 134
Meadow Lake, 32–33, 41n29
Mechling, Tom, 165
Melton, Marilyn, 163
Memorial Day, 138
Mexican War, 55–56
MGM, 142–43
MGM Grand Hotel–Casino
(Las Vegas), 197
MGM Grand Reno, 197
Miller, Arthur, 159
Miller, Heine, 92
Miller, William, 175, 176–77
Minneapolis Arts Commis-
sion, 214
Minneapolis Artspace,
214–15
*Misfits, The* (film), 159
Mission Revival style, 72
"mis-spots," 185
Mix, Tom, 143
Moana Line, 79
Money Honey slot machines,
184, 186
Moon, Winfield, 187, 188
Moore, John L., 14
Mount Davidson, 107
Munley, Emmett, 174
Munley, Harold, 173, 174, 175
Murphy, Joseph, 81–82

Nada Dada Motel, 219
Nash, Richar, 61, 62
Nataqua Territory, 6
National Automobile
Museum, 233
National Environmental Pol-
icy Act, 212
National Register of Historic
Places: Reno Post Office

and, 139, 230; Riverside
Hotel and, 121–22, 199,
210; Virginia Street Bridge
and, 78, 199, 205
National Trust for Historic
Preservation, 216
Nature Conservancy, 230
NDOT. *See* Nevada Depart-
ment of Transportation
Nelson, George (Baby Face
Nelson), 133
Nevada: depression of 1880–
1900, 71; divorce business,
85–86; divorce laws, 85,
110–11, 128; divorces in
1931, 136; divorces in the
1940s, 142; Great Depres-
sion and, 131; high-tech
business and, 236; legali-
zation of casino gambling,
128–29; Lincoln Highway,
108–9
*Nevada: A History of the State*
(Mack), 28
Nevada-California-Idaho
Stagecoach line, 37
Nevada Club, 148
Nevada Day, 62
Nevada Department of
Transportation (NDOT),
212, 224, 225, 229
Nevada Gaming Commis-
sion, 173–74, 175, 176, 177,
182
Nevada Gaming Control
Board, 169, 184–85
Nevada National Guard, 66
Nevada State Fair, 111
Nevada State Militia, 62
Nevada Supreme Court, 46,
54
Nevada Transit Company, 79
Never Sweats, 6
Newlands, Francis G., 65, 99
news media, 130
Ng, Peter, 200–201, 208, 209,
210, 211, 213
Nicholls, Owen Winslow,
135
Nitschke, I. E., 168–69
North Virginia Street, 99

O'Connor, D. W., 74
O'Connor, Donald, 175
Oddie, Tasker, 111
O'Donnell, Don, 195
O'Keefe brothers, 60
Oliver McMillan firm, 213, 215, 220
Olsen, Edward A., 161, 165–66, 182, 185–86
Olsson, Margaret, 162
Olympics Room, 176–77
O'Neill's Station, 10
"One Sound State" campaign, 134
Oritz, Louis, 60–62, 63
outdoor public art exhibits, 152
Overland Hotel, 114
Overland Hotel–Casino, 197
Overton, Del, 52

P. J. Walker Company, 121
Palace Hotel, 110
Panasonic, 236
parabolic bowstring bridges, 58
"Parisian Follies, The," 160
Pavlovich, Steve, 131–32, 133
Petricciani, Silvio, 131
Phares, William Bonner, 191–92
Pig 'N Whistle restaurant chain, 188
Pincolini, Ernesto, 82
Pine, Daniel Hickey, 33, *98*
Pine Grove, 8
Pine Street, 33
Pittman, Key, 143–44
pogonip, 15
Pony Express, 44–45
pony truss bridge, 226–27, 232–36
Porter, H. Hughes, 179–80
Potato War, 24
Powers, Roy, 163–64
Powning, C. C., 64, 66, 68, 79
Pringle, George C., 18
Pritzker, Don, 180
prohibition, 110
Project Huckleberry, 236
Prospectors' Club, 151

Prouty, Annie Estelle, 13–14, 28, 30
public art: outdoor exhibits, 152; projected for the Virginia Street Bridge, 228–29

Q&D Construction, 232–35

racism, 163–64
Ramage, Walter, 182
Ramsey, Alice, 95
Ram's Head dining room, 180
Rappaport, Marvin, 188
Raymond, Elizabeth, 120, 122
Raymond I. Smith Truckee Riverwalk, 204
Read, John T., 62
Reconstruction Finance Corporation, 131
Redd, William Silas, 184, 186
Redwood Room, 151
Regional Transportation Commission, 229
Reid, H. E., 91
Reno: in 1875, 52–53; African Americans and discrimination, 163–64; anti-divorce militants, 110–11; architecture and public building in the early twentieth century, 71–72; Bi-Centennial Fair and Exposition, 205; boxing matches, 112; bridges over the Truckee River in the 1930s, 139; casino gambling and, 129, 130–31, 144–45, 199, 209–10 (*see also* casino gambling); C.I.T.Y. 2000 Arts Commission, 218; decline in the downtown area in the 1990s, 209–10; depression of 1880–1900, 71; divorce business, 69, 85–86, 110–12, 128, 135–38, 142, 154, 159; in the early 1920s, 114; electric trolley system, 79, *80*; fire of 1879, 53–54; floods (*see* floods); Folsom Prison escapees of

1903, 81–82; founding of, 34–39; Fourth of July Celebration in 1949, 149; C. W. Fuller and the origins of, 7, 12–20, 23; gambling and alcohol prohibitions in the 1900s, 110; Great Depression and, 136; growth in the 1950s, 154; growth in the early twentieth century, 106; growth in the late nineteenth century, 57; high-tech business and, 236; T. K. Hymers and, 82–83; incorporation/de-incorporation contentions, 68–69; labor disputes, 149; Lake Mansion, 30, 54, 55, 205; Las Vegas and, 154, 173; Lincoln Highway and, 109; loss of the Nevada State Fair, 111; lynching of Louis Ortiz, 60–62, 63; marriage business, 69; naming of, 38–39; national news media of the 1930s and, 130; premiere of *Virginia City* in 1940, 142–43; promotions in the late nineteenth century, 64; purchase of the Mapes Hotel, 211; revitalization in the twenty-first century, 229–30, 236–37; Riverwalk, 96, 99, 140, 204, 208, 209; slot machines and, 184, 186; Virginia & Truckee railroad and, 45–46
Reno Carnegie Public Library, 72, 106–7
Reno City Council: Riverside Artist Lofts and, 215; Riverside Hotel and, 208, 213; Virginia Street Bridge replacement and, 223, 225, 226, 227, 228, 232
Reno City Development Agency, 210
Reno City Planning Commission, 208

Reno Guards, 62

Reno Post Office, 72, 106–7, 139, 230

Reno Press Brick Company, 90

Reno Press Club, 180

Reno Redevelopment Agency, 213, 215

Reno Securities Company, 118

Reno Service League, 205

Reno Ski Bowl, 166

Reno Traction Company, 79

*Reno Twenty Years Ago* (McClellan), 28–29, *98*

RENOvation project, 204

Resorts Casino–Hotel, 198

*Reunion in Reno* (film), 159

revue shows, 176–77

Reynolds, Donald, 163

Richards, John P., 182–83

Richter, Bernard, 183, 185, 186

Rickard, George Lewis, 112

Riddick, Bert, 131–32, 133

rigged dice, 184–86

Risley, Nancy C., 193

River Room restaurant, 221

Riverside, Inc., 180, 181–82

Riverside Artist Lofts: awards received, 221; centennial celebration of the Virginia Street Bridge, 223; conversion of the Riverside Hotel into, 213–16; historical significance, 3; opening and description of, 218–21

Riverside Bank, 131, 133

Riverside Buffet, 132

Riverside Café, 134

Riverside Casino Corporation, 179

Riverside Hotel: in the 1930s, 129–30, 131–35; annex added in 1897, 68; Jessie Beck's ownership and management, 193–97; Norman Blitz and, 134–35; bunco scam by Bill Graham and Jim McKay, 133; casino gambling and, 129, 131–32, 145, 148–49, 184–86, 194–95; W. R. Chamberlain's renovations, 56–57; cheating at the casino, 184–86; competition in the 1970s, 197; condemned by Reno in 1997, 213; conversion to the Riverside Artist Lofts, 213–16; corner bar, 132, 164–66, 178, 179–80; death of Key Pittman and, 143–44; death of mascot Cleo, 108; divorce business and, 85, 86, 121, 122, 125, 142; in the early 1900s, 43, *100, 101*; in the early 1920s, 114–15; encroachment on Island Avenue, 94; entertainment at, 160–64, 176–77, 180, 183; excursion packages in the 1960s, 178; expansion in the 1940s, 145, 148, 150–51; famous visitors of, 130; fifth anniversary in 1932, 130; fire of 1922, *102*, 115–17; floods of 1950 and 1955, 155–58; C. W. Fuller and the origins of, 7, 12–15, 19–20, 23; Harry Gosse and the rebuilding of, 1901–1907, *87*–94; Harry Gosse becomes owner of, 91–92; Harry Gosse sells to George Wingfield, 118; Harry Gosse's management of, 66–68, 86–94, 108, 109–10, 114–15, 118, 120; historical significance, 3; Richard Hobson's ownership and closing of, 197–200; Jim Crow and, 163–64; as Lake House, 25–26 (*see also* Lake House); level of service at, 94–95; C. E. Mack and Anna Warren as owners, 68; marriage business and, 69; Pat McCarran and, 165–66; National Register of Historic Places and, 121– 22, 199, 210; Peter Ng and plans for resurrecting the hotel, 200–201, 208, 209–11; I. E. Nitschke's management of, 168–69; ownership groups, financial problems, and closings in the 1960s, 172–83, 186–88; parapet controversy of the Virginia Street Bridge and, 106–7; William Phares and, 191–92; premier of *Virginia City* in 1940 and, 143; prohibition and, 110; promotions in the late nineteenth century, 64; purchase and sale by the Wertheimers and Ruby Mathias, 167, 168; registration desk in the early twentieth century, *87*; Reno boxing matches and, 112; restaurateur R. Scott Weaver, 125; Charles Sadleir's management, 124; soda fountain in the 1940s, 146–47; special guests in 1909, 95–96; William Thompson's ownership and sale of, 56–57, 63–66; traveling sales agents and, 145; Truckee riverfront and, 209; Lou Wertheimer and, 159; George Wingfield rebuilds in 1927–29, *102*–3, 120–24; George Wingfield's expansion of in the 1950s, 166; George Wingfield's ownership in the 1930s, 129, 131, 135; George Wingfield's ownership in the 1940s, 144, 145, 148–49, 150–52; George Wingfield's planned expansion of in 1929, 125–26; George Wingfield's sale of, 166–67; Mary Davis Winn's description of, 129

Riverside Hotel Company, 91, 93, 116

Riverside Hotel Enterprises, 200–201
"Riverside Starlets," 162
Riverside Theatre Restaurant, 150, 158, 166. *See also* Olympics Room
Riverwalk, 96, 99, 140, 204, 208, 209
Riverwalk District, 209
roads: C. W. Fuller's wagon road, 16–17; Myron Lake's toll road, 30; Lincoln Highway, 108–9
Roberts, E. E., 106
Rocha, Guy, 144
Rock Boulevard, 155
Rock Street Bridge, 80–81, 139, 155
roller rink, 109–10
Roop, Isaac, 5
Roop, Susan, 5
Roop's Fort, 6
Rosen, Burton, 188
Ross, Silas, 95
Rowan and Martin, 162
Rowley, William, 69
Royle, William and Dorothy, 124
Rush to Washoe, 10
Russell, John Francis Stanley (Earl Russell), 85–86

Saccomanno, J. J., 187
Sadleir, Charles J., 124
Sage Brush War, 6
sales tax: supporting the Virginia Street Bridge project, 229
saloons: prohibition and, 110
Sanford, Clifford, 180
Sanford, John, 130
Scardino, Anthony, 188
Schieve, Hillary, 232, 236
Schnitzer, William, 86
Scott Ranch irrigation ditch, 74–75
Scrugham, James, 139
Sebeline family, 116
Sellers, J. S., 34, 42
Shapiro, Chuck, 220–21
Sharon, William, 45

Sheehan, John, 184–85
Ship and Bottle Club, 131
Siegel, Benjamin ("Bugsy"), 160
Sierra Arts Foundation, 213–15
Sierra Nevada: passes across, 9
Sierra Street Bridge, 139
Sierra Valley Road, 22n49, 31, 38
Sievers, Ferdie, 180
Sinatra, Frank, 160–61
Sinatra, Nancy, 160, 161
"Site of Reno's Beginning, The," 210
*Six Months in Reno* (booklet), 115
Sky Room, 148, 160, 169
Slide Mountain, 166
slot machines, 184, 186
Smith, Patricia, 214, 215
Smith, Raymond, 159
Smith, Ron, 160
Smith, Virgil, 169, 172, 173–74
Smith family, 179, 192–93
soda fountains, 146–47
Sommers, John, 180
south Reno, 10
South Virginia Street, 31
Spalding, Zetus N., 6, 23
Spector, Raymond, 177, 178–79, 179
Spencer, Harry, 161, 162
squatters, 13
Squaw Valley, 166, 173
Standard Computers, Inc., 188
Starr, Kay, 162, 200
Statcher, Joseph, 174
Status, Edwin, 15
Stevens, Elisha, 9
Stevens-Townsend-Murphy wagon train, 9–10
Stewart, Thomas K., 73–74, 78, 81, 204
Stewart Street, 204
Stoddard, Richard, 118
Stone, John, 11, 19
Stone & Gates Crossing, 11, 19, 34

Stratosphere Hotel–Casino, 211
Streeter, Jack, 180
strikes, 149
Stupak, Bob, 211
Sullivan-Kelly irrigation ditch, 74–75
Summa Corporation, 193
Summit City, 32. *See also* Meadow Lake
Sun Mountain, 10, 107
Susan River, 5
Susan River Canyon, 5
Susanville, 5
Swift, Calvin, 180
Switch data center developer, 236
Switch SuperNAP, 236

tariffs, 44–45
Taylor, George H., 91
teamsters, 44
Teamsters Union Pension Funds, 177–78, 186, 187, 191, 192
television, 163
Tesla Motors, 236
Thanksgiving Day flood (1950), 154–59
Theatre Restaurant. *See* Riverside Theatre Restaurant
The Lancer restaurant, 167
Thompson, Florence, 13–14
Thompson, William, 54–55, 56, 57, 63–66, 88
*Thompson & West's History of Nevada, 1881*, 13
Toadtown, 7
toll bridges: C. W. Fuller's petition for a charter, 18; Lake's Bridge and Myron Lake, 30. *See also* Fuller's Bridge; Lake's Crossing Bridge
toll roads, 16–17, 30
Toogood, Mona Kay, 66–68
Topaz Lodge, 198
Toronto Restaurant, 64
*Tough Little Town on the Truckee* (Townley), 14

Tourism Development
  Award, 221
Townley, John M., 14, 17, 37
"TRAction Visioning Proj-
  ect" report, 223–24
trading posts, 15
Trocadero Club, 134
trolley system, 79, 80
Truckee Lane Building,
  230
Truckee Livery, Feed, and
  Stable, 99
Truckee Meadows: ArkStorm
  of 1861–62, 26–28; description of, 8–9; early trappers, 9; floods (see floods);
  C. W. Fuller's arrival, 8;
  Gold Rush period to 1860,
  9–11; Myron Lake, Central
  Pacific Railroad, and the
  founding of Reno, 34–39;
  squatters, 13
Truckee Meadows Water
  Authority, 236
Truckee River: ArkStorm of
  1861–62, 27–28; beautification projects, 201–4, 208,
  209; cattle bridge of 1887,
  57; description of, 8–9;
  floods (see floods); C. W.
  Fuller and Fuller's Crossing, 12–20 (see also Fuller's
  Bridge); Lake's Crossing
  (see Lake's Crossing); Reno
  bridges in the 1930s, 139;
  restoration efforts, 230;
  storage and management
  of drought reserves, 236;
  Virginia Street Bridge (see
  Virginia Street Bridge);
  Virginia & Truckee Railroad bridge, 45–46; wedding ring myth and,
  136–38
Truckee River Flood Man-
  agement Authority, 223,
  229, 230
Truckee River Flood Project,
  225, 229
Truckee River Island Park,
  202–3

Truckee Turnpike Com-
  pany, 17
Tutto Ferro metalworking,
  228–29, 235

United Press Association, 161
Universal-International Pictures, 159
U.S. Army Corps of Engi-
  neers, 222, 223, 225
U.S. Department of Defense,
  196
U.S. Department of Hous-
  ing and Urban Develop-
  ment, 215
U.S. Postal Service, 230. See
  also Reno Post Office
Utah Territory, 8

Valley Bank of Nevada, 199,
  200, 201
VB Liquidation Corpora-
  tion, 199
Veil, Duster, and Tire Iron
  (Ramsey), 95
Verdi Bridge, 96
Very Special Arts of Nevada
  (VSA), 30, 205
Vesey, Edwin A., 52, 53–54
Vesey, Horace M., 52
video poker, 186
vigilantes, 61–62
Virginia City (film), 142–43
Virginia Street: floods of
  1950 and 1955, 156–57; origins of, 12, 17; Sierra Valley
  Road renamed as, 38
Virginia Street Bridge: in
  1868, 98; 1877 iron bridge,
  47–52, 57–58, 72–73 (see
  also Rock Street Bridge);
  1940 premiere of Virginia
  City and, 143; 2007 decision to rebuild, 223–24;
  ArkStorm of 1861–62 and
  the rebuilding of, 28, 29;
  centennial celebration,
  223; Circus Day in 1915,
  107; city celebrations and,
  107; construction and
  opening of the 2015–16

pony truss bridge, 232–36;
  deaths on, 82; demolition
  of the concrete bridge in
  2015, 105; electric trolleys
  and, 79; facelift in 1970,
  204; featured in Reunion
  in Reno, 159; fiftieth-fifth
  anniversary, 204; flood of
  1907, 96; flood of 1997, 212;
  flood of 2005, 223; floods of
  1950 and 1955, 155, 157, 159;
  Folsom Prison escapees of
  1903, 81–82; C. W. Fuller
  and the origins of, 7, 12–13,
  15–20, 23; historical significance, 3; historic relics of
  the 1877 iron bridge, 233;
  T. K. Hymers and, 46–47,
  48–49, 73–74, 83; as Lake's
  Crossing Bridge (see Lake's
  Crossing Bridge); in the
  late nineteenth century,
  99; lynching of Louis
  Ortiz, 60–62, 63; National
  Register of Historic Places
  and, 78, 199, 205; outdoor
  public art exhibits, 152;
  parapet controversy of the
  concrete bridge, 106–7;
  planning and building
  the concrete bridge of
  1905, 73–75, 76–79, 100–1;
  planning and funding
  for 2015–16 replacement
  bridge project, 225–28, 229;
  public art for the 2015–16
  replacement bridge project, 228–29; public cere-
  monies in the 1930s, 138;
  rehabilitation debate in
  the 1990s, 212, 221–23; re-
  location of the 1877 iron
  bridge, 75–76, 80–81; repairs and modifications
  in the 1930s, 138–39;
  seventy-fifth anniversary
  celebration, 139–40; skew
  in, 48–49, 75; sobriquets,
  138; Washoe Indians and,
  62–63; wedding ring myth
  and, 136–38

Virginia & Truckee Railroad, 44, 45–46
Virginia & Truckee Railroad bridge, 45–46, 47

Wadsworth, 10, 38
wagon roads, 16–17
wagon trains, 9–10
Waldorf Club, 148
Warren, Anna, 91, 92
Warren, Anna Mudd, 68
Washoe, 8
Washoe County: casino gambling and, 130–31; Lincoln Highway, 108–9
Washoe County Bank, 47, 109
Washoe County Commission, 46–47
Washoe County Courthouse, 35, 45, 72, 100, 121, 136, 138
Washoe County Health inspector, 210
Washoe Hotel Corp., 177
Washoe Indians, 62–63
Washoe Landmarks Preservation, Inc., 205
Weaver, R. Scott, 125
wedding ring myth, 136–38
Wertheimer, Lou: death of, 169; joins brother Mert at the Riverside Hotel, 159; Mapes Hotel and, 148, 159; personality of, 160; purchase and sale of the Riverside Hotel, 167, 168; Teamsters Union pays off the mortgage of, 177

Wertheimer, Max, 150
Wertheimer, Mert: brother Lou joins at the Riverside Hotel, 159; closed-circuit broadcast of the 1952 baseball World Series, 163; death of, 169; flood of 1955 and, 158; gaming concession at the Riverside Hotel, 148–49; marquee entertainment at the Riverside Hotel, 161–62; purchase and sale of the Riverside Hotel, 167, 168; reputation and personality of, 159–60, 169–70; Teamsters Union pays off the mortgage of, 177
West, Elmer G., 149, 167, 168
Western Nevada Clean Committees, 201
Western sophisticate style, 151
West Street Plaza development, 204
Wheeler, S. H., 91
White Curtain, 164
Wild River Grill, 220–21
Willis, Rev. F. M., 13
Will Mastin Trio, 200
Willows nightclub, 132
Wilson, Lucille, 183
Wilson, Thomas Cave, 137–38
Wingfield, George, 103, 119; 1922 plans for a new hotel in Reno, 116–17; biographical overview, 117; Norman Blitz and, 135; closed-circuit broadcast

of the 1952 baseball World Series, 163; expansion of the Riverside Hotel in the 1940s, 145, 148, 150–51; expansion of the Riverside Hotel in the 1950s, 166; floods of 1950 and 1955, 158; Great Depression and, 126, 131, 135; later life and death of, 167; ownership of the Riverside Hotel in the 1930s, 129, 131, 135; ownership of the Riverside Hotel in the 1940s, 144, 145, 148–49, 150–152; planned expansion of the Riverside Hotel in 1929, 125–26; purchase of the burned-down Riverside Hotel, 118; rebuilding of the Riverside Hotel in 1927–29, 120–24; Riverside Bank, 124–25; sale of the Riverside Hotel in 1955, 166–67
Wingfield, George, Jr., 144, 150, 177
Wingfield Park, 120, 201, 204
Winn, Mary Davis, 129
Winnie, Don, 184–85
Winter Olympics (1960), 166, 173
Wiseman, Dick, 201, 208
Wolf, Joe, 179
Works Progress Administration (WPA), 201, 202–3
Wren, Thomas, 62–63
Wykoff, Leonard, 180

YMCA building, 72